GOLDSCOPE
and
The Mines of Derwent Fells

by Ian Tyler

BLUE ROCK PUBLICATIONS
2005

Copyright © Ian Tyler 2005

ISBN 0 9548631 3 5

Published by BLUE ROCK PUBLICATIONS

Keswick Mining Museum,
Otley House,
Otley Road,
Keswick.
CA12 5LE

Printed and bound in Great Britain by:

SMITH SETTLE

Ilkley Road, Otley, W. Yorks LS21 3JP

Contents

Acknowledgments   5
Foreword   7

Setting the Scene   8

Small Mines and Trials of the Newlands Valley

Littletown Mine   19
Parrock Gill Trials   19
Barnes Gill Trials   19
Near Broad Gill & St. Thomas Work   20
Castlenook Mine   21
Dalehead Mine   22
Two Trials on High Spy   48
Longwork   48
The Eastern Valley of High Snab Bank   52
Littledale Crags & Scope End Workings   54

Goldscope Mine

1 Copper Cradle   57
2 Settling In   62
3 Stamping and Smelting   71
4 Treasure Island   82
5 Awesome!   86
6 Stride Wide and Lift the Leg   89
7 Daniel Dies   92
8 Sudden Death!   111
9 The Breadth of a Sheet   116
10 Copper Bottomed   123
11 The Great Bunch   126
12 Goldscope - Goodbye   146

Yewthwaite Mine

1 Home of the Wild Cats   150
2 A Grand Level   152
3 A New Partnership   157
4 Vercoe the Villain   159
5 Into the Scrap Man's Hands   162

Rowling End Trials 186
The Stonycroft Smelters 186
Stonycroft Mine 187
The Cobalt Mine 191

Barrow Mine

1 The Golden Mountain 195
2 East, West, which is Best? 198
3 Candles & a Good, Strong Rope 201
4 Across the Road to Uzzicar 203

Bassenthwaite Area

Ladstock Mine & Rachel Wood 235
Old Rachel Wood Mine 237
The Rachel Wood Crosscut 237

Thornthwaite Lead Mine

1 Engine Shafts & Deep Mining 241
2 Gold Fever 245
3 Gleaming Galena 249
4 Laal Joe 252
5 Battered & Bleeding 256

Windy Hill, Woodend & Barf 261
Beckstones Mine 262

Wythop Silica Mine

1 The Secret Valley 265
2 A Serious Project 267
3 Friends Step In 270

Miners & Personnel 273
Glossary of Terms 287
Production Figures 291
Bibliography 299

Acknowledgments

The vast amount of research for this book has not been achieved without the help of numerous people who we would like to thank here:

The Lords of the Manors

Thanks must go to Lords Lonsdale, Inglewood, and Egremont for permission to use their archives, without which this book could not have been written, and to Lord Rochdale for permission to enter his estate and take photographs.

The Friends

Naturally much field work has had to be done to eventually uncover the complexities of the Newlands Valley, Goldscope Mine and the Derwent Fells. A whole team of willing hands has, after much discussion, attempted to solve the mystery and thanks must go especially to Ian Hebson, Kirsten Crowther, Donald Angus, Mike Lugton, Albyn Austin, Martin Thompson, Bill Walker, Peter Blezard, Stuart Clement, Billy Griffin, Martin Willey and Rudy Devriese. Rudy has also supplied details from various sources in Europe. Jean, my wife, who revels in all that is ancient, has had a field day. All the aforementioned are members of MOLES (Mines of Lakeland Exploration Society).

To Michael Anderton of Rochdale Estates for permission to visit Copper Heap Bay on Derwentwater.
To Mary, Ian and Eric Hindmarch for their information and photographs of their family.
To my friend George Hall who has once again supplied invaluable information from his archive.
To Mike Davies Shiel for all his valuable knowledge and his time and patience in explaining the intricacies of the Keswick smelters.
To Sam Murphy and Richard Smith for their help and information about Goldscope and Stonycroft.
To Robert Hudson for local information.
To Andy Lowe of the LDNP for information from his vast knowledge of the Lake District in times gone by.
To Arthur Bennett for his diagrams of Goldscope, likewise to John Crompton for his plans of Goldscope.
To M. Faulkner, P. Baggley, Russell Weir, and Nimrod Lockwood for helping with information on the silica mine and providing various surface plans of the area.
To Les Bennett of Furness for information on Dalehead Mine, also to Nick Stuart for his various snippets of information and photograph.
To Bonita Cawood for supplying information and photocopies about Mr. Sanders of the Thornthwaite Mines.

To Peter Holmes for his detailed information about the Jung locomotive.
Photographs have been submitted for inclusion by Ian Hebson, Stuart Clement, Peter Stanier, Bill Creighton, Martin Thompson and the Keswick Mining Museum Archive.
A special thanks must go to Ian Hebson for his input and thoughts on the workings of Goldscope, both on surface and underground, gained through his many years of study and exploration.

The Cumbrian Archive Service

The Archive staff at Carlisle headed by David Bowcock and Robert Baxter and the team at Whitehaven have been brilliant, as usual, in producing and copying vital information for this book: D/Lec Box 290, D/Lec S/L 29/5, D/Lec MB 6/8 and D/Lec 81.

The Libraries

To Stephen White and the team at Carlisle, who have helped in providing information on Thomas Robinson.
To Jackie Fay at Kendal, Catriona MacKenzie at Keswick and the staff at Penrith all of whom have provided an excellent service.

The Museums

The Keswick Mining Museum (Ian Tyler, Private Archive).
To Harvey Wilkinson of Abbott Hall Museum, Kendal for details from the Collingwood Papers.
To Stephen Hewitt of Tullie House Museum, Carlisle for permission to use photographs.
To Beamish Museum, Stanley, County Durham for their assistance.

The Forestry Commission

To John Bates, Senior Forester for all his help and assistance regarding the mines of Thornthwaite Woods.

WARNING

Derelict mines are in many instances, places of extreme danger and are out of bounds to the inquisitive amateur. Some sites are on private property and therefore, entry without permission constitutes trespass.

Foreword

Now that the Carrock book had been safely delivered to the printers, we began to mull over ideas for our next one. Our thoughts were certainly on the Caldbeck Fells but years ago, we had done a lot of research on the Derwent Fells area and decided to take this as our next subject.

This fascinating story covers the vast mining area of the Newlands Valley, perhaps the best known of the German sites, and also the surrounding territory of the Derwent Fells. Beneath Catbells are huge veins bearing copper, lead, zinc and baryte and in the northernmost part of these fells lies a silica mine, hidden in the dense forests of Wythop and Thornthwaite. Here the land has been torn asunder and although the area has been covered in thick foliage, we will reveal its secrets. To the west, further secrets lie hidden in the gill of Stonycroft, and beyond the summit of Causey Pike lay the remains of the cobalt mine, secure in the secluded clefts of Scar Crags. This rich mining area was under the ownership of the Earl of Egremont, and the Manor of Braithwaite and Coledale covers most of the mining sites within this book.

The problems of writing about history so far back are the lack of available source material, and the fact that that which can be obtained is not always accurate. Our little German Clerk of Works back in 1564 was not always the best writer - and most of it was written in his native tongue! We are hugely indebted to W. G. Collingwood, who took on a monumental task when he translated the original company documents for his classic 1912 book on the subject. There are large gaps in the documentation, particularly for the 16th. and 17th. Centuries, and in some parts of the book we have had to make educated guesses as to how things went. No doubt, many of you who are experienced in the subject, will have drawn different conclusions from earlier reading, but much of it must still remain a mystery to us.

Ian Tyler December 2005

Setting the Scene

Very little has been written about the early metalliferous mining in the country, and even less on this industry in the north of England. Having said that, sources of information are somewhat difficult to collate. In an attempt to lay a basic foundation, we have assembled the following details in order to present to our readers a background to mining in the country as a whole. We must add that this accumulation of facts is incomplete and has been laid out chronologically, so that one can see the involvement of overseas interest prior to the arrival of the German miners in Keswick, and the formation of the Company of Mines Royal.

The northern occupation of England by Hadrian commenced in AD122 and had ended by AD409, and there is much evidence of this occupation in Cumberland and the Borders. Although the thought of Roman mining in Cumberland is certainly an exciting prospect, despite the extensive mining fields adjacent to Hadrian's Wall and numerous archaeological digs and excavations, no records have come to light to reveal involvement during the occupation. However, one snippet of information reveals that the lead mines of Dufton on the Pennines could be a possibility. At the nearby Roman encampment, only a few miles away at Long Marton, sited just west of Penrith, a discovery of pigs of lead at a furnace at Temple Sowerby gives rise for speculation.

One of the most interesting records of early mining in Cumberland was the discovery of coins struck during the reign of the King William II, the red-haired "Rufus", (1087 - 1100). A miner called Joseph Winskill is reputed to have found the coins and some ancient tools at Thortergill, which is on the Browngill Lead Vein near Garrigill, Cumberland. Another early reference is recorded during the reign of Henry I (1130-1135) when the silver mine at Carlisle (Alston) was leased, in 1130, to William Hildert of Carlisle for £40. These workings are again mentioned during the reign of Henry II (1154-1189) and it appears that, in 1158, a German adventurer, William Erkenbald paid £100 a year to operate the mines but fell into arrears and was soon owing £333 6s. 8d in rent. Another report confirms that in 1166, an adventurer by the name of William Holdegar had paid a sum of 500 marks to work two mines in the area. William Erkenbald was still operating his mine but by 1174, the rent was still in arrears and had risen to £2,106 13s. 4d.. He was certainly raising lead ore during this period and he sent 55 cart loads, via the Sheriff of Northumberland, to Caen in France and a further 100 cart loads for a church in Clarevall. Despite ore being raised and dispatched however, further arrears had accrued by 1182. During his tenure it appears that he paid some £2,154 out in rent for the mines - a huge sum in those days. Six men are recorded as mining in 1183, Humfrey, Richard, Adam, Henry Estreis, Richard Edmond Eshalla and William Erkenbald. By 1189, in the reign of Richard I (1189-1199), there is a further record of a rent for mines in Cumberland of £10, and the name on the lease is again our old friend Erkenbald. It is also recorded that an Erkenbald was involved in mining in 1222-1226 and it seems likely that this latter working was by

William's son. There is some evidence that these foreign miners had been given letters of protection during 1229.

Miners are recorded as working the mineral veins in Newlands during the reign of Henry III (1216-1272) and although there is no specific location for the very early workings in this area, we do know that by 1266, the nearby lead veins of Derwent Fells were already being exploited. This is substantiated by the annual royalty of 6s. 8d being collected from the mines in 1266/67 and this had risen to 40s. by 1272. One of the earliest recordings of foreign involvement in this country is during the reign of Edward I (1272 -1307), when it is recorded that Jews had been involved in the exploitation of some of the Cornish tin mines with some success. During 1278, it was stated that the King should receive from the mine at Alston, a 1/9th. royalty, this being as much ore as a man could lift from the ground. Local miners are quoted as saying that there was enough ore to last "till the end of time" Later working followed when, in 1318, John Le Balaunce and Richard Champion were prospecting and later still, in 1324 and with a new partner, Thomas of Almayne, they obtained the right to investigate the veins of Cumberland. We find that Richard Champion was still working at the mines eleven years later with a Robert de la Furse, and held a lease in 1331. By this time also, Edward III had begun to establish a code of practice for mining in the country and he created the position of Keeper of the Mines for the region of Alston and at Minerdale and Silverbeck. in Cumberland, and at Westmorland Harcla. Edward appointed one Robert de Barton as Sergeant of the Mines, in an effort to try and prevent illegal digging, extraction and prospecting. A similar appointment was made in the south of the country when a Keeper of Mines, Mathew de Crawthorn, was appointed in Devon in the year of 1338.

The next recorded Cumbrian activity was in 1356 when the lead mines of Alston were being worked for a rent of 10 marks and three years later, in 1359, copper mines were added to those of gold, silver and lead in Letters Patent.

In Devon, workings were let to John Balancer and Walter Goldbeter and at Alston in the north of England, to a Tilman of Cologne; this was under a royalty payment to the King of 1/5th. Tilman was engaged in some serious prospecting in the region, in particular specializing in attempting to separate the silver from the lead ore. It is also reported that in 1385, the first brass cannon was manufactured using locally mined ore, ordnance which was commissioned by the Sheriff of Cumberland.

The search for minerals continued, and in 1394, during the reign of Richard II, Hugh de Burnfell allowed James Mynour of Derby to work Wenlock Mine, and Nicholas Wake was given permission to mine in Devon. These workings were continued five years later by Henry Derby, and later his son John continued to work mines for a further ten years. In 1401 another Keeper of the Mines was appointed by Henry IV; this was Fitz Wauter who was to carry out the task of prosecuting and convicting illicit mining operators. As we can see, mining was now starting to expand across the country and on the 13th. of November 1414, William Stapleton agreed to pay 10 marks a year for the right to prospect. Later, in 1427, Henry VI granted John of Lancaster, Duke of Bedford, a 10 year lease for the mines in his kingdom, the period being extended, in 1433, by a further 12 years. Around this time, Henry also allowed thirty three miners from Bohemia to come to England to prospect and work his mineral veins to procure precious metals by the art of smelting, but unhappily this venture ended in failure. Unperturbed by this, the King then granted John Solers permission to mine in Devon on a 20 year lease, and continued the policy of tighter controls by appointing John Botright, in 1452, as another Controller of the Mines in Devon and Cornwall.

Another small snippet of information confirms that during the reign of Edward IV (1461- 1483) a charter was granted for mining and a further report states that the town of Keswick, sometime during this period, was "full of miners". This clearly indicates the presence of a mining work force in the heart of the Lake District, with Keswick as a mining centre. Further to the south, in 1462, Edward 1V gave Gallias de Lune, William Maryner and Simon Spert license to work the mines of Somerset and Gloucester and again, on the 20th. of December 1468, he allowed Richard Neville, Earl of Warwick, mining rights north of the river Tweed at a royalty payment of 1/12th. It appears that for many years, trading with Europe had been problematic and in 1475, a trade treaty was established with Holland and Germany which would hopefully allow free trading patterns.

In March of the same year, land was leased to John Marchall and William Goderswyk of Cologne for a 15 year term at a royalty of 1/8th. A report was made by George Willarby that the only three mines of any note in the north of England were Blanchland and Shildon in Northumberland, Fletcheras at Alston and Keswick in Cumberland. These ventures were supported by the very powerful Earl of Northumberland and the Duke of Gloucester. Three years later, in 1478, the mines of Cumberland and Northumberland were again leased for a period of 10 years at a royalty of 1/15th. by Henry Van Orle, Arnald Van Anne, Albert Millyng of Cologne and Dederic van Riswyk of England. This lease specified copper for use in the manufacture of ordnance. Perhaps this was one of the first real attempts to mine Longwork and Goldscope however, the venture was short-lived and lasted for only 6 years before it was suspended.

It was Henry VII, in 1486, who stated the importance of the miners and decreed they be paid reasonable wages and they be allowed wood for smelting at a fair price. Likewise they should not dig in gardens or under houses!!

Over in Germany, in 1492, we hear for the first time of the Hechstetter family when it is recorded that Ambrosius Hechstetter headed the firm in Augsburg, a firm which was expanding its interests, and in 1526, his son Joachim was to come to prospect for gold in Scotland. This venture failed miserably and some of the miners and prospectors had to be assisted back to Germany, having competely run out of money. However, Joachim stayed on and worked in the west country. During this period, it is estimated that around 10,000 men were employed in Germany in the production of ore and the smelting of metals.

By now, Henry VIII had attained the throne and it was he who introduced Breton and Dutch miners to smelt the ore at the Cornish tin mines. These were the mines to which Joachim Hechstetter had gone and by now he was a gentleman with considerable mining experience; in consequence he was given the grand title

"Principal Surveyor and Master of all Mines in England and Ireland". The initial venture was commenced with 6 experts and 1,000 men! It can perhaps be assumed that this number of men is somewhat exaggerated. Despite Henry's efforts, England was still very much reliant on imported copper, but time and again the failings were in the smelting processes. The King's chief advisor, the Duke of Suffolk, registered his displeasure at Henry's apparent inability to develop our own resources and his words did not go unheeded, for a law was passed in 1529 to stop the export of copper or brass. This created a home trade for ordnance, bell metal, wire and the cards and combs essential for the woollen industry. Despite Henry's efforts however, many of the workings throughout the country had fallen idle and by 1538, most had been abandoned. Henry VIII had, in the past, had dealings and communication with the House of Fugger, which at the time, amongst other commercial interests, was operating the Neusohl mines in Hungary.

In 1542, the debasement of silver coinage was under great scrutiny in order to generate funds for the privy purse. Reducing the silver content by 9.2% and replacing this with copper, would prevent the practice of clipping and filing down the currency by fraudsters. Once the copper had been amalgamated with the silver it was a finite solution as there was no known way of separating it, thus making it more difficult for would-be counterfeiters to work any defaced currency. A further premium was put on the value of copper in 1543, when copper and brass were required for the defence of the realm in the manufacture of cannon and arms which became a major priority. It was decreed that it was essential that copper be mined within our own country, and there was no reliance on foreign imports. A report in 1545, indicates that some coinage had been debased by as much as 17.5% and the situation was to continue as a means of creating funding for the crown.

After the death of Henry VIII in 1547, the throne passed to Edward VI who, in an attempt to generate the mining of minerals within the country, invited Joachim Gundelfinger to work the silver mines in Wexford, Ireland. He also established contact with another company in Augsburg, the merchant house of David Haug, Hans Langnauer & Co. who were entrepreneurs in all manner of products including mining and who, in 1550, took over the mining operations at Neusohl from the House of Fugger. These initial contacts were, as we shall see, to have a lasting effect on our country's mining exploits.

During the reign of Mary I (1553-1558), Burchard Kranich was given a grant to exploit the silver deposits in Cornwall, however it was early days and these ventures provided poor results. By this period, 100,000lbs. of ore had been raised from Newlands Valley in the Lake District and in 1557, Queen Mary granted the land and the mines to Thomas Percy, Earl of Northumberland.

With the accession of Queen Elizabeth I (1558-1603), private enterprise was encouraged in all manner of activities, including the art of mining and smelting. The English had not fared well in these arts however, and at this time the Germans were considered to be the leaders in this field in Europe. The debasement of silver coins continued meanwhile, and by 1560 a 6d., for example, became worth only 4½d., a devaluation of 25%. If one can imagine that the mint was making around £7,000 of coins per week the savings in real terms would be £1,750, a vast amount of money in those days.. The situation became so acute that in July 1561, Sir Thomas Gresham invited Daniel Ulstat of Augsburg, who was later to become Deputy Governor of the Mines Royal Company, to help in the project of debasing the country's coinage, thereby cementing Anglo-German relations further. The results for the German experts, 220,227lbs. of coins, were predictably higher than the English effort of 96,450lbs. The amount of silver recovered was 244,416lbs. worth £3 per lb., a total saving of £733,248. The Germans were paid 6% of the silver recovered for their efforts - it is no wonder that they were eager to be involved in the forthcoming Mines Royal venture.

It is fair to say that the coming of the German miners in 1564 would alter our methods of mining by virtue of their expertise. They had, as we know, been here earlier and had already created a foundation for the future. It is considered that the initial successes of these early ventures laid the foundation for the creation of the Mines Royal Company.

It was one Thomas Thurland who, in his position of Master of the Savoy in London, had befriended mining expert Johann Steinberg in 1561 with a proposal for a Royal Grant for mining. The proposition was taken back to Germany and brought to the attention of the merchant house of Messrs. Haug and Langnauer, in Augsburg. The prospects of the charter appeared to have many plusses, and they dispatched their mining agent Daniel Hechstetter to investigate the matter further.

The initial plans and agreement were endorsed by Daniel Hechstetter, Ludwig Haug and Hans Loner, all prominent men in the Haug & Langnauer company, but the plans then lapsed for a period of three years. At last, however, these men and their entourage arrived in Keswick bringing with them several expert miners from Gastein in the Tyrol mining area. The outcome was that the original negotiations with Steinberg and Thurland were transferred to Hechstetter and Thurland, as representatives of both Germany and England. A new lease allowed them to search for copper in Yorkshire, Lancashire, Cumberland, Gloucestershire, Worcestershire, Devon, Cornwall and Wales.

It was not until the advent of the Company of Mines Royal in 1564 that we can take up the thread of our story. At the beginning of Elizabeth's reign the debasement of coinage had become a necessity, and it was William Cecil who considered creating a patent for the production of copper in this country. But, why was Keswick destined to become the centre of the German mining operations? Ecton, Cornwall, Anglesey and the Orme had, on face value at any rate, larger deposits but perhaps it was because of the nearness to the coast, the ready supply of wood and coal or that it was more accessible, that Keswick was chosen. It has also been suggested that there was perhaps a similarity to the landscape in their own country which drew them, and that the sparse population would maybe mean less aggression from locals. Whatever the reasons, it was indeed Keswick that was to become the centre of the German mining operation which was to last upwards of 80 years in one form or another.

The initial company was formed with 24 shares valued at £1,200 each and the Hans Langnauer company held 11 of them. A variety of English noblemen and business men took the remaining 13, although over the next few years, portions of these shares were disposed of to others, almost tripling the number of shareholders involved. No shares were ever held by the Earl of Northumberland on whose land the mines were operated.

Shareholders from 1564 to 1569

Haug, Langnauer & Co.	Augsburg
Thomas Thurland	Master of the Savoy
Edmund Thurland	
Sir William Cecil (Lord Burghley)	Secretary of State
Robert Dudley, Earl of Leicester	
William Herbert, 1st Earl of Pembroke	
Lord James Mountjoy	
Lionell Duckett	Alderman
Anthony Duckett	Grayrigg
Jeffrey Duckett	
Richard Springham	Alderman
Roger Wetheral	Barrister
John Dudley	Stoke Newington
George Nedham	Liaison
William Patten	
Jeffrey Wolcheton	
William Humphrey	Assay Master at the Mint
Thomas Smythe	HM Customs, Port of London
Benedetto Spinola	Merchant
Cornelius de Vos	Alum and Copperas works.
John Tamworth	Clerk of Windsor Castle
William Burd	Treasury
Admiral William Wynter	Master of Ordnance
Mathew Field	
Edmond Wurschopp	
Richard Barnes	Alderman

The Germans made their entry into England via London or the port of Newcastle, which was a bustling and most important coal port, handling 33,000 tons per year, much of which was sent by sea to London. For the miners, the 1,000 mile journey across Europe was a long and painstaking affair using, wherever possible, the huge rivers of the Rhine, the Meuse and the Elbe, then by horseback and carriage until eventually arriving at the ports of departure of Rotterdam, Antwerp or Calais, depending whether they were coming via London or Newcastle. Indeed, the final leg of their journey could indeed be the most perilous if coming via Newcastle, for here the marauding ruffians north of Hadrian's Wall posed a life threatening danger, and so a detour was often made south via Barnard Castle. This irksome detour could extend the journey time by a few days and the whole trip, provided there was good weather for sailings and horses were quickly available when needed, took about three to four weeks.

The advent of German miners under the stewardship of Daniel Hechstetter in 1564 was the renaissance of mining in the Northern Fells and from that time until the Civil War of 1642, the industry flourished. The pastoral valleys of the Derwent Fells became a hive of activity, there was work for all in what had been a poor and isolated community, and the foreigners soon became part of the local scene.

There were problems to begin with when the local townsfolk of Keswick saw the influx of these foreigners as an intrusion into their way of life. At that time, Keswick was no more than one muddy street with a few mean yards running off it. Still a town of mediaeval building, the houses were timber framed and thatched with burgage plots running behind them. Only important buildings such as the church and almost certainly the Moot Hall would have had slate roofs. Life was frugal, and basic rural industries were the only means of support in the area; the arrival of these able men from the Continent was a threat. The local girls however looked at things in a different light, and it was not long before some of them had selected partners and were indeed married.

After a while, it began to dawn on the local population that due to the setting up of the mining industry by these men, a considerable amount of paid work was available, and before long all was running smoothly. Work began initially by the shores of Derwentwater, but our story is of Newlands Valley and the Derwent Fells.

Top: The Arms of the Company of Mines Royal, granted 26th. of August 1568.
Bottom: The Arms of the Society of Mineral and Battery Works, 1568.

Similar type wheel was pumping lower workings at St. George Shaft, 16th. C. De Re Metallica, Georgius Agricola.

Top: Ambrosius Hechstetter c1529, father of Daniel Hechstetter who brought the first German miners to Keswick in 1564.
Bottom: Cottages at Bridge House, Keswick 1890, pulled down many years ago. In the left hand one was discovered a private chapel complete with black oak altar, inscribed with the name Daniel Hechstetter. M. Birbeck.

*Top: Moot Hall, Keswick used by the Germans to store copper 16th. C. Clarke.
Bottom: Crosthwaite Church, Keswick where some of the Hechstetters are buried.
J. Clark*

Small Mines and Trials in Newlands Valley

Littletown Mine

This is a small German open working on an eastern extension of the Goldscope E/W copper vein and has been driven on the exposed vein on the north western shoulder of Maiden Moor. Two workings have actually been made, a surface trial around 20ft. below the main working and a more serious effort above, which was worked around 1569. A considerable amount of vein material has been taken and the open cut is approximately 35yds. long, at least 20ft. deep, and around 4ft. wide along its length. Here can clearly be seen the hand-chip marks in what is thought to be the forehead, although it is possible that in the sole of the working there could be a level where the vein has continued at depth. Due to the trial now being filled with alluvial debris over almost its entire length, it is nigh on impossible to establish the total extent of the working.

Situated in the same crag and a few yards to the north, there appears to be a series of trials in the base of the crag and the vein has also been tried on a parallel stringer. Here also is a series of stemple holes cut into the crag - perhaps they were for supports, or for a small hut.

Directly below the workings are two flat cleared areas of ground, the higher of which is the larger and a good track leads directly to it from the main mine road which serviced the Newlands Valley and Goldscope Mine; from this area a trod leads straight to the openwork. The lower area is half the size of the higher one and both appear to have been for wooden buildings, possibly stores or a bothy.

Parrock Gill Trials

Two small surface trials on the eastern side of the Newlands Valley have been made on the vein which has been exposed by Parrock Gill. Here the early prospectors have diverted the stream from its original course, to allow the work to continue without the hindrance of water in the beck. Production here would have been minimal and no details can be found as to who worked the venture. The trials are not easy to spot as they are completely overgrown, particularly during the summer months when the bracken is high..

Barnes Gill Trials

On the far side of the Newlands Valley, virtually opposite the Goldscope Grand Level, is a single trial level for lead, a crosscut to a N/S lead-bearing vein on the eastern flank of Maiden Moor. The trial was commenced around 1872 and was later inspected, on the 30th. of December 1873, by Mr. Davison, of Goldscope Mine and a visiting mining engineer who made a report on the mine. One would surmise that his expertise lay in the field of coal mining as all his terminology relates to the industry, his report peppered with words such as overman, drift, slide etc. His report reveals that the crosscut had been driven 80yds. where it had intersected the vein and here headings had been driven north and south. The north had been driven 12yds. and after a promising start had intersected a fault which was producing a great deal of water. There were 6 men working in the southern drive which was also in 12yds. and had just 16yds. to go before it would intersect a promising copper vein seen on the surface. It appears the venture did not extend beyond these efforts.

The last record is that of two men clearing out the level in 1920, but no further work was done and certainly no ore was removed by these men. During the vicious storms of January 2005, the power of Barnes Gill became very evident when a huge deluge literally ripped out the side of the fell taking part of the dump with it.

Near Broad Gill Trial & St. Thomas Work

It has been accepted for a long time that the St. Thomas work refers to the two openwork sites, above and south east of Castlenook lead mine. On Thomas Robinson's map of the Newlands Valley workings, however, we find that it is this working which is the St.Thomas work.

Four hundred yards south of Castlenook Mine lies one of the largest gullies on the western shoulder of Maiden Moor; this is Near Broad Gill and for millions of years it has discharged thousands of tons of scree and alluvial debris down the fell, its waters crashing through the crags, spewing spoil and rubbish across the valley floor. It is precisely this action which allowed the earliest adventurers to see the exposed N/S veins which carry lead and mispickell.

The first miners to try this area are confirmed as being the Germans, by the records of Thomas Robinson, who held the lease in 1698, and it is in his records that we find the proof that some of these workings are earlier than originally thought. The positions of the workings are clearly marked on his plan dated 1698, one of them being listed as St. Thomas Work. A German working of 1566, he describes it as follows, "Water filled much work wrought hard and narrow all filled, below the Old Men have cut about 4 fathoms in rock to let out the water".

The German miners first of all attacked the vein by a series of surface pits and open works directly on the back of the vein, and nearby, to the south and slightly lower, are to be found more surface pits and trials. Whether or not these workings were further tried by Thomas Robinson whilst he was operating the sett is unclear.

It seems that the next period of working was by the adventurers of the period of 1830 to 1850 when, on either side of the gill, workings have been made. On the southern side, a substantial 6ft. square shaft has been sunk to a depth of around 35ft. (this is now choked) while to the north of the gill and below the early St. Thomas Work, another shaft has been sunk to around 20ft. (again choked). Both these shafts have certainly proved the vein to a good depth, and it seems at the time this work was done, the adventurers were satisfied with what they recovered from the workings, only probably being defeated finally by water.

The large spoil heap around 60ft. below the above workings is the result of a crosscut level being driven around the 1860's, and its purpose was to de-water the two, now flooded, surface shafts. Certainly these adventurers would not have missed the mineralization on the dumps, and probably thought a quick killing was possible. The mine adit was secured by a timber entrance and after about 10yds. the level hit bedrock; the drive went forward virtually due east for around 70yds. and here a short level was driven to de-water the northern shaft. The level was then driven south, but in so doing hit the old Thomas lead vein and here, the miners followed a strong quartz vein for around 20yds. but no mineral of any note was discovered. The drive continued for another 35yds. where the men holed out into the southern shaft, but no mineralization of any worth was encountered. The level continued for a further 28yds. or so in the vein, but nothing of any value was found. The level was cut to a good size, around 6ft. 6ins. high and 5ft. wide and it appears that it was also railed out, indicating that the miners were expecting a good strike; overall the level was driven a total of around 180yds.

In about 1920, two adventurers were reported to have re-opened the workings but this was more of an exploratory venture and no commercial mining took place.

Today

Over the past year we have looked very closely at this site and the records available, and we are satisfied that this is the correct site for the location of St. Thomas Work. The huge spoil heap cannot be missed by walkers as they plod up the valley but this is a site of which little is known by either mines historian or explorer. We know that Newlands Valley was a place of work for hundreds of years and for many miners, but where did they live? Here, directly below these workings, is one possibility, the stout remaining dwelling of the Carlisle Mountaineering Club hut and this building, now recently renovated and re-roofed, would have been an ideal dwelling for our early adventurers. Only a few years ago a substantial growth of mature trees was cut down from the southern side which had protected the dwelling for many years. It is also a fact that man is a creature of habit, and tends to build his houses on old foundations, if convenient.

Castlenook Mine

The mine is to be found on a bluff of rock which protrudes from the western flank of Maiden Moor and here, an E/W vein known as the West Castlenook Lode is clearly exposed in the crag face from which the mine has taken its name. To the south, behind the bluff of the crag, is much evidence of trenching and crude trials made on the back of the vein where it had been tried by the German miners. Again we must thank Thomas Robinson, who clearly records these workings as already being established by 1698. Thomas himself did not show any interest in the working during his tenure although he does state that mineralization was evident.

It is known that a lease was held from the 5th of August 1835 by Isaac Sealby, John Reed and John Tebay at a royalty of 1/8th. but as to their efforts here, nothing is known. These were all experienced men and it is hard to think they would have totally ignored this sett and the possibility of making a good trial.

It was 14 years later when adventurers Richard David Holland and George John May took a 21 year lease on Goldscope Mine on the 25th. of December 1859, and the following year they decided to investigate and open up the old workings at Castlenook. A considerable amount of work was done, at least four men were kept in employment, and by the end of the year the miners had driven a 62yd. crosscut level which intersected the lead vein. The vein now proved, the men were engaged in sinking a shaft, and once down to a depth of 10fms., a level was driven out in the vein 8yds. proving the lode with lead ore in the forehead worth 15cwt. per fathom. In the first few months, four tons of lead ore were raised valued at £13 per ton; work went well and a further 10 tons of ore were raised valued at £118 10s. 0d.

The vein had indeed proved better at depth than on surface, and plans were soon afoot to extend the workings, so from the sole of the shaft a level was driven 76yds. south in the 10fms. Level and 20fms. 64yds. north in the vein. The internal jack-roll used for pumping and hauling was totally inadequate, so the workforce was increased to eighteen men and the shaft was taken the 30ft. to the surface. Huge wooden timbers were brought up the valley to support the new 16ft. waterwheel which would be used for pumping, and leats were constructed to it, the longest of these bringing water 400yds. from Newlands Beck just below the Longwork, to the south. Other leats were constructed to feed the dressing floor by means of a sluice off the main leat, the beck being at a lower horizon than the dressing floor. The new hand-dressing floor was a relatively simple affair with crude hand jiggs and slimes ponds to ensure the beck was not soiled; up to now 30 tons of ore had been processed.

With the wheel now operating, the pumps kept the workings dry and further headings were driven giving the adventurers a modicum of success, 55 tons of lead ore being produced to the value of £620. By 1863 it is thought a further 30 tons of ore were raised, and it was during this year that this company ceased its mining venture at Castlenook.

In 1917, the Heywood partnership looked at the old working and decided to make a further trial high up in the crag at OD1200ft., near to the junction of where the NE/SW Castlenook vein could intersect the N/S vein, which had already been tried at Broad Gill and other places. The trial was pursued and driven on both headings, initially south, then due east as a crosscut to the N/S vein. A total of 42yds. of level were driven but certainly no riches were found. Undeterred by their failure, the miners made a further trial just 40yds. to the north and at roughly 50ft. higher. The miners worked in the black rock directly into a good showing of quartz for a distance of 27yds., but at this point the adventurers gave up and no further work was done and no ore was raised.

Dalehead Mine

Dalehead Mountain towers at OD2473ft. and lies directly across the southern end of the Newlands Valley, in fact its summit cairn can be seen from Littletown Church some 3 miles away. Directly beneath the summit of this famous mountain lies a series of workings on a NE/SW copper vein. These consist of at least three adit workings, and on the back of the vein, a series of early surface works can be traced right across the broken and shattered northern face of Dalehead mountain.

Below the plateau, at OD1750ft., are the earliest workings of the sett which are on the back of an E/W vein referred to in early papers as the "Gluton Vein" and here, at least two openworks have been made by the German miners c1570. This vein, if traced east, is cut by the higher reaches of Newlands Beck. but no workings appear at this point.

In around 1680, picking up where the German miners had left off 100 years before, mining entrepreneur David Davies leased the area from the Duke of Somerset, but it is unclear as to whether or not he actually prospected here. He was a man of considerable skills, and it is more than likely his other commitments in the valley occupied his time.

Ten years or so later, around 1690, the Rev. Thomas Robinson of Ousby had acquired the lease and was investigating the possibilities of reworking the copper vein, which was referred to as the "black copper vein", hading NE/SW. The vein is bright with malachite and chrysocolla but the copper ore here is bornite, which tends to be very dark and does not appear a gold/yellow as one would expect. However, Thomas turned his attentions to the lower workings of Longwork where he thought his trials would be more rewarding.

Over 100 years were to pass before the next company of workmen was recorded as operating here in June 1805, when William Evells Sheffield of St. Pancras, London who was employed as the mineral agent of the Duke of Devonshire, took up a 30 year lease from Lord Egremont. His agent was Mr. John Bennett of Manesty. Production of around 150 tons a year was achieved and it is recorded that they in fact constructed their own smelt mill (1806-1809) to deal with it. Unfortunately its exact location is unknown although they may well have been the last occupants of the old Newlands Smelter, the site of which is a mile to the south.

It is to this company that all the levels and underground work must be attributed, and also the development of the sled and pony routes. The company was working hard and enjoying success for, after all, they had prospected skillfully and found a strike which the German miners had missed, as had David Davies followed by Thomas Robinson.

The success of this venture however, was to be marred by a tragedy which occurred on Saturday, the 25th. of February 1810 when John Bennett was returning home to Manesty accompanied by a friend, from the market in Keswick; it was about 8 o'clock in the evening and dark and to reach his home he had to cross the River Derwent at Grange Bridge. On this Saturday night the river was in full spate, the road was covered with brown, swirling water and the bridge was in an appalling state of repair, having no parapet. Undeterred, John told his friend that he would go first as he was mounted, and he started across the bridge. He had nearly made the far side when his horse stumbled and poor John was thrown instantly into the fast moving water and was swept downstream, his cries for help lost in the howling of the wind and the din of the rushing torrent. His friend commenced his journey across the bridge unaware of the tragedy which had just taken place in the blackness of the night, arriving at the far side unharmed. He went to look for John but found only his horse wandering thirty yards downstream, so the alarm was raised; John Bennett's lifeless body was discovered the following day on the riverside, his watch still ticking in his pocket! A verdict of Accidental Death was recorded at the inquest which was held locally before the Coroner Robert Benson on the 27th of February. John Bennett's untimely death left his pregnant wife widowed and two small children fatherless.

In June 1818, John Barker inspected the workings and another miner in the employ of the Newlands Mining Company had, by this time, driven 3 levels into the near vertical face of Dalehead Mountain. During November 1819, a letter was sent to the office of Lord Egremont cancelling the lease and this was re-assigned to Messrs. John Tebay, Isaac Sealby and John Reed, and they continued to work the mine along with Brandlehow and Brandley Mines. The royalty payment was 1/8th., however, although ore was being removed, they were in financial difficulties and the rents for 1831 of £26. 6s. 0d. and for 1832 of £7. 17s. 0d., were in arrears. The company's attentions were now obviously being directed elsewhere and consequently the operation closed in 1833.

Over the past 28 years the northern breast of Dalehead Mountain, with its commanding view of the Newlands Valley, had been transformed into a complete industrial landscape. A substantial bothy had been built on a small plateau at OD1750ft. for the use of the miners and this was a lonely outpost, the nearest farm or habitation being a good 3 miles away. The climb was in the region of 1,300ft., which would be impractical to walk in winter months or in bad weather, and consequently the bothy was a good, solid building. It was 17ft. long and 16ft. wide complete with slate roof, and walls 2ft. thick, and had at least two rooms and a fireplace; with plenty of local peat and heather nearby to supplement the coal, the men would be warm and cosy in inclement weather. Attached to the southern end of the bothy was the smithy which measured 12ft. x 11ft. and outside this was a large stone on which the blacksmith tested his steels. There was another building nearby, 6ft. x 6ft. which was possibly the ore store and directly below this was the ore washing and dressing floor. This was a large, tapering, angled paved area 16ft. long, 15ft. wide at the top and 13ft. wide at the bucking end. Water for this essential job was channelled from an underground spring and all dressing here was done by hand-bucking, no luxury of waterwheels and stamps here. To access the plateau area and bothy from the valley, an engineered road was constructed for the transportation of both mined ore leaving for the smelter, and essential tools and chattels being brought in from Keswick, 10 miles away - a day's journey in those times. The steep zig-zags above Far Tongue Gill have been duplicated, so that sleds or pack mules could pass one another unhindered, but the fords and bridges across the Newlands Beck and Far Tongue Gill have now been swept away and lost in the mists of time.

The lowest of the three levels is the No. 1 at OD2040ft. and was almost surely the first to be driven; this was the easiest to locate, the vein being exposed directly in the vertical rock face, and the level driven directly in on the exposure. It was accessed by a precarious engineered trod from just above the bothy across the face of the fell, and in wooden clogs and high winds this would not have been a journey to work one would have taken lightly ... one slip would almost surely bring death or severe injury. The adit is cut in solid rock and emits a vast quantity of water, being the drainage level for the two higher workings. The No. 1 is driven to a good size, over 6ft. high and around 3ft. 9ins. wide, and it follows the twisting and meandering vein. This must have made life difficult for the miners when they railed the level out using elm wood with iron strips on top to prevent wear. The level branches after about 80yds. to the connecting rise to the No. 2 Level, and the main drive then carries on for at least another 130yds. on a S/W heading. All the spoil and development material has been discarded straight down the front of the crag hundreds of feet below, its dispersal ensured by the cascade which continues for most of the year. The removal of ore from here must have been difficult, for the trod is narrow, unsuitable for barrows or tubs and ore must have been raised through the rise or carried out in leather bags to the dressing floor a ¼ mile away.

The No. 2 Level is around 60ft. above and the miners have laid a good road from the bothy plateau to the entrance of the level, where a substantial working area has been made from the development material. The entrance to the working is protected by a heavily timbered bunning section, and the miners here would have experienced serious problems in driving forward through yards of alluvial scree to find solid ground. Once into the bedrock, the miners commenced driving the level which they cut to a good size, larger than the No. 1, being over 6ft. 3ins. high and 4ft. wide and again it has been railed out. The level is driven virtually dead straight on a S/W heading and numerous trials have been made on stringers by the old men in an effort to find the lode, which does not appear as strong here. Undeterred, the miners have pushed the working on, and at around 140yds. a stope has been commenced in the roof and a few yards further on, a vertical connecting rise has been put up to the No. 3 Level, 60ft. above. It is at this point that it seems that the miners have encountered the orebody. On the left hand wall, a parallel level has been driven back 32yds. towards day and at the end of this drive, connection has been made down to the No. 1 Level (this is now choked). From this point the level continues on a virtually straight heading for around another 260yds. and appears to be totally barren. This drivage alone was a substantial commitment and must have taken at least five years to achieve, but to what end? After the rise to No. 3, the host rock changes and there is no sign of any mineralization.

The No. 3 Level lies at OD2160ft., the portal of which again was driven through oceans of scree which must have been a nightmare for the hard pressed miners, working on the exposed face just 300ft. under the summit of Dalehead. The level entrance (now totally run in) was made from huge stone blocks and was driven on the same S/W heading and extends 80yds., but again this is totally barren.

Interest in the mine after this venture was basically nil, and although small amounts of ore are recorded these were minimal. A further Take-note was issued in June 1845 to J. Dixon at a royalty of 1/12th. but this venture seems to have failed and another Take-note was issued in November 1847 to Messrs. W. Clemence, W. Clemence Jnr. and J. Floyd at a royalty of 1/15th. The final lease was in November 1848 to Messrs. Andrew Clarke, C. N. P. Chapman, G. W. Horn and T. Hart. Again a royalty of 1/15th. was required for both lead and copper raised, but the main interest seemed to lie in Goldscope and not Dalehead Mine which was by now totally worked out.

Dalehead Mine is passed by walkers almost every day of the year, on their way to the summit by a route up the old engineered trod, oblivious to the back-breaking work which went into the making of it. Beneath their well-shod feet lies the work of men who walked day after day the 4 miles into work in clogs, hessian and wool jackets, moleskin trousers and flat hats to ward off the weather; these hardy men worked by the dim light of tallow to create half a mile of tunnels. This is possibly one of the most evocative mines in the Lakes ... the view from the No. 1 Level down the Newlands Valley is one never to be forgotten ....and these old timers saw it every day of their working lives!

Littletown Mine, 16th. C. working, Newlands Valley. Ian Tyler Collection.

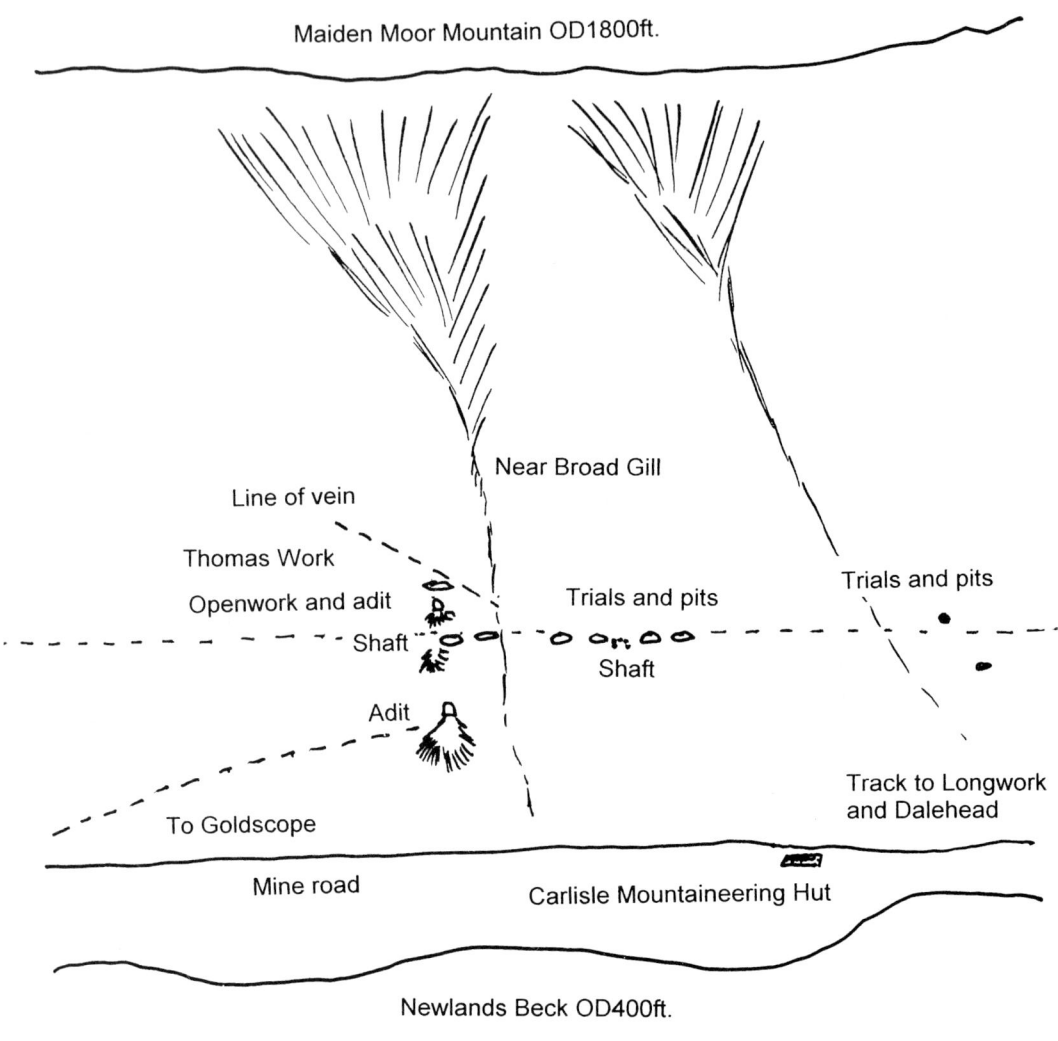

Mine sett near Broad Gill. Drawn by Ian Tyler.

Near Broad Gill. Stuart Clement Collection.

Hand-chipped 16th. C. working on Goldscope vein overlooking Yewthwaite Mine. Ian Tyler Collection.

Top: Newlands Church, Newlands Valley c1600. Stuart Clement Collection.
Bottom: Sportsman's Inn, landlord Mr. Lowden, manager at Goldscope Mine c1840 . Abrahams

*Top: Dalehead Mine dressing floor and mine shop. Stuart Clement Collection.
Bottom: Dalehead Mine and miners' track on the front of Dalehead. Courtesy of Peter Stanier.*

No. 1 Adit in crag face, Dalehead Mine. Stuart Clement Collection.

No. 1 Adit, Dalehead Mine - note wooden rails in situ c1840. Ian Tyler Collection.

The 16th. C. Pluckhor openwork. Ian Hebson Collection.

Longwork Mine sett looking west from High Spy. Stuart Clement Collection.

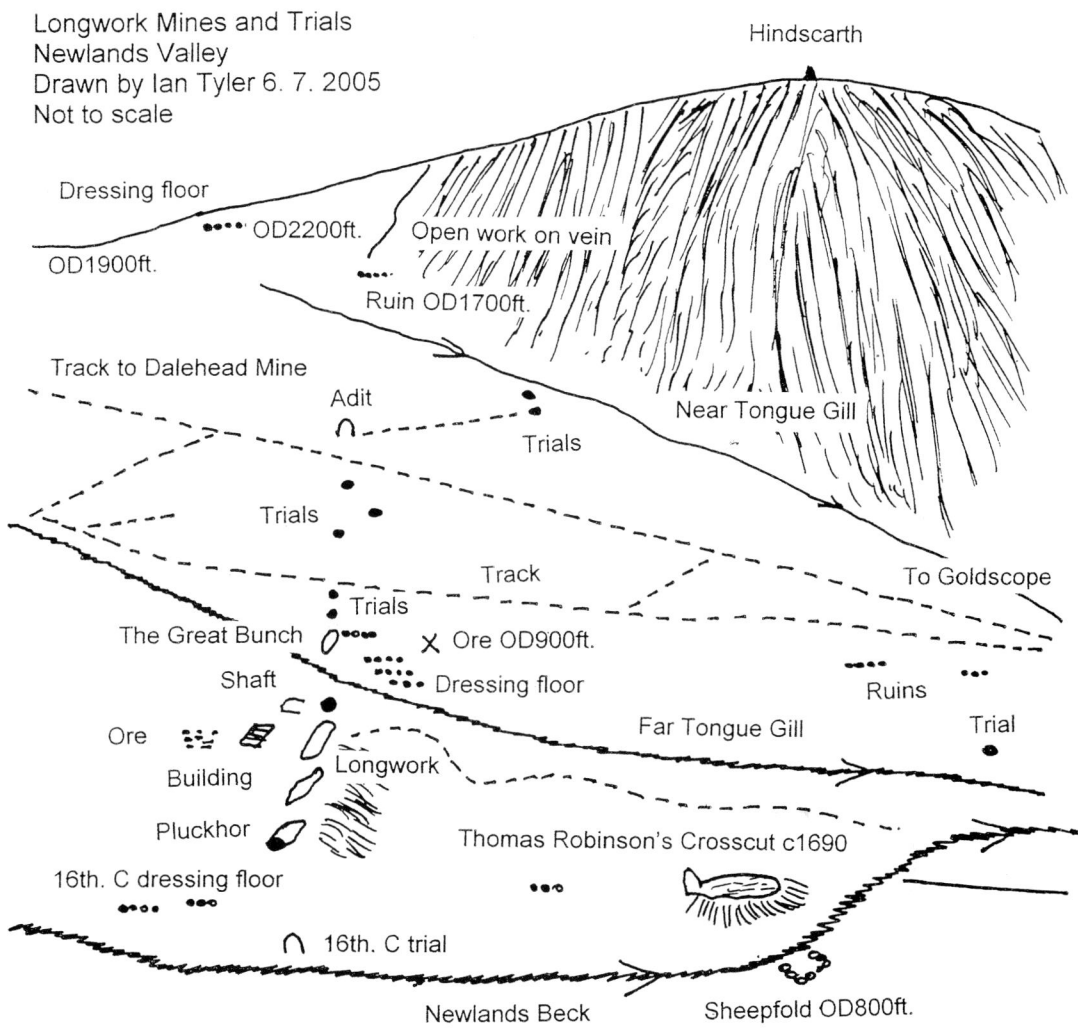

Longwork Mine and Trials. Drawn by Ian Tyler.

Bucking stones on 16th. C. dressing floor at Longwork. Ian Tyler Collection.

Longwork, 16th. C. openwork. Ian Tyler Collection.

Longwork, the Great Bunch, a 16th. C. working on the back of the copper vein. Ian Hebson Collection.

Top: Longwork, compacted copper mound near the Great Bunch dressing Floor. Ian Tyler Collection.
Bottom: Longwork, 16th. C. work and c1690 crosscut by Thomas Robinson. Ian Tyler Collection.

Longwork, crosscut driven by Thomas Robinson 1690 and copper stope c1910. Ian Hebson Collection.

Longwork, crosscut - rise driven beneath to de-water Longwork in 1920. Ian Hebson Collection.

Top: Miner Thomas Barnes of Braithwaite looking towards the head of Newlands and the possible re-opening of Longwork.
Bottom: Looking north to Castlenook and Goldscope from ancient house on Dalehead. Stuart Clement Collection.

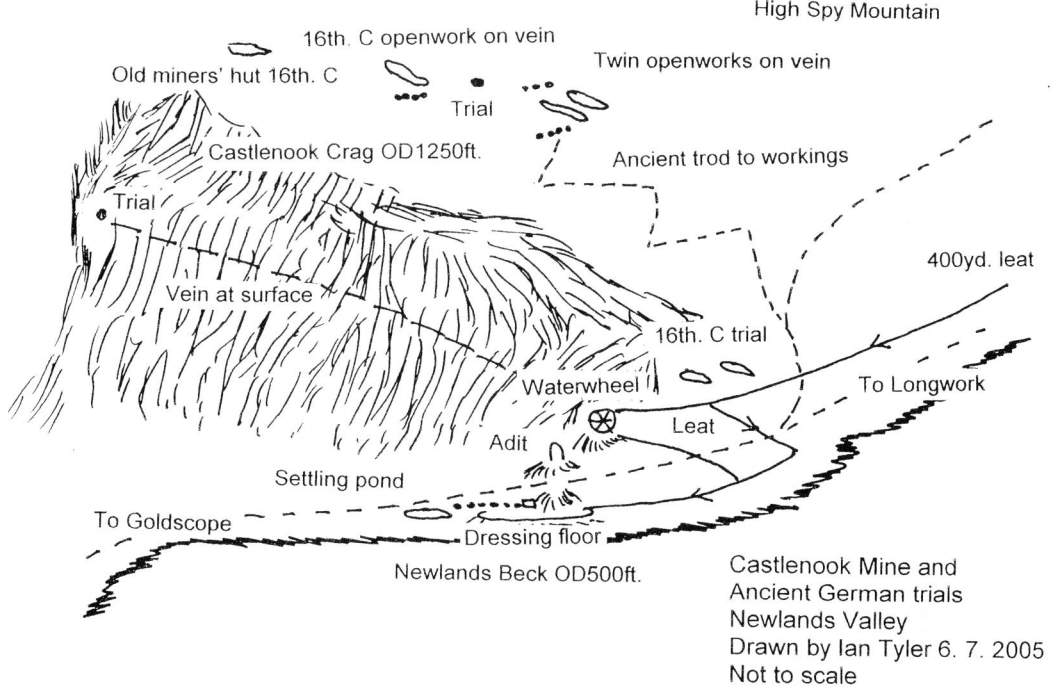

Top: Castlenook Mine sett. Drawn by Ian Tyler Collection.
Bottom: Castlenook Mine sett. Ian Tyler Collection.

Site of Castlenook Mine shaft and wheelpit area. Ian Tyler Collection.

Top: Remains of old 16th. C. German house on ridge of Castle Crag near old workings. Stuart Clement Collection.
Bottom: Openwork on copper vein near house, sometimes referred to as Thomas Work. Ian Tyler Collection.

Two Trials on High Spy

These are the trials which, in the past, have generally been referred to as the St. Thomas Work. The workings are to be found high up on the western flank of High Spy, a few hundred yards north east of the Longwork sett but hundreds of feet higher. The first is at OD1000ft. up the sheer steep mountain side, and was accessed by a steep zig-zag track. The working here, under the looming crags of High Spy, consists of two large openworks which are parallel, having worked two separate veins about 30ft. apart. In the right hand vein the miners have picked their way forward, and eventually they have advanced far enough to be underground, where they have commenced a shaft in the sole of the level; the hand worked level continues another few yards to a forehead. In both cases the full width of the vein has been taken out on its exposure, forming two large slits in the rock and both workings were done in about 1565. These are more than speculative trials and would have taken years rather than months; it is more than likely that in the forehead of the northern slit, a level has been driven to pursue the vein further, On a small plateau above is what could be the remains of a small stone hut, and across the entrance of the working a substantial dressing floor area has been constructed.

From these workings the track continues up the fell to where the Old Men have tried another section of the vein exposed in the open crag, but this is no more than a trial. Still higher, and directly on the vein, the German miners have worked a considerable open cut to a depth of around 30ft. and again, a proper dressing floor has been constructed directly in front of the works. These are the highest works and are at around OD1300ft. Higher still on the exposed summit shoulder of Castlenook at OD 1500ft. are the remains of some ruined buildings, where a buttress of rock has been used to create the back wall; the side walls extend 12ft. and are 3ft. thick and the front wall is 16ft. long. This building is more than likely one of the remains of the early German settlers' dwellings, although we do not know how long they operated this site, and it was 127 years before the workings were revisited. Thomas Robinson raised 1 ton of ore from here in March 1692. By his plan of the area, this site is not the St. Thomas Work, as it has been traditionally referred to. As previously mentioned this may be ½ mile north further down the valley at Near Broad Gill.

Longwork

It soon became obvious that trying to distinguish the various dates of the numerous workings in the Newlands Valley would prove difficult, in fact almost impossible, the reason being that the original workings are referred to collectively as the Newlands mines, with little individual identification. The valley of Newlands derives its name from the fact that Uzzicar Tarn, existing in Viking times, was drained thus creating "New Lands".

At the head of the valley and in the shadow of Dalehead mountain is to be found a whole series of mine workings of a great age, and the largest and possibly the oldest of these has become known as Longwork, although in fact this only refers to the middle section of the workings which span the valley floor. These workings are deep cuttings down on the back of the exposed vein, and cover a distance of nearly half a mile east to west across the valley .

To the east are Pluckhor and Longwork and further to the west a trial shaft, then the Great Bunch, all of which could have been originally worked in the 13th. Century, during the reign of Henry III. In my opinion, this vein was re-worked on subsequent visits from the German miners to Newlands probably in the 15th. Century, during the reign of Edward the IV. Certainly by the early 16th. Century, the copper and lead veins in Newlands were known and had in many cases been worked. Within a few years of the inception of the Mines Royal, many workings had been established, and in the records available we have numerous miners working but not identified with a particular place of work. For the sake of convenience, the production figures of the various mines in the early days were amalgamated, and it was not until a few years later that particular workings became individually recognized and recorded.

Certainly the discovery of the vein by the early German prospectors would have been relatively easy. The sheer force of Newlands Beck which cascades down from the plateau of Dalehead Tarn, hundreds of feet above the valley, has simply bared the rock and exposed the 5ft. quartz vein running E/W and its mineral content of chalcopyrite, revealing just what the adventurers had been searching for. Nearby on the sett are at least three other mineralized veins apart from the Longwork, all of which run parallel across the valley floor and all have been tried, some with more success than others.

In 1569, we find it recorded that nine German miners under Hans Haring, an experienced mine foreman, were dispatched to work the exposed vein which extends around 400yds. across the valley floor. The initial work would have been reasonably easy and the copper ore raised was cobbed by hand and sorted beside the Newlands Beck. Nearby and just to the south of the open work, a group of small huts was built for storage and protection against the elements, the foundations of which are still evident. Goldscope was literally only 40 minutes walk to the north where good accommodation and food would have been readily available; some miners lodged in local farmhouses of which there were several in the valley at this time. These farms would not only offer accommodation but also the land here had been cleared hundreds of years before by the Norsemen, whose settlement now provided some fertile agricultural land. Evidence of rigg and furrow working can still be seen in and around High Snab and Low House and these lands would no doubt provide some produce for sale to the new settlers.

The works were diligently pursued, but as they opened up along the back of the vein, problems began to present themselves. The raising of the ore from a depth of at least 40ft. could be easily overcome, and the miners could lift the ore in stout leather bags either by hand or jackroll. Water however, created its own problem and the hade of the vein was such that kibbles or buckets would spill the contents before arriving at the surface; a system of pumping by rag and chain or similar method would have to be employed by Hans Haring and his men. Over the period of working the miners had leap-frogged from one exposed section of the vein at surface to the next, leaving a rock barrier so as to prevent the working either side becoming flooded. Interestingly the actual hade of the vein provided some natural cover, and the creation of a drainage ledge in the foot wall prevented any casual water from entering the workings. The ore here was all hand dressed at three different dressing floors, and at the eastern end of the workings are the remains of the bucking stones and the leats taking water from the end working, Pluckhor, to wash the ore. It may well have been that Pluckhor was the original working and was later allowed to flood for use as a reservoir.

Foreman Hans Haring was still in charge of the working in 1573 and had as many as seventeen miners working, some of them engaged as pumpers for de-watering the working, which at the Pluckhor had reached a depth of nearly 20fms. These miners were being paid 3/- a week for their efforts and Hans was paid 10/-. Water of course, was a continual source of trouble to any mining venture and was costly to pump out but once clear of the mine, it would be channelled to the dressing floors for use in further processes. Ironically a shortage of water in mining was just as critical as too much, and the Germans had solved part of the problem by creating a dam and reservoir high up at the head of Far Tongue Gill. This would, in the dry season, conveniently provide water for the dressing floor beside the Great Bunch and the nearby shaft work; here, a considerably large boulder has been used as a bucking stone. Directly under the huge buttress Gable Crag, is what appears to be a further attempt to construct a reservoir and nearby, hidden in the jumble of rocks, is a very small ancient dwelling.... I wonder who built this?

As far as we can tell, these were the last recorded workings of the Mines Royal Company here, and it would be over a hundred years later when David Davies applied to the Duke of Somerset to work the mines of Newlands. It is not clear however, whether he actually worked the Longwork Vein or if he confined his efforts only to the area of Goldscope and Littledale Brow.

The next recorded prospecting was during 1690 by Thomas Robinson, the Vicar of Ousby. He was an amateur geologist with a keen interest in mining, and he arranged to lease the workings from the Duke of Somerset, taking the sett over from David Davies. Over the next two years he was engaged in exploring and crudely sketching the workings, and in some cases recording their extent. He confirmed that the first working, Pluckhor open work, was down to a depth of 20fms.; the next working, Longwork, was flooded and this was pumped clear of water proving the depth of the workings to be 70ft. Further exploration however, was hindered by debris and as a result, the sole of the workings and foreheads or the extent of the underground workings were not seen. In an effort to establish any remaining copper reserves, Thomas Robinson, decided to drive a crosscut adit which, on connection to the sole of Longwork, would provide permanent drainage and a simple means of bringing the ore out to day. The adit commenced from beside the Newlands Beck and was driven along a fault a distance of 50yds. at which point the work was halted, although this was not even half way to cutting into the bottom of the Longwork stope. Thomas reckoned that it would cost around £300 to complete the work, and there were richer and easier pickings in the area.

The next working along the vein westwards was the shaft work which, as far as we know, has no name but judging by the amount of spoil, it has been sunk to a reasonable depth. It would have been ideal to extend from the sole eastwards back to Longwork and west into the Great Bunch to prove the vein at depth, and make an underground connection. The Great Bunch was commenced on steeply rising ground beside Far Tongue Gill, and here the German miners had worked the vein by means of a level and sunk down deep in the sole. The vein was pursued west and further deep surface excavations were made; certainly good ore was found here by the Germans over their tenure, and they had also created a substantial tiered dressing and washing floor on the western bank of Far Tongue Gill, just below the workings. To prove the vein further west there is a series of shallow workings up the hillside, but these appear to have been unproductive.

Further north by 300yds., another vein running parallel to Longwork has been tried by the German miners and subsequently by Thomas Robinson where, just to the east of Newlands Beck, a small shaft has been sunk and some ore raised. Nearby, in the lee of a large rock, a building has been constructed and there are also the remains of a smaller hut. The exploration of this vein continues up the steep fellside, where a series of opencut trials can be seen at 1,300ft. and crossing Near Tongue Gill, the vein continues up the southern shoulder of Hindscarth where, at the base of the crags, is a small ruined building. From here the vein continues up in steep, broken rock for around 400ft. to the summit ridge. Clean ore can be seen still in situ and there are hand drilled holes in evidence. The adventurers have created a hand-cobbing floor at around 2,100ft. beside the summit ridge; this working could be the one referred to by Thomas Robinson as Littledale Crag. It is perhaps the most precarious site we have discovered and is not for the faint hearted!

Thomas Robinson was not a mining engineer and having neither the knowledge and skill of his predecessors, it wasn't long before he ran into monetary trouble as a result of which, his venture was to collapse. Thomas however, was not a quitter as we shall later see.

Further interest was shown in the workings by Thomas Ackersley in 1713 when he proposed taking on a 21 year lease with the Duke of Somerset. The lease, however, included Goldscope, which was not producing as he had envisaged, and he asked that the rent and royalties be waived in lieu of a percentage of the profits from ore sold. This apparently did not suit the Duke and the venture came to an end

The works, after many years of idleness were taken on in 1910 by J. Burns on a Take-note for 1 year at a rent of £5 and a royalty of 1/20th. After further investigation, he took a 21 year lease on the sett which still included Goldscope, and in 1912, the rent was £20 on the first year and £50 the second and subject to a royalty of 1/30th. which was in his favour. Possibly because of the intervening hostilities in Europe, this venture collapsed.

The next interest was shown in 1919 at the end of the Great War, by Mr. Bennett Johns of Keswick and W. H. Heywood who began by de-watering the Longwork, which entailed continuing the old crosscut driven by Thomas Robinson all those years before. The work commenced by hand drilling forward in the traditional manner, the muck being cleared by wheelbarrow. On cutting the Longwork vein, the miners passed through the copper lode and followed a barren stringer due south, but why this was done is a complete mystery. They then returned to the main E/W vein, which at this point is directly underneath the flooded German workings. The men commenced to rise hard in the vein and brought down a considerable amount of copper-bearing ore, which was removed by wheelbarrow out to the dump. After rising 20ft., they drove a short way south and again started to rise; all this work was done by hand drilling and using gelignite explosive. Eventually the second rise was up around 25ft. and from here a final charge was set off. Much to the consternation of the miners, this blew out the bottom of the flooded stope above and the thousands of gallons of stored water cascaded all around them, but at last they would see if the Germans had left them the dreamed of riches. Alas, on inspection of the stopes it appears there was little ore to be seen but one artifact remained: a hollowed out log, presumably one of the pumps from either the German or Thomas Robinson eras, but this was never recovered.

A further trial was made at OD1250ft. above the Great Bunch just above the track to Dalehead Mine, where the miners have driven a level directly on the higher reaches of the vein. This was cut to a good size and a small amount of chalcopyrite was encountered, but not enough to pursue the venture further. The level was driven in the vein for a distance of 115yds. to a height of 6ft. by 4ft. wide, and a small, stone hut for tools was constructed outside. Despite their enthusiasm however, financially stretched and with their operations at Glenderaterra failing, the company was wound up and no further work was done.

Mining engineer Bill Shaw of Chestnut Hill, Keswick naturally knew of all the local workable deposits of ore and was aware of the previous company's efforts at Longwork. He had mulled over the idea of trying to re-open the mine just after the last war, but this did not come to fruition. A survey done by Mr. Thomas Barnes, the last surviving miner of those working at Longwork when it closed in 1922, revealed that from every 100 tons of copper-bearing ore, 4 tons of pure copper could be obtained. In the 1960s, the price of copper was £450 per ton, and this was to attract the attention of a Canadian consortium based in Toronto. It was anticipated the company would employ around 50 men and Bill. Shaw was handling the project locally. However, the Development and Control Committee of the Lake District Planning Board turned down the request saying it would spoil the valley. The Derwent Parish Council strongly recommended that the mine go ahead as there was already a 400 year old tradition of mining in this valley, and it would be worth it to produce the 50 jobs. Unfortunately, the Planning Board could not be swayed and the project was stopped before it started.

The Eastern Valley of High Snab Bank

Littledale is the valley on the western side of Hindscarth mountain wherein lies Goldscope Mine, cutting through the lower part of the mountain, Scope End, between Newlands and Littledale. On the western shoulder of Hindscarth are Littledale Crags, from which the upper part of the valley has taken its name, and opposite is Robinson mountain and the continuation north is High Snab Bank.

These fells and crags form the Littledale Valley through which flows Scope Beck. Both sides of the valley have been extensively mined by the Old men and Scope Beck was to be an essential source of water power for the mines for nearly 300 years. In the valley bottom are two substantial tracks which come from the direction of Low High Snab Farm. The slightly higher one leads directly to the mine, the other is an old pony route and continues beyond the site of the dam. This ancient trod is still discernible, leading up the steep-sided gorge between Robinson Ridge and Littledale Crags. Besides being the direct route to Buttermere for travellers and peddlers, it would also have served to draw peat from the head of the valley for local usage and also for the sledding of stone for the building of the dam by the Old Men.

On the western side of the valley there are at least three veins coursing through the shoulder of High Snab Bank, most of these appear to be NW/SE bearing and are for lead. Again we are indebted to Thomas Robinson for the records and plans he drew up during his tenure of the mines in 1698, when he took the time to record and map the area. In some cases he was also able to investigate underground and had access to some of the original Hechstetter papers. This source of information has allowed us to prove earlier dates for some of these ancient workings than were previously known.

The earliest workings here were certainly pre-gunpowder and excavated by the German miners prior to 1600, where they have followed what appears to be the largest of the veins on the eastern flank of the hill, up onto the summit ridge. Here, at OD1300ft., a substantial hand-chipped opencut working has been made along the back of the exposed lead vein. The ground cover at this point is very thin and the vein would have been easily spotted by the German prospectors in the rock outcrops. This visual situation however does not continue on the western side of the High Snab Bank ridge, where the peaty ground cover increases dramatically, and the miners have prospected here with trenches and pits for at least 150yds. in a north westerly direction, but found little to justify a proper working.

Just below the workings, on the summit ridge at OD1200ft., the German miners have chipped their way forward on an E/W heading in an attempt to cut the vein at depth. In this lofty and exposed outpost they have driven a distance of around 18yds. and near the forehead, they have sunk down on a pocket of ore. It appears the sole of the level has been understoped over some of its length.

Beneath this, at OD1050ft., is a series of pits and a substantial opencut working, again on the back of the vein; these extend around 40yds. on possibly the same lead vein as are the higher workings. It is more than likely that these are the early trials of David Davies in the 1680s. Unfortunately the side of the fell here is very steep, and loose rock has filled most of these workings in, but judging by the amount of spoil along the length of the vein, it is evident that some lead ore was raised. At the southern end of this working are the remains of two bothies and a dressing floor; there is another little building in the lea of a small crag, and just above is another surface trial. All these workings are confirmed by Robinson, who states they were first opened up by the Old Men and later re-worked by David Davies. After this first opened up by the Old Men and later re-worked by David Davies. After this period, some further activity was reported, stating that mining was continuing, but no production or other information was revealed.

The efforts of the Old Men had not gone unnoticed by adventurers of around 1850, when a trial crosscut was driven at around OD950ft., beneath the above mentioned surface trials. The drive intersected the vein after around 20yds., then continued north, however the extent of these headings cannot be established as the ground is fallen in, presumably from the old open stope workings above. The amount of the spoil would indicate a drivage of 100yds. or so and the initial drive is of a reasonable size, but further in the level reduces considerably in size inferring the level could have been widened by this last company. Below this point and near the track is a small bothy and hand-cobbing floor which was used for ore sampling, and to the south another surface trial has been made on the eastern side of the beck.

Littledale Crag and Scope End Workings

The Littledale Valley has been worked for lead and copper on both sides of the valley over many years. The German miners have prospected numerous veins on the western flank of Hindscarth mountain in the region of Littledale Crags which are about a half mile south of the main Goldscope Mine. The vein structure on this side of the valley is somewhat complex and it is thought that at least 4 veins have been tried. One of these is the Goldscope lead vein which runs nearly N/S and according to later plans, it is confirmed that south of the main Goldscope workings two parallel veins/stringers run off obliquely SE/NW. Another vein further south is to be seen coursing NE/SW and the flashes of quartz would have been easily spotted by the early adventurers; the mineral content of this vein however is copper and it later became known as the Baker Vein.

The ground here is steep, bare, cold, hard rock and the rewards for the labours of the early miners were little. The early workings are openworks on the back of the vein although one or two short trials have been driven and are pre-gunpowder. Because these trials are quite numerous and some have been re-worked, the actual dating and naming of the sites by their original German names is impossible (see photographs and plans).

Again we are indebted to the papers of Thomas Robinson who clearly states the location of some of the works in his report of 1698. Starting at the most southerly workings, which are hidden high in the Littledale and High Crags at OD1500ft., is a small hand-chipped open work on a NE/SW vein and some pyrite material has been removed from here. There is a small dressing floor nearby and this working is certainly from the German period of c1600. This could well been have been re-worked by Thomas Robinsons's own employee, a man named Baker who was engaged to smelt ore for him during his tenure and for whom the vein he worked was named.

A few hundred yards further north, a lead vein (later named Sealby's Vein) coursing NW/SE across the flank of Scope End, has been worked over a

1680, and again later by Thomas Robinson himself. The extent of the workings continues for nearly 400yds. and can be traced right over the ridge of the fell and into Newlands Valley. The lowest working is at OD1400ft. where a level has been driven and a rise put up to surface. Following the exposure of the vein, another trial has been commenced about 50ft. higher in solid rock, but little ore appears to have been won here.

Higher still, the SE vein intersects a natural gully at its head at around 1,500ft. and a considerable amount of lead ore has been removed by the ancients from where the vein has been exposed in the face of the crag; here a small hand dressing floor has been established.

On closer inspection of this site it appears that the early miners have attempted to divert water in a "Y" shape, the water being funnelled from two points on the ridge and then allowed to cascade down towards the dressing floor area, thus scarring and baring the whole rock face below, as one would effectively hush a site. Above this point, on the southerly branch of the "Y", three further trials have been made still following the vein to the SE which eventually intersects the actual summit ridge at OD1550ft. The last two workings are to be found just over the ridge on the Newlands Valley side, and nearby are the remains of a small stone hut in the lea of a rock face. Where the northern branch of the "Y" reaches the ridge, another trial is to be found.

Just below the dressing floor, sited at OD1500ft. and slightly south, hidden in the crags is another group of hand-worked German trials, extending only a few yards but all appearing to be driven towards the NE/SW Baker Vein.

Near this working, at around OD1400ft. and to the north, is another vein bearing NE/SW and containing black sulphurous ore; this has been tried and is referred to by Thomas Robinson as the Gluton Vein. It was worked by David Davies during his years of tenure in and around 1680. The workings on the whole of this inhospitable and remote landscape would have tested the early prospectors' skills of detection as well as their mountaineering abilities.

Below the aforementioned workings and running virtually N/S is the Goldscope lead vein, worked to the north of the last working by a series of 5 ancient trials directly on the back of the vein, and which contour around the OD1100ft. horizon. All are hand-chipped and are certainly in the style of the early German masters. The most important of these and the most northerly, has been put down in the sole to a considerable depth, at least 30ft. It is this working which, years later, was driven towards by a crosscut level at OD1050ft. by David Davies in the 1680's in what is referred to as the Sand Vein. Directly above the openworks and in line with the Davies trial, is another short trial level at OD1250ft. This has been driven virtually due NW/SE and the extent of the level is no more than 20yds. It is not a hand-chipped level but is very small in its dimensions, which would indicate a working date of around the late 1800s, but who actually made the trial we are unable to say. Certainly no fortunes were made here. Directly above this point is a steep grass gully, and near its head is an exposed quartz vein which has been tried during the pre-gunpowder age. Below the leat from the dam, another crosscut trial has been made; this again is just a few yards and never intersected the vein and was worked by much later adventurers of c1840. In contrast to the previous trials, the Sealby lead trial was certainly the most sustained and rewarding effort which was to be made by the owners of the Goldscope sett in c1840, and was given its name for one of the investors. The level was started in a solid rock face at OD805ft. and a small bothy was built at the left of the portal for tools and storage. The level from the start was cut to a good size, being 6ft. high and 4ft. wide, and follows the lead vein as it twists and turns. The company had obviously intended to invest heavily here by taking the decision to rail the level with wood and iron strip rails. After about 60yds., the good sound rock gives way to poor sugary quartz, but here the actual mineralized lead vein became clearly visible, and it was at around 130yds. inbye that the first stoping was tried. Timbers straddle the level which enabled the Old Men to work the roof to a height of 20ft. and directly below, in the sole, a shallow shaft was sunk. Further inbye, more ground had been stoped and this must have given the men encouragement. Beyond this, two small stopes have been worked in the roof further along the level, and all along this section the rock is friable and the men must have found it easy to work. At around 280yds. inbye, the vein splits and the rock returns to solid and better ground and efforts were made on both branches. One was worked 16yds. east to a forehead and the southern drive was driven on to where the rock became even harder. The men pushed on, now in over 300yds., and here the stench of the tallow and sweating bodies in this confined space must have made for exhausting work. The final gunpowder charges were laid and fired, but the lead vein had disappeared from the face of dark, grey rock and all their efforts and toil had come to an end. All the elm rails laid to the face were removed, apart from the final few lengths, but the wedges and hammers and the remains of tallow candles in knobs of clay were left just where they were, when extinguished by the last shift.

Certainly a few tons of lead were removed, some reports mentioning 20 tons, which would have been won from the shaft and the stopes above, where the vein was rich. However, the cost of railing out and driving a level of 336yds. plus stoping and the payments made to the men, would not have been covered by the sale of the ore raised. The time spent here by the workforce to create the drivage must have taken at least 4 years. Unfortunately the records for this venture have been totally overshadowed by the developments at Goldscope and Yewthwaite and all details have been lost.

Finally, the last trial to be located on the Scope End Ridge bisects the ridge E/W and runs parallel to the main Goldscope Vein. This is a German openwork around 30ft. long and 2ft. wide where the vein has been removed (some of the working has been filled in as it cuts through the ridge path). Nearby, on the western side, is a cleared area suitable for a small shelter.

Goldscope

1. Copper Cradle

Most people who visit the ancient valley of Newlands cannot fail to see the huge twin spoil heaps lying at the entrance to Goldscope mine, reminders of a long ago time when the valley rang with the clatter and clang of mining and resounded to the crashing thud of the stamp mill crushing the hard-won ore. This is an area of huge historical importance and Goldscope was one of the oldest mine sites in Cumberland, its magnificent exposed copper vein running over Scope End, unmissable to the early adventurers. The Mining Journal reports that the first mining took place here in this valley during the 12th. Century and certainly, by the 13th Century, this is verified by an entry in the Close Rolls of Henry III when it is stated that "Keswick Town is full of miners". Still later the mine was again confirmed as working under a Charter decreed by Edward IV.

The copper vein here courses E/W directly over the shoulder of Scope End, and the early adventurers have laid it bare over much of its 400yd. length, creating a great gash over the fellside where the glowing copper ore was extracted.

There have been many interpretations of the name Goldscope conjured up by mines historians over the years: that it originated as Goldscalpe, a reference to the flaxen haired men who worked it or that the copper lustre was indicative of the presence of gold. It seems likely that the true meaning stems from the German name "Gottes Gab" meaning God's Gift, a name used often for mines in Germany, Austria and Hungary at the time, no doubt referring to the extreme richness of the vein uncovered, indeed a gift from the Almighty.

At this time here in England, we were importing large amounts of copper which we were desperately in need of. We had a huge wool industry needing brass pins for carding, a basic requirement for copper utensils and a silver coinage which was being quickly eroded by the illegal method of clipping the coins. In 1558 we were also re-arming for the defense of our realm and needed copper to make bronze for our ordnance. William Cecil, secretary to Queen Elizabeth I was promoting the manufacture of arms in this country and was supported by Sir Thomas Gresham, who, in fact, already had his own ordnance foundry at Mayfield. Due to the necessity of the nation's security, Cecil did not want to have to look abroad for resources. It is important to realize that, in the known world at this time, Germany led the field in mining, ore processing and smelting. We had copper in abundance in the Northern Fells of the Lake District but we had not the expertise to mine or smelt it satisfactorily - for that we needed the Germans.

By 1561 negotiations were taking place with a mining expert, Johann Steinberg to form a company and, with around thirty men, to prospect the Lake District. An indenture was granted by the Queen to Steinberg and Thomas Thurland to form a mining company. Thomas Thurland was a Rector of the parish of Gamston near

Nottingham, and at that time held the not unimportant position of the Master of the Savoy Hospital in London.

Steinberg however, was not prepared to allow the English to see the German methods or in fact to see how their engines worked. Indeed Hans Loner, the leading brass manufacturer in Germany, had refused to show how his battery works operated despite a request from William Humphrey, who had just been appointed Assay Master at the Royal Mint in the Tower of London; the German fears were indeed justified as Humphrey had brought together his best workers to observe the German techniques! In fact so protective of their advanced technology were the Germans, that it was actually their intention to export the copper ore to Germany for smelting, however, the old act of 1530 forbade this.

Three years later at Thurland's request, on the 10th. of September 1564, the grants were transferred to Daniel Hechstetter and partners. There were some very odd covenants attached to the agreement indeed! They were not to tunnel under castles, houses, gardens or orchards unless the owner approved; if there was any dispute with the landowner this was to be settled by a jury of six men, and should the decision go against the company the fine would be £100; the erection of water engines etc. would be allowed for a 20 year period and failure to remove them without a further agreement would result in them being forfeited or a £200 fine enforced. Tin, pearl, lead or precious stones attracted a 1/10th. royalty, gold would be at 8d. an ounce and silver at 1d. ounce. There was a royalty of 2/- per cwt. for copper, or 1/20th. for 5 years and after this time, 2/6d. cwt. or 1/15th. Should the Queen not require the copper this could be sold abroad after export duty of 40/- a cwt. was paid. The responsibility for the behaviour of the work force lay with Daniel Hechstetter and Thomas Thurland and the company would be formed with twenty four shareholders.

This then was the agreement, and in 1564 Letters Patent were granted with Daniel Hechstetter as the agent for David Haug, Hans Langnaur & Co. of Augsburg, empowering these men to search, dig, roast and melt all manner of ores of gold, silver. copper and quicksilver in the counties of York, Lancaster, Cumberland, Westmorland, Cornwall, Devon, Gloucester, Worcester and Wales. The brass manufacturer Hans Loner became the London agent for the company, and was already a member of the Hechstetter family having married Regina Hechstetter in 1556. The stage was set and the principal actors all in place - now all it needed were the extras!

At last, in June 1564, Daniel Hechstetter and Hans Loner came to England, accompanied by twelve miners; these were the advance party and soon mining in the Northern Fells would begin in earnest. While Daniel and the men made the difficult journey north Hans settled in London as the Company's agent. The men, all experienced, arrived after a long and arduous journey, many hundreds of miles by land and sea to the small town of Keswick. They had travelled by carriage and on horseback from their native towns, through the Low Countries, across the English Channel and finally into the port of Newcastle. From here it was a long and tortuous journey across the wild north eastern moors into the town of Carlisle and

Daniel Hechstetter makes his plans. J. Tyler

from there to Keswick. Some of these men had left wives and children back home in Germany and must have been very homesick here in a desolate, foreign place, unable to speak the language and receiving a hostile welcome in some instances. The men were housed in lodgings in and around Keswick and began the difficult task of settling into an alien way of life. During this period the Crosthwaite parish register recorded around 1,600 souls dwelling in 320 houses, farms, smallholdings etc., spread around the areas of Keswick, Borrowdale, Newlands, Braithwaite, Thornthwaite and Thirlmere. Daniel, however, being the boss, stayed in the George Hotel until a house was available for him!

Up until this time, Keswick had been a small, unremarkable town consisting of one muddy street with a few yards running off it. There were two inns on the main street, The George and Dragon and The Oak. The first of these later had the 'Dragon' dropped from its name at the accession to the throne of King George I and the second gained 'Royal' in its name to commemorate the escape of King Charles II, after the battle of Worcester, by hiding in an oak tree. There were likely to be also several pot-houses in the town and there was a Saturday market which had gained its Charter in 1276 and which is still in existence today. The market would have drawn many people into the town and weekends would have seen Keswick full of hustle and bustle, farmers and their families coming to sell their produce, the children playing street games, and people watching the bear-baiting and betting on the cock-fighting.

The houses of this period were still in the mediaeval style of timber framing and thatch and had burgage plots running behind them containing middens, livestock, pig sties and orchards etc. Usually, at this time, only the more important buildings such as churches were of local stone with slated roofs. On the main street of Keswick, the houses were placed so that they came across the ends of the street with lanes and yards running between and in the centre was the Moot Hall. This was the court house in Mediaeval ages but was falling into ruination at this time as was the Keswick Bridge, which was the main way through to the west of the county and was hardly usable. The arrival of the Germans was to breathe new life into the little town as the miners brought jobs and prosperity into this isolated area.

Although the strangers were not well received by some at first, the local girls were certainly not complaining and were soon courting these hardy men from beyond the sea. They must have seemed very exciting, being well travelled, well paid and foreign, speaking a different language and having different customs. In little more than a year after their arrival, several of these men had married local girls and many more were to follow suit as time passed. Some of the miners of course, had families back home and would return to them at intervals.

By the time the second party of 20 men arrived, mining had already commenced in the veins beside Derwentwater, and while the German miners concentrated on applying their skills to opening up the ground, local tradesmen were employed in all manner of basic construction.

The planning and forethought of the mining operations was meticulous and the need for fuel for smelting had not been underestimated. Keswick was a well wooded area but these woodlands were owned by various parties who could, if not restricted in their actions, see fit to make unfair gains, which of course was against the Crown's wishes. These mining works, so heavily backed by the Crown and involving shareholders from the great and good of the land, would take precautions against unfair profiteering and decreed that dispensation to cut timber was sanctioned provided realistic prices were offered. Indeed it was realized that this was going to be a very long term project and the possibility of acquiring timber from as far away as Ireland was considered.

During 1565, the Augsburg firm of Haug and Langnauer, impressed with the initial prospecting, were prepared to invest £20,000 with Daniel Hechstetter heading the operation. To assist in attracting a skilled workforce from Europe, permission was sought from the Crown to allow a maximum of 400 foreign workers into the country. The number was capped to 300 and another group of around fifty German miners arrived via Newcastle, and by July the adventurers had arrived in Keswick. Now that there were a considerable number of foreign workers in the area, the local people were made aware that they must accept these men with respect and hospitality and do them no harm. Because they were here at the request of the Crown, they had permission to demand timber and even to impress wagons and horses. They were also given dispensation to report disorderly conduct of English workers and this obviously gave rise to bad feeling.

The month of July, 1565 was most significant for this was when the Company of Mines Royal was ratified and by the end of this year, the mining developments under the guidance and the plans laid down by Daniel Hechstetter, were well forward. The amount of progress achieved by a workforce of 80 or so was quite staggering and a testimony to the work ethic of the German nation.

A scandal involving one of the shareholders and the Master of the Mint no less, occurred also in 1565, faraway from Keswick at the Tower of London. William Humphrey was involved in some sort of robbery and scandal at the Royal Mint ... it appears £400 was taken from a strong room box, the door having not been forced but unlocked, and a long slender footprint was left, which fitted perfectly the shoe of Humphrey!! He was also accused of clipping ingots and at one time there had been seen 6 pots of silver and 1 of gold in his cupboard. He had apparently also been lavishly entertained by the Germans and had overpaid them for their silver.

2 Settling In

Accommodation in the area was a problem as there were few houses, and some locals were particular who they took in, although probably the sound of the "chinks" would alter their thinking somewhat. The company was also building accommodation and barrack type dwellings in Newlands were erected becoming know locally as the Dutch Huts. Lodgings had to be found for some workmen, there was a house for the smelters and a smith was lodged in Borrowdale. Two of the higher managers had a room at the parsonage for a rent of 19/- a year and the company had a house in Keswick Town where Thurland lived and which later became the home of the Hechstetters. Other miners were lodged at Low Snab, Gillbanks, Stair, Swinside and Braithwaite, these being the nearest habitations. The accounts ledgers were filling up and every item of sale or purchase was annotated by the Clerk of Works.

The first miner actually recorded by name in the accounts was Matheus Suess who travelled to England in September 1565, then came two more miners later in September followed by Michael Thurer. In the same year, Israel Waltz reached Keswick, an important arrivee as Israel was the Company surgeon and stayed in Keswick for many years. It may well have been that some of these men were travelling in loose groups on horseback rather than by carriage and were arriving at staggered times due to the exigencies of the journey. The favoured route was from London to Newcastle by sea, then overland via Barnard Castle and on to Keswick, but the journey was no picnic and took at least 5 days; overnight stays cost around 4/6 a night plus 2/6 for dinner.

Many of these men were young and single and would have taken their relaxation in the taverns and inns in and around Keswick. Soon several of them had met local girls and the first marriage to take place was between Hans Haring and Isabella Atkinson on the 17th. of September 1565. They were soon followed by Simon Buchberger and Janet Fisher of Grange who married in November and approximately 27 unions between German miners and local girls were blessed in Crosthwaite Church over the next 2 years.

There was of course the age old problem of the unwed mother and unhappily there were many illegitimate children born to German miners, some of whom very likely had wives and families back home to whom they returned. Orphans and fatherless children were "on the parish" so these poor, unfortunate "base-begotten" mites were afforded at least some rudimentary care. The story also exists that some of the men took their pleasure at the colourfully named "House of the Harlot"- this is the translation of the name of the village of Portinscale (apologies to the residents) and the house itself apparently stood beside the Miners' Trod close to Nichol End. Generally speaking, however, the men seemed to be anxious to lead a fairly ordered way of life.

Fuel was still a major concern and another officer, a Mr. Denton was sent to Ireland for further reports on the import of more wood, or the setting up of charcoal burning stations in Ireland to support the industry; charcoal of course would be lighter and the volume in transportation would be more economical. Meanwhile, it appears there were problems with the complexity of the mineral being raised and some samples of copper were sent back to Augsburg for analysis which proved high quality metal, however the matrix of the ore was creating complications in the actual smelting process. The word copper is freely used but the ore that was being mined was in fact chalcopyrite, not native copper which requires less processing, and chalcopyrite in these early days taxed even the skills of the German smelters.

By the spring of 1566, work had begun on mining the veins at the head of Newlands Valley and a small smelter had been established at Brigham near Keswick on the western bank of the Greta to test smelt the ore being raised; this would later be replaced by the huge complex, Smelthouses.

Then, in the August of 1566, the great copper lode on Scope End was discovered and by late 1566, 500,000lbs. (223 tons) of ore had been raised from Goldscope mine. Thomas Percy, Earl of Northumberland, who owned the land and the mineral rights and was entitled to the rents and royalties thereof, was justifiably incensed. He sent in his troops to stop the miners working only to be rebuked by none other than his Queen, and informed that he must allow the mining to continue in the Newlands Valley. Thomas insisted that the ores removed from the Newlands workings belong to him and he was later again complaining of ore being removed from the Copper Plate Mine near Ellers in Borrowdale.

Daniel's plans for Goldscope were soon underway; in principle his plan was to mine the area at the western flank of Scope End (the area now referred to as the Pan Holes) following the vein down from the surface, and what we must realize is that this was a solid area of fell side which has fallen away *since* then, to expose what were then deep workings. Naturally, as they went deeper the extraction of water would prove more and more difficult. Daniel Hechstetter had already solved this problem and a new low level, the St. George, today referred to as the Grand Level, would be driven in the vein from the eastern side of Scope End. This level would be 247yds. long at which point it would reach the St. George Shaft, the engine shaft for draining the lower workings. A 22ft. waterwheel for pumping would be installed here in the heart of the mountain, and the water to drive the wheel would be brought in from the western flank through the Water Level (referred to also as the Back Level), down 60ft. in the Water Shaft, to be collected into a huge wooden cistern and from here, channelled by an intricately angled rock tunnel onto a series of wooden boards, directly above the wheelpit chamber, which would allow the water to be distributed evenly across the 4ft. breast of the wheel. The water would be contained by a substantial dam at the head of Littledale and channelled by a 1,200yd. leat down the valley to enter the mine by the Water Level via stout boards and trunking. At this time twelve miners were working 16 hours a day and producing 20 kibbles of ore a week (around 28½ cwt.). The men were paid 8d. a kibble for the ore produced, for sorting it, 6d. a kibble and for tunnelling forward 40/- a fathom. This would be hard and difficult work, hand-chipping, splitting and prizing the rock from its underground hold, and the advancement would be no more than 3ft./4ft. a week.

The 29th. of September was a great day for Thomas Thurland, Daniel Hechstetter and Hans Loner... they had actually made copper! A sample was sent to the Queen, and trials were being made to see if it contained gold or silver. It required around one hundred weight (112lbs.) of charcoal to produce 2lbs. of copper and the heat required to smelt chalcopyrite is around 1,200degs. C. The process was far from easy and involved numerous stages lasting days, and requiring virtually exact temperatures to ensure the production of copper. George Nedham estimated that that one furnace could produce 16cwt. of copper a day, which meant that, based on a 282 day year, £13,536 worth of copper could be produced.

Although the integration of the workforce was by all accounts reasonable, there was still resentment from some of the locals and things came to a head on Saturday the 10th. of October 1566 when Leonard Stoultz, a German miner, was viciously attacked and beaten up by a mob of 20 men. The ringleader was a man called Fisher, by all accounts well known for his violent and threatening behaviour. Another of the thugs, John Wood, struck Leonard so viciously that he could not defend himself and the ensuing beating killed him. The following day in Grasmere, a group of 50 men attacked Hans Matzcler but fortunately Mr. Fleming (probably of the well-known Rydal family) arrived to intervene and saved him further injury and possibly death. These were dangerous times and on the following Sunday in Kendal, a jeering mob collected threatening mayhem and murder! The responsibility for law and order and dispensation of penalties in the event of trouble lay with Henry, Lord Scrope, the Governor of Carlisle and John, Bishop of Carlisle. The Bishop thought the offenders should be executed, whereas Lady Radcliffe called for clemency. When the Queen heard of the attacks she was furious and ordered Lord Scrope to advise the Justices of the Peace in Westmorland and Cumberland to repress this behaviour at all costs and by whatever means.

During this period, disaster struck when a storm of the most violent proportions struck the town and both Newlands Valley and the Keswick smelter suffered severe damage. Much of the work recently done at the smelter was ruined by the River Greta as it crashed down from the Glenderaterra Valley, tearing away the coal store, dams and sluices and work had to begin again repairing everything to its former state

In March 1567, the Duke of Northumberland was even more angered by the German invasion when he had to allow 200 bucket loads of ore to be taken from Borrowdale mines and in August the Germans were given permission by the court to remove ore from Copper Plate Mine. Here, Northumberland insisted the ores be weighed and valued to his steward's satisfaction and proving to him the weight and value of the ore. Regarding Northumberland's obstruction of the mining activities, Daniel Hechstetter wrote to Sir William Cecil, a man who had the ear of the Queen, who was a major shareholder in the company and who was later to become the Lord High Treasurer. The end result was a law case which began in the Michaelmas Term of 1567, to determine whether or not the Newlands Mines were Royal mines (i.e. containing silver or gold to a greater value than the base metals therein) and as may be guessed, Thomas lost the case but we will hear more of him later.

The Death of Leonard Stoulzt. J. Tyler

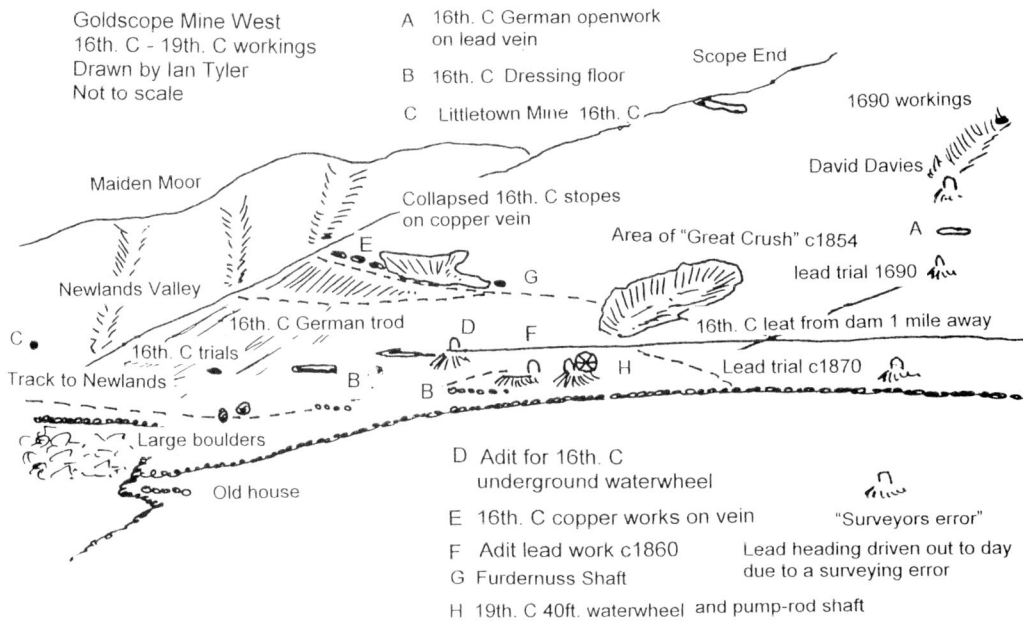

Goldscope West. Ian Tyler Collection.
Goldscope West. Drawn by Ian Tyler.

16th. C. German workings on copper vein, Goldscope West. Ian Tyler Collection.

Example of early 16th. C. shaft/pit on back of copper vein, Goldscope West - note the twin hand-chipped grooves to prevent water running into the workings. Ian Tyler Collection.

16th. C. German copper workings and collapsed stope area on Goldscope West. Ian Tyler Collection.

Top: Very old dwelling house, store and smithy below Goldscope West workings. Stuart Clement Collection.
Bottom: 16th. C. dressing floors below Goldscope West - the old house is behind the wall. Ian Tyler Collection.

3 Stamping and Smelting

At Goldscope the mine was still expanding, a new area in the Pan Holes over the crest and on the western slope of Scope End, known as Bagpipes was being worked and a 36in. vein was being opened up in two places. Apart from Goldscope, the company was now working 18 mines and trials in the immediate vicinity which reveals how active the men were in prospecting for new veins.

Expenses 1564-1568

Mines		*Smelting*	*General*	
Newlands	£4485	£5908	Travel	£2326
Borrowdale	£1489		General	£2214
Grasmere	£ 967		Petty cash	£ 483
Caldbeck	£ 204		Furniture	£ 204
Fornside	£ 74		Draper	£ 93
Stonycroft	£ 55		Wine	£ 74
Buttermere	£ 27			
Minersputt	£ 9			

Overall spending

1565	£2884
1566	£3927
1567	£5076
1568	£6722
1569	£6908
1570	£5647

To complement the workings a new company was set up to operate a battery works; this was to make all manner of things, in particular wire for the woollen industry, pans and utensils, castings for various necessities etc. The newly formed company, entitled the Mineral and Battery Company, was ratified on the 28th. of May 1568 and had a splendid coat of arms. With the title came certain privileges, the right to prospect in all areas, the right to mine calamine (essential for the manufacture of brass) and an exclusive monopoly to manufacture wire using a water driven machine which was of German design. The Company of Mineral and Battery Works was a much smaller affair than the Mines Royal Company and there was as little as a tenth of investment. The new company did not have a board of directors but was administrated by two governors, two deputies and eight others, however it was foreseen that the two companies would work together for their mutual benefit and success. The Mines Royal had the sole right to mine for precious metals and copper, whilst the Mineral and Battery works had the sole right to mine calamine and manufacture brass. It would, however, be several years before the battery works came into operation.

The foundations for the new smelter were laid in 1568 but building was to continue all through 1569 as various ancillary buildings were erected on the site. Production from the mine was increasing all the time and it was planned to have six or eight furnaces to cope with production, the original smelter having only three.

Smelter Buildings at Brigham

Vessel dressing house
Store house
Carpenters store
Melting house three stories high with three furnaces 78ft. x 54ft.
Stamping house with ten headed iron stamps
Assay house
Stove and bathhouse
Blacksmithy
Dwelling house 66ft. x 18ft.
New building 33ft. x 21ft.
Charcoal house
Peat store

This was to be no small affair; when finished the site would consist of at least ten buildings. The smelthouse itself was 78ft. long, 54ft. wide and was built of local stone with a slated roof.; many of the slates were brought from the nearby Applethwaite Gill on Skiddaw by Gilbert Warton and his men, and the long and winding sled tracks from these ancient quarries are still in evidence today. Some local reports said the smelting works looked like a small town, especially at night when the dull red glow could be seen rising up from the Greta Valley. The smelter chimney was raised in height to alleviate the problem of noxious, sulphurous fumes affecting the local folk, and to increase the effectiveness of the draw of the furnace; nearby, John Scott and his men were finishing the refining ovens.

Ore was heaped and waiting to be smelted and speed was of the essence so twenty four local carpenters were employed to ensure the job went ahead quickly. Daniel however, could not believe that the men worked so slowly... in his opinion, twelve German carpenters could have done the work at twice the speed! For the workings of the smelter, the technical parts for the six furnaces were dispatched from Germany along with other revolutionary and secret equipment to be used in the venture. The water was transferred from higher up the Greta and here, at an elbow in the river, a weir was constructed from which a substantial leat 3ft. wide and 3ft. deep was taken off which passed 15yds. through a bluff of rock. Here the miners drove a tunnel 6ft. high by 3ft. wide to allow the water through and this became known as the "Hammerhole". The distance from here to the smelter site was 180yds. and the fall on the 220yd. leat was 10ft. overall, allowing the water to travel at a velocity of one foot per second to drive the waterwheels on site. The fuel initially for this huge operation was supplied from the nearby forests, but due to the insatiable need for fuel, it had to be brought from farther afield and peat was delivered from Skiddaw and wood from Borrowdale, Isel Park and Calgarth on Windermere. Later, coal was brought from Bolton Low Houses at Wigton and charcoal from Furness and of course, the expectations of bringing a fuel source from Ireland had not been shelved. The logistics of transporting all these materials the distances involved is mind-boggling and all this in the days of no instant communication, of long and arduous journeys on horse back to see that all was being done correctly, and the immense cost to the company in payments to the carriers.

On the home front as it were, there was again an undercurrent of dissatisfaction. In the past the Duke of Northumberland had treated the Germans with hostility although he had been happy enough to profit from their need for wood purchased from his land. Lady Radcliffe acted in much the same way also. She appears to have been no champion of their cause, and in some records it is said she opposed the construction of the smelter, although she also was happy to profiteer from the German company, and the price for essentials such as wood, peat and land was higher than average. It was during June 1568 that she was approached by the Germans with a proposal to purchase the freehold of the smelt mill site, as opposed to the original agreement of a 21 year lease for which they were paying the extortionate sum of £20 to £30. This was not acceptable to Milady, who certainly knew on which side her bread was buttered!

In February 1569, Vicar Island (formerly known as Stallion Island and now Derwent Isle) was purchased from John Williamson for the price of £60. Men were put to work clearing away the shrubbery etc., and they set about constructing a piggery and brewery and planting apple and pear trees.

At God's Gift, the Furdernuss adit to the water shaft was being driven forward, the water shaft was being cleared and boards for troughs were being installed. All the areas below this were being worked, and a shaft was being sunk in the Bagpipes. The work was under the supervision of Hans Reitter, the mine manager, who was paid 10/- a week. Hans Haring was the foreman, Bartelm Moser was foreman sorter and Steffan Murr was the foreman washer. The surveyor was Martin Kendler and Wolff Hund was the blacksmith. There were about fifty miners working in the area at this time.

Meanwhile, the St. George Level was being driven in from the eastern side of Scope End. This was a drainage level to carry water from the wheelpit and was driven both east and west simultaneously. A team of miners driving in from the east commenced at approximately OD710ft. in good rock following a copper vein already exposed and worked on the surface above them (Pan Holes). The men working from the wheelpit end were restricted as to where they could dispose of the rubbish. Any ore removed from the vein would have to be hauled in stages to the surface 260ft. above, via the Furdernuss Shaft and out to the hand dressing floors on the western shoulder; the rubbish would have to be removed either by the same method which would be costly, or stacked and used as backfill in disused workings.

The level, because it uses the weakness of the vein, meanders slightly and the vein hades N/S but the adit was cut to a generous size being roughly 3ft. 6ins. wide at the base to 8ins. wide at the top of the adit and around 7ft high. The point at which the two converging drivings meet is about 30yds. east of the wheelpit where there is a noticeable kink in the level, and the pick marks can clearly be seen coming from opposite directions. One can imagine the relief of the miners when the connection was made; the men driving from the east had come in a distance of 220yds. where the lack of air must have made conditions intolerable, and the only consolation would have been the dryness of the working. By comparison the men on the wheelpit side had connection to day by at least three different ventilation sources, and the breakthrough now meant that ventilation for the whole mine was assured and the disposal of ore, water and debris would all be through this level to the east. In May 1569, local carpenter and builder John Scott was making a set of wheels to carry the huge axle for the waterwheel. The patent for the design of the water engine was officiated with a seal in London at the end of May, and the cost of this was £5 17s. 5d. including a special box for the seal. If this was for the main wheel, one can only assume that the St. George Adit was nearing completion and also the waterwheel pit was well under construction.

By the end of 1569, around 300 working shifts had been completed over a period of 487 days; the work had entailed the digging of the water leat and the head German carpenter had worked 15 days on the waterwheel at 8d. a day. English carpenters worked 91 days making two axles and cutting big posts for the Stamp mill and another 4 months had been taken up in making planks. The big augers were brought from Grasmere Mine to bore out wooden pipes which, when completed would be, we assume, for pumping out the new shaft. It is this information which leads us to believe that Daniel, at this time, was now ready to sink below the sole of St. George's Level, and commence the St. George's Shaft. During this time much equipment had been brought from Germany, of which the German engineers were very proud and secretive about.

The workings established at God's Gift by 1569 were the Furdernuss Adit, Furdernuss Shaft, Bagpipes, Bagpipes Nick, St. Peter, Windenburg, New Cut at St. Daniel, Third and Upper Workings, Middle Workings, St. Lienhart's at Veldort, St.Lienhart's Upper Working, Franckenstein, Hamblin, St. Joseph, St. Joseph Crosscut, Littletown New Cut and Littletown Cut Below.

By this time, at Goldscope Mine, a stamp mill was under construction; this measured 61ft. x 33ft. and contained sixteen stamps, four of which were shod with iron; it had sturdy timber walls and a slated roof and was capable of treating 120 kibbles of ore per week (at 150lbs. per kibble this equalled 9 tons). The stamps would be driven by a 16ft. waterwheel which would also service the smithy built at the south end of the stamp mill. This was 30ft. x 22ft. also with a slate roof under which were housed two forges where all the necessary iron work could be done on site; to take away the fumes and smoke, a stout chimney topped the building. Lofts were boarded out in the roof space of the buildings to afford some basic accommodation for the men working in Newlands Valley. Local man John Scott supervised the construction with his workforce of twenty five men who were being paid around 6d a day and the buildings were being slated under the supervision of Robert Kirkby. By the end of 1569, the building work was completed and by way of appreciation for the hard work, Wolff Prugger and Wolf Hochholtzer were each presented with a pair of breeches as a bonus. Whilst the mill was under construction, the men had been bucking the ore by hand beside the mill site. Now fully operational, the sluices could be opened and water allowed to run to turn the wheel, and the real operation of crushing the ore could begin. The new stamp mill here would employ a foreman, twelve stampers, five washers and five sorters making a total workforce of twenty three men; women are also recorded as working the washing floors at this time. The location of this site was probably just below the entrance to the St. George Level on a plateau atop the low spoil heap. Here, footings still remain which accord with the measurements of the mill and smithy, and the 1580 inventory records the wooden trough used to transport water onto the waterwheel of the stamp mill. Again the measurements of this agree with the distance from the level entrance whence the water issued.

Generally the miners were paid on the production of ore by kibbles and after it was cleaned and graded the price was 1/10d. per kibble of best ore. The ore was classified into three grades: pure, shaley and inferior. Sorters were paid 4/5d a day and for development work, contracts were bargained for. Wages could be boosted by finding a new vein, and for this 10/- would be paid and then a further 4d. a kibble paid should the mine prove lucrative for the next two terms.

The smelter at Keswick was now fully operational and was claimed to be bigger than anything in Germany, and indeed the known world. On this site there were of course, many valuable tools and equipment, and for security the Germans had acquired a large and fearsome guard dog to protect their chattels and also to prevent prying eyes from seeing how they operated. It must be emphasized that many of the methods employed by the Germans were known only to them and were very advanced for the time, and it was their intention things would remain like this. It was now producing 10cwt. of copper per day and it was estimated that 6,000 seams of coal would be required to ensure the works could stay operational.

At Fawe Park (Copperheap Bay) a pier had been constructed at the water's edge both for the dispatch of ore and the transportation of personnel to the eastern side of Derwentwater. A large boat was used for this purpose and was also employed for other means such as bringing wood and materials from Borrowdale at the southern end of the lake, to Keswick, and there were three other boats in use also. Besides the pier at Copperheap Bay, there was a building measuring approximately 8ft. x 20ft. As this was such an important area, the building would have been a shelter for the boatmen and carriers, and probably have contained a storeroom and an office for the recording of lading, goods etc., and may even have provided overnight accommodation. The stamped and milled copper was transported from Goldscope via Littletown to the lake shore, and with a laden pony train the journey would certainly have taken 2 to 3 hours. It was then taken the short distance across the lake by boat from the water's edge at Fawe Park to the landing stage at Keswick, called then the Middingstett; it then went onwards by cart or pony train to the smelter. Not all went smoothly however and after a boat load of copper ore sank, the dispatch point came to be known as Copperheap Bay. When, at various times, the boats were unavailable, the ore was brought to the smelter by road and this entailed the use of the all important Keswick Bridge. The increased activity of haulage had created more of a problem with the already unstable structure, and it was decided the company would go ahead and repair the bridge, benefiting both themselves and the townspeople of Keswick.

During September, Nedham was negotiating with Messrs. Curwen for a parcel of ground at Workington to construct their own Company wharf for the mineral trade. A 12 acre site was found for which Henry Curwen required a rent of £13 6s. 8d. The Irish timber situation was still a possibility and all eventualities were still being considered. The cost of fuel is illustrated in the fact that 92 horse loads were transported from Workington via Cockermouth at a cost of 19d. a load of around 120lbs. The output of around 60 tons a year seems very low by today's operations, however the initial requirement for copper for the manufacture of bronze for cannon had deteriorated, due to cheaper and inferior cast iron cannon being introduced. Copper was still in demand however, and a embargo was placed on all exports.

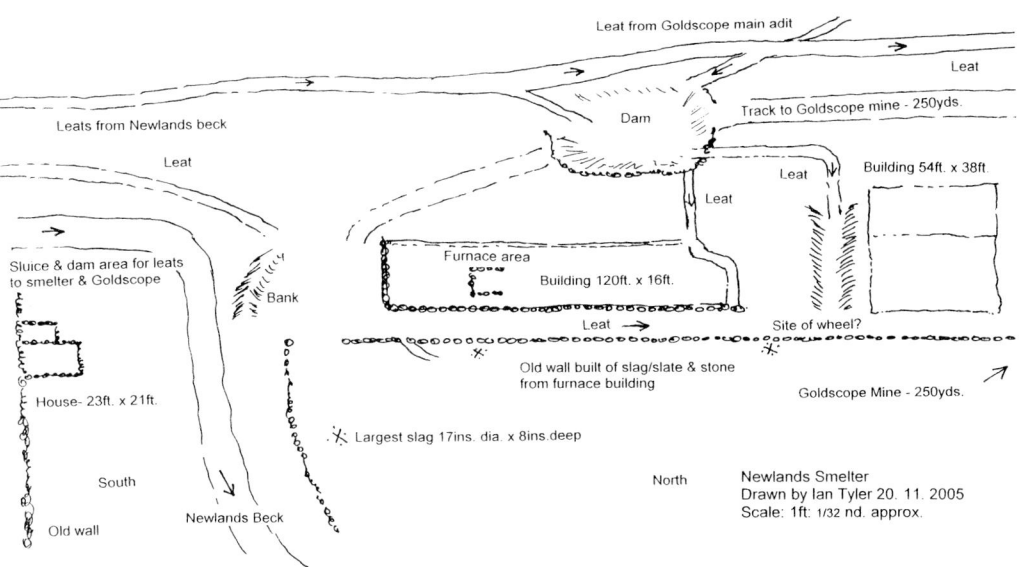

Top: Site of Newlands Smelter 17th. C. 250yds. south of Goldscope Mine. The wall contains slag, slate and stone from building. Stuart Clement Collection.
Bottom: Plan of Newlands Smelter. Drawn by Ian Tyler.

Top: Slag on site of Newlands Smelter. Stuart Clement Collection.
Bottom: Compacted heap of 16th. C. copper ore at Copperheap Bay ready for dispatch to Brigham Smelter. Ian Hebson Collection.

Top: Copperheap Bay on western shore of Derwentwater, Catbells on left. Stuart Clement Collection.
Bottom: Vicar's Island (now Derwent Isle) bought by the Germans in 1565. Stuart Clement Collection.

The weir on the River Greta to supply water via the Hammer Hole to Brigham Smelter. Ian Tyler Collection.

The leat entering the Hammer Hole taking water to Brigham Smelter. Ian Tyler Collection.

4 Treasure Island

The acute shortage of coal fuel was rapidly becoming apparent, and one Anthony Dediman was given £20 to prospect for coal within a radius of 1½ miles of Keswick but, alas, to no avail. However, Ralph Carr located it at Blindcrake, where two shafts had been sunk 12fms. and later coal was discovered at Bolton Low Houses. To ensure a good supply of coal from here, the company supplied the colliery with rope and candles, timbered the shaft and had it covered to stop water going down; they also encouraged the local colliers to look for other seams nearby. The Company even paid for 15 days and 15 nights pumping the mine dry.

It appears that ale and wine were freely dispensed among the men, for mining is a hard and thirsty job and some leisure time had also to be made available. Fishing and game shooting were certainly on the agenda and it would be likely that much free time was spent in Keswick playing games and getting to know the local population, particularly the girls! From time to time Lord Mountjoy's players came to entertain them with various productions and Lord Scrope's servants presented a comedy and music for them. Bear-baiting was also a popular attraction in those days, as was cock-fighting which attracted some serious gambling.

The German community used the Crosthwaite Church in Keswick for their worship although they still were waiting for their own preacher, and so here they said their prayers in their native tongue, were married and had their children baptized.

During this year, some copper was being sold to the Crown but by 1570, the Crown could not accept the total amount ready for purchase, reflecting that production at this time was exceeding expectations. Within a very short time it became apparent that the rapid expenditure was crippling the company. Daniel Hechstetter was an obvious target for the failure to bring home the goods to the shareholders however, his emotions ran deeper than concern for what anyone may have thought of him. Although the expenditure was high, assets stood at £12,055 and copper was being produced but alas, a ready market was not to be found. Three options were open to Hechstetter to try and save the day:

1, To be allowed to export copper to Europe.
2. To be allowed to manufacture copper utensils.
3. For the state to purchase the copper produced.

The truth was that the expenditure for trials and plant had snowballed out of all proportion and without a major success. The English were apprehensive and the Germans were in a cleft stick having entered into an agreement and being now practically insolvent. There was only one thing for it - Daniel and his family would have to leave their homeland forever and move to Keswick permanently, so that he could stay on top of the business.

As well as the problems experienced by the company in its English venture, the ground swell of other troubles far away was going to have disastrous repercussions. To begin with, the Lowlands of Brabant, Flanders, Zeeland, Holland and Friesland suffered freak tidal flooding and the ramifications of this with regard to trading created a catastrophic loss for the Haug company. The Turkish Venetian war still raged, and the Netherlands was having a huge religious struggle. Whilst all this was well away from our shores, our northern Earls had started an uprising led by the Earl of Northumberland and Lord Dacre.

Within just five years the unbelievable sum of £31,167 had been spent on the mining venture and a further call of £850 per share was made on the already jittery English shareholders, a total of £20,400 extra. Rumours abounded and were directed at Hechstetter speculating that he was the only person benefiting from this venture; his salary, incidentally, was £150 per year plus expenses. Hans Langnauer had invested £8,287 in shares and he had in fact borrowed money from Antwerp, but news of the lamentable results of the company's performance had reached the ears of the big German finance houses and no further money was available. The situation was further aggravated by the lack of the English investors to accept the share call and in October 1570, Hans Loner, who had been back in Augsburg returned to London on behalf of all the German investors who had paid up their share dues, and appealed to the Queen to buy copper.

The January of 1571 saw the Newlands Valley and the surrounding area in the grip of a vicious winter. Derwentwater was completely iced over and the essential power source for the stamp mill was now like cast iron in the ground, everything was literally frozen to a standstill. The Smeltmill was faring little better, although the sheltered nature of its position was allowing some work to continue, however, the eventual thaw came and things returned to normal. There were other problems to contend with though and not least of these concerned the despatch of copper. By May of this year, of eighteen different ships sailing with a cargo of copper from Newcastle, on berthing at London all were recorded as having short weight to the manifest.

Not all the news was poor and a cash investment from the Crown of £2,500 was indeed well received. On Daniel Hechstetter's 46th. birthday, a large party was organized where wine was freely given to the seventy four German workers, and both they and thirty six English workers were also each given a quart of ale.

At last, in July of the same year, Daniel brought his pregnant wife Radagunda and their children to England to settle permanently in Keswick and later in the same year, Emanuel, their eldest son arrived also. The Hechstetter Dynasty was now being firmly founded here in Cumberland and as the years passed and generations came and went, they were to prove a highly prominent and successful family. It seems that they settled in a house in Keswick situated where the local supermarket now stands. Many years later, work was being done on the house where some of the plaster had fallen off a landing wall. The builder found a door behind the plaster, opening onto a passage which led to another door. Behind this was a small room, a chapel, containing a black oak altar inscribed with the name Daniel Hechstetter.

Vicar Island became the scene of much activity when, in 1571, work began on making the island a place of productivity for the day to day living of the miners. An 11ft. square windmill was being erected with canvas sails along with a grind house, a mill stone for grinding arrived from Penrith, and manure was being brought to cultivate the land. Two stone houses, a pigeon house and pig sty were being built and 5,400 slates were brought from Skiddaw for roofing. Foundations measuring 39ft. x 20ft. were being dug out and a cellar, a stone-floored bakehouse 12ft. x 20ft., a dovecote 17ft. high, a peat house and a bathhouse were being built. In Germany, apparently, baths were frequently taken but only the well to do had them in their houses. The public stoves or hot-houses were usually heated on Saturdays and were used by the women for cleanliness and by the men "to repair their health crazed by immoderate drinking"! A garden 50yds. square was laid out and 300 apple and pear trees were being planted in an orchard measuring 80yds. x 90yds. Altogether a total of £1,360 was spent on developing the island and although the miners were never resident on the island, they probably spent a fair amount of time there. Legend has it that the miners were actually paid on the island for although the greater part of their wages was given in credit, they needed some coinage for day to day expenses. It is likely that there was a degree of secrecy about what they earned - this way, the good people of Keswick would never know!

At this time, the mines working in Newlands were Goldscope, Franckenstein, High St. Daniel, St. Lienhart, St. Peter and the Hamblin and these were under the direction of foreman Hans Harmer.

In September of this year, a serious accident happened at the crusher at Newlands when Robert Banke was severely injured and needed the attention of the surgeon Israel Waltz, for which service he was paid 6/3d. Israel had married Jane Wood in 1567 and they lived in Keswick; his services would of course have been required here and there, especially if a miner was so injured as to have necessitated the surgeon going to him on site. It may also have been that Israel also afforded his treatments to the local townsfolk.

The provision of fuel for the smelter a costly job and at this time there were delivered to Brigham 973 loads at £24 6s. 6d. and a further 651 loads at £19 0s. 0d. Such was the demand that the coal mine at Bolton Low Houses was assisted in working by the Company, the shaft being sunk a further 48ft. to retrieve more coal. The transport manager was Hans Reinbrun and the responsibility of all the toing and froing must have been a nightmare. Meanwhile, new methods of smelting were constantly being researched and in 1572, a gentleman by the name of Henry Pope had submitted plans for a new method, but it was evidently not enough of an innovation for it to be taken up.

In this year of 1571, Good Queen Bess must have brought some colour to Hans Loner's cheeks when she purchased copper at £4,000 but, nevertheless, finances were still very strained. Between 1565-1572 the amount raised in copper sales for the seven year period amounted to £38,449 with expenses standing at £24,351.

Two years earlier, it had been pointed out that a considerable amount of copper was lying here and there, waiting to be checked and marked, and it was decided to seek a building for storing it. Richard Dudley of Yanwath was elected to deal with this and was authorized to weigh, mark and coin the copper at a rate of 3/- per cwt. To store the copper, Richard rented the old court house (the Moot Hall) in Keswick from Lady Radcliffe and set about repairing it. This was quite a costly affair but to have built a new house altogether would have been even more expensive. The 24 stamps which Richard received for marking the copper would not actually make an imprint on it as it was, as Richard said, "so hard and rough" and he was obliged to pour a small amount of lead into the rough part and stamp that.

Finally, we hear again, in this year, of the ill-fated Thomas Percy, Duke of Northumberland who had already had one run-in with the Queen and had, not unexpectedly, come off the worse for wear. His subsequent disaffection for Her Majesty led to his later instigation of an armed uprising, the Northern Rebellion, against the Crown. The results were draconian: his rebellion was quashed, he was incarcerated in a Scottish jail and then brought to trial for treason against the Crown. The outcome was predictable... one does not attempt to usurp the throne of England and expect to live when the ploy fails! Poor Thomas, at only 34 years of age, was beheaded and his head displayed on a spike on one of the gates entering York - a salutary lesson!

5 Awesome!

Although perhaps an Americanism has no place in the history of the 16th. Century mining of the Lake District, the only word to describe the chamber and wheelpit in the heart of Goldscope Mine is 'awesome' - it is truly breathtaking. The size of the work that those German miners did without the aid of gunpowder is staggering. The chamber is huge, and high above can be seen ancient timbers, stunning green flashes of copper in the rock and beyond that a deep, impenetrable blackness. The pit itself curves smoothly and precisely down the sides of the chamber and the perfectly circular scrape marks from the wheel can be seen against the rock wall.

In 1573, a shaft was being sunk in St. George's Level and it would be logical to assume that the working below the sole would now require de-watering. All the external work had been completed, the dam and the leat to bring water from Littledale were ready and internally the connection had been made so as to bring the water via the water level, then down through the water shaft, into the cistern and onto the wheel. The spent water from the wheel, and the raised water brought up by the pumps from the lower workings, would now run out through the St. George Level adit. Here, the water was then diverted into a trough standing on stays of wood which fed it onto the 16ft. waterwheel operating the stamps in the mill below. From this time on, the centre of operations would be on the eastern side of Scope End and the workings on the western side would be virtually worked out. In fact the miners were now working in the sole and to raise ore up through the old workings was impractical and unnecessary. Although the only record available to us regarding the construction of a waterwheel at Goldscope is for the one erected in 1602, this must have been a replacement for an earlier one. The inventory taken by accountant Richard Ledes in 1580 clearly described the trough on stays to conduct water to the stamp mill wheel and although this may have been just for the water make coming through the mine, the depth of the working by this time would surely require the use of a wheel. There were also five pumps for the mine lying beside the stamp mill, and at Smelthouses, in a storage building was " *1 bellowe bourde prepared for St. georges Myne or Sumpe in Newlands by gods gift Myne*".

The St. George Level was not just a drainage level for the mine but an exploratory level which would also prove the copper vein ran the full width of the mountain a distance of 400yds. In fact a considerable amount of stoping and extraction took place along its length of 250yds. from the wheelpit out to day. The position of the wheelpit was centred right at the heart of the copper orebody, and here the lode was proven from the surface to this point, a vertical height of at least 350ft.; evidence suggests it was up to 10ft. wide here and was continuing downwards. The chamber was hand-picked out of solid rock at right angles to the lode and here the 22½ft. diameter wheelpit was excavated, its width 4ft. 6ins. To support the main axle bearings, long ledges were precisely chipped to take the huge twin main 9in. x 14in. timbers which spanned the width of the chamber. To absorb the vibration from the turning wheel, 9in. vertical timbers were set in the side walls of the wheelpit directly under the centre of the axle boss, which has left its wear marks on the pit wall. The actual shaft was situated about 4ft. on the outbye side of the chamber at OD724ft., and the level gave an 14ft. fall to the adit. Directly above the chamber are all the huge timbers required to support the gear work and pumping system which was probably the rag and chain method. Because the waterwheel spanned the full width of the workings at this point, a by-pass level was created giving the miners direct access to the water level, 180ft above and other levels back to surface on the western side.

On Vicar Island things were expanding and in 1573 we find that there were now two goats in residence along with a cow and Indian fowl. The brewery was in the capable hands of Martin Harris and the produce, bread and beer were providing a useful supplement to miners' diet.

During the month of July, another ship sailed from Newcastle and on board were 46cwt. 93lbs. of copper, however on its arrival the copper was weighed and, once again, the weight from leaving the smelt mill in Keswick was different, the copper weight was short again. In this year also, the Queen paid £2,000 for 666cwt. of copper which was to be used for ordnance.

In 1574, one of the original orchestrators of the Mines Royal, Thomas Thurland, died. Altogether, Thomas seems to have been somewhat of a shady character and had been in some fairly serious trouble with the Church and the Royal Court over his administration of the Savoy Hospital in London. Thomas's problems had all been financial and he had converted considerable amounts of Church plate and valuables into cash for his own use. In June, 1561, when St. Paul's had caught fire, Thomas had been given some of the Church plate for safekeeping and had pawned it at 5s. the ounce! Creditors were chasing him but Thomas was enjoying a good standard of living and kept on ducking and diving. He was finally deprived of the mastership of the Savoy on Saturday, the 29th. of July 1570.

Drawing water from the bottom of the mine. J. Tyler

6 Stride Wide and Lift the Leg

During 1574, there appears to be have been much coming and going among the German workers, some going back to Germany and some leaving to work elsewhere. Some left because they were homesick and when their contracts ended they were happy to return to their homeland, and some possibly were not happy with 'the truck' system of payment. This meant the miners were paid a wage on paper and the company would then feed them, clothe them, provide lodgings and send back increments to their wives etc. in Germany. The men of course could draw money for personal needs, pleasure, ale, gambling etc., and of course this could over the years generate into a debt situation, as in the case of Jorg Siber. He had been nine years in Keswick and had obviously been given every chance, but Jorg was in debt to the Company to the tune of £30 19s. 0d. (living beyond his means on 'the truck') and was dismissed. Perhaps the taverns of Keswick Town, or the local lovelies, had been too much of an attraction but he did, however, leave a Lutheran Bible to his mates on his departure. Although the actual cash flow generated by the miners in Keswick may not have been great, for the local traders, carters, foresters and other resident workers the mines did create new wealth. In fact the company had no fewer than 338 local traders registered in their account books by this time.

On the home front, many men had by now taken English wives and their children were attending Crosthwaite School, the boys preparing to follow their fathers into mining, smelting and other jobs at the mines when they finally left schooldays behind them. No Lutheran minister had been brought from their homeland but apparently the miners were content enough to accept the local ministry at Crosthwaite Church. Their domestic lives seemed to have been harmonious and peaceful and a settled home life seems to have been important as, when a husband or wife died, the remaining partner re-married fairly soon. There seems to have been considerable trade of fabrics and varied foodstuffs brought in by the German investors who, as we have said, were general merchants in Europe, trading with the East for certain items.

The general diet of the working class at this time was mainly porridge, oaten bread, whey, beans, hard cheese and clapbread (oatcakes). Oats were the only cereal food eaten then as rye was susceptible to "ergot", a kind of fungus which had hallucinatory properties - the LSD of the 16th. Century! Fresh meat was unknown and was all salted and smoked. It seems the German miners also brought certain of their traditions with them and indeed, it is said that the world famous Cumberland sausage originated from these men who must have found our English sausage very bland compared to their spicy version! Several of the local women were employed by the company and worked mainly at washing and sorting the ore. The usual occupations of women at this time were spinning, weaving, clothes-making, knitting, sewing quilts and linen and making rugs, soap and rushlights. These last were the means of lighting in houses, the streets being lit publicly in the larger towns but in Keswick, the little main street was probably illuminated by light streaming from the houses and taverns, and folk abroad after dark would carry their own lanterns; in the rural dwellings, a lantern was hung at the gate on dark nights for latecomers. These guiding lights would have been a boon for those men who, after their tough daily toil, needed rest and relaxation - a night on the town in Keswick! Apparently when first arriving in this country, the German miners found our beer not to their liking and drank only wine with their food, but it could be assumed that they did become accustomed to English ales. For these hard working men, in Keswick Town there was heady ale and beer which went by such wonderful names as Father Whoreson, huffcap, the mad dog,, go-by-the-wall, merry-go-round, angel's food, dragon's milk, stride wide and lift the leg etc. (Would that we had such colourful language today!)

In comparison to the diet of the working class of the period, that enjoyed by the Hechstetter household was considerably better. Whilst they were staying in London on their way to Keswick as a family, there was entertainment for the children such as bear-baiting and going to see the lions, it cost 2d. to see a curious calf and there were purchases of white candy and brandy and a washerwoman to do the laundry. When they were settled in the house in Keswick they had three maids, a cook and a kitchen boy and certain groceries were sent from London, obviously being unattainable in little Keswick Town. Among these items were sugarloaf, plums, raisins, figs, almonds, pepper, ginger, cloves, cinnamon, saffron and nutmeg. There were silver spoons and glasses, bed linen and cushions, feather beds and bolsters for the house, and *"15 ells of coarse canvas over the dining room to keep bats out"*!

A great variety of fabrics also came from the Augsburg company, they being general merchants, and the folk of Keswick must have enjoyed their shopping at the market. There was *"velvet, taffeta, macheyar, fustian, half silk ticken, frieze and cordovan leather"* and some of this was purchased by the miners themselves. Daniel himself was the recipient of a spun gold and silver lined hood from his wife, Radagunda, and when Rochius Franckh returned to Germany, he sold on a purple dressing gown, a good black riding coat with fringe, a cotton-lined white linen jacket and a black jerkin lined with fox-skin... quite a dandy!

To identify an accurate wages structure is difficult but at the higher end, Mark Steinberger who was in charge of smelting was paid 180 florins (£18) a year whilst mine manager Hans Reitter received 10/- a week (£25) a year. The smelting foreman was on 13/6 a week (£35 a year) but the miners' wages varied greatly depending upon how much ore was extracted and of what grade it was, bonuses etc. Piecework and contract workers were all paid on production of agreed amount of ore per day or the amount of newly developed ground at a fixed rate. Tributing was a system of working where the miner chose to work underground and then sold the ore to the company, having of course to pay for his own tools, candles etc.

In August, a commission of two men, Fredrick Schwartz and George Chezter, arrived from Germany to assess the situation and meet with some of the English shareholders. The outcome was predictable - no more money would be invested. The shareholders were out for blood and Loner and Hechstetter were condemned for the losses. The situation was critical, and Loner was replaced as the Company agent by Jorg Kozer. Daniel meanwhile carried on, insisting the way forward was to mine the ore and find a market for it.

During this year the Queen paid £500 for copper and £100 for silver from the Company but this was a drop in the ocean compared to what was needed and by October, the German company was ailing; excessive spending coupled with poor returns are a recipe for disaster and the situation was looking critical.

There was a glimmer of hope however, in the shape of a battery for the production of sheet copper and a variety of vessels which, it was expected, would stem some of the shortfall in profit. The Copper Hammer House, which had been discussed six years before, was now under construction and was 39ft. long by 27ft. wide by 17ft. high with 3ft. thick walls; it was built of stone to absorb the pounding vibration of the huge hammers and the slate roof was supported on stout timbers. Inside the building were two forges for casting copper, two huge iron shears for cutting copper sheeting and Lady Radcliffe had supplied ten ash trees for the copper hammer beams.

Soon a further influx of imported specialist labour to operate the new battery arrived from Germany: coppersmiths and polishers Hans Roslle, Celles Rosten and Conrad Zinnagel. These experienced men would head the team who would manufacture a whole spectrum of items from pins, thimbles, buckles, buttons, wire, nails, kettles, pots and pans to copper sheets, rods and copper ingots for disposal to other industries. The battery was under the watchful eye of the foreman Sebastian Dibler and two more coppersmiths arrived, Bartleme Kornman and Melchior Moser, both of Augsburg; they were to be paid 9/- and 5/- per week respectively. Five of the coppersmiths lived nearby in the Master's House at Brigham for which board was deducted from their wages. By 1575, the smelter was now operating with fourteen men; a new refining furnace and copper shop were being constructed and four new copper moulds had been made for the lead ingots.

Around this time 31cwts. of copper were exported and sold to the Muscovy Company and to France, whilst the local market and London were not forgotten. By April, the first copper goods were produced and a total of £1,622 was realized on the sale of them; by the end of the year, 763 cwt. of copper had been made.

7 Daniel Dies

Meanwhile, in Newlands Valley at God's Gift, work continued in the St. George and a new mine was being opened up called Vogelsang (Bird Song). It was at this time also that Emanuel, Daniel's eldest son commenced working at the mines in return for his board and for a quarterly payment of £1 15s. 0d.

At about this time the church was built in Newlands. This is a beautiful little church and both the miners and the locals would have found it a God-send, particularly in bad winter weather, not to have to make their way to Crosthwaite.

The copper utensil trade was now a valuable part of the trading pattern and 896lbs. of copper utensils were sent to Kendal at a charge of £62 12s. 4d. Indeed some accounts were being paid in the value of the pots they were manufacturing, for instance two tons of French wine valued at £29 was paid for with copper pots, candles and iron goods and various charcoal dealers were prepared to accept payment in this fashion. The battery had now three copper smiths and five beaters plus three other workmen in the battery and such was their success that they were paid a bonus of £2 10s. 0d. at Christmas 1576.

In 1576, we find that Hans Loner was finally brought to book and castigated for his failure to send detailed accounts, his neglect of sales, his lack of effort to reduce costs, the misapplication of funds etc. His accounts were completed by the 12th of October and he was sacked with the blame for the Company's dire financial situation firmly laid at his door.

Disaster befell the operation completely, when the Haug Langnauer Company went bankrupt in 1577; half the original capital had been supplied by them and this threatened to destroy the Mines Royal Company and halt the ongoing operation. It was up to the remaining shareholders to take up the challenge. By now however, the English shareholders were in arrears to the tune of £17,561 including £3,125 unpaid by Lord Burghley and £2,634 by the Queen, whereas the German investors were £9,268 paid up. The Haug Company officially withdrew from the company in this year after having invested £10,916 since its inception in 1564. They had poured money into the business, borrowing from other finance houses, and the gamble had not paid off.

Failure stared the company in the face and by 1578 it was in dire straits with old Daniel still at the reins. Since the beginning the Company had not made a profit, and in spite of everything, copper was still being imported. Although the mines were ailing, Daniel Hechstetter was still convinced that the project was worthwhile and approached the Queen with the suggestion that he could re-float the company with a loan of £1,000 and bring in 500 men to make the mines profitable. Rumours were rife and there was much bad feeling in the town; some of the miners had not been paid and there were outstanding accounts with local traders. Richard Ledes, the resident book keeper, naturally took the brunt of the anger.

In 1579, Hechstetter recommended that there be a further share call of £41 per share, or the mines should be leased to him forthwith. However, at Christmas 1580, a joint 5 year lease was issued to Daniel and Thomas Smythe who was already a shareholder in the company and an extremely clever financier. The lessees were to pay an annual rent of 500 marks (£333 6s. 8d.) and every 7 weeks were to pay the equivalent of the ninth kibble of ore raised. They were also bound to keep twelve principal mines operating and to employ 20 labourers gathering the ore. They also had to continue with a drainage scheme for the mines.

By 1581, the projected figures that copper production at the smelter would achieve over past 14 years, had failed to materialize, having been perhaps, rather over optimistic and were based on all the furnaces working flat out. In point of fact, most of the time two were always out of commission due to repairs etc., consequently the initial figures were totally unrealistic.

On the 14th. of May 1581, Daniel Hechstetter, the man had who had been the driving force behind the mining operations in the Northern Fells, died. He had been in poor health for some time and the strain of running this complex and difficult business had taken its toll. He was buried in Crosthwaite Church in Keswick, his adopted home, far, far away from his native Augsburg. Daniel was succeeded by his two sons Daniel the Younger and Emanuel and it was Emanuel, the elder son who, at 25 years of age, became director of the mining operation. Thomas Smythe continued to hold the lease on his own for the next few years and also took leases on the Cornish mines, sending Ulrich Frosse down to Treworth near Perin Sands to manage them.

Following the death of Daniel, George Nedham who was a liaison officer between the Crown and the Company, brought in Joachim Gaunse who was living in London to sort out better smelting techniques; Joachim was a man of the Jewish faith, born in Prague in Bohemia. and had brilliant new ideas for mineral smelting.

Smelted Copper Produced (in cwts.) 1567 - 1584

Year	cwts	Notes
1567	10	
1568	293	
1569	791	
1570	1248	Some reports state (1261) value £3 cwt. £3744.00
1571	1023	
1572	1197	
1573	1200	
1574	532	
1575	105	
1576	574	
1577	285	
1578	60	
1579	360	
1580	150	
1581	660	
1582	-	
1583	810	
1584	1050	10348 cwts. of refined copper

During 1587 there was a return to further violence when the Sergeant of the Mines Royal of Grasmere was beaten up on a street in Kendal, during a riot led by a Robert Sleddel. These were raw and rough times indeed.

In 1589, Thomas Smythe was granted a 10 year lease on the mines, and in 1590 he was joined by Emanuel Hechstetter and Mark Steinberger, paying a £600 share. The venture was a disaster producing a meagre 900 quintals of coppers in two years and then, in June 1591, Thomas Smythe died and his son John took up his share.

It was in this year also that young Daniel married Jane Nicholson and they settled in a house near Keswick Bridge. During the reconstruction of this house, many years later, oak wainscotting was uncovered and over the fireplace was a carved oak shield with the initials DH and JH on either side of it.

In order to expand the business, in 1592 John Smythe decided that a new hammer mill should be constructed at a location about a quarter of a mile downstream from the site of the previous mill. A very dry summer had meant that there was insufficient water coming down the Greta to work the first one and the re-location would improve the situation. Unfortunately, at about this time, the huge charcoal store in Keswick burnt down.

Meanwhile, in the heart of Scope End, in 1593, the German miners were working hard, oblivious of the problems of their masters, and this is reflected in the great depth that the engine shaft (St. George) was down to. It was now 30fms. down from the St. George Level and here the miners were enjoying the benefits of a good copper strike.

Various scant reports indicate the Germans had started to vacate Goldscope during 1595 at about the time the plague began to spread around the Lake District. The word "plague" in these early days would have struck terror into the hearts of the local inhabitants and from 1595 to 1599 there were 569 deaths, only a handful compared with other parts of the country, in particular of course, heavily populated towns, but a frightening situation nonetheless.

Certainly during this time, little mining appears to have been going on, however, when the time came for renewal of the lease in 1596, a Thomas Acworth applied for it but his application was unsuccessful. On the 4th. of July in the following year, Emanuel Hechstetter, Mark Steinberger and Richard Ledes were ordered by the Company to appraise the mines. They pointed out that the time was inappropriate for such an undertaking, as the smelting of accumulated stock of ore had been very much delayed due to the wet weather, which had affected the supply and quality of the peat. The stock-taking was postponed until the autumn when the stock pile of milled ore would have been reduced, a situation which was much more favourable for the Company; they estimated that not less than £2,020 a year would be required to generate a profit.

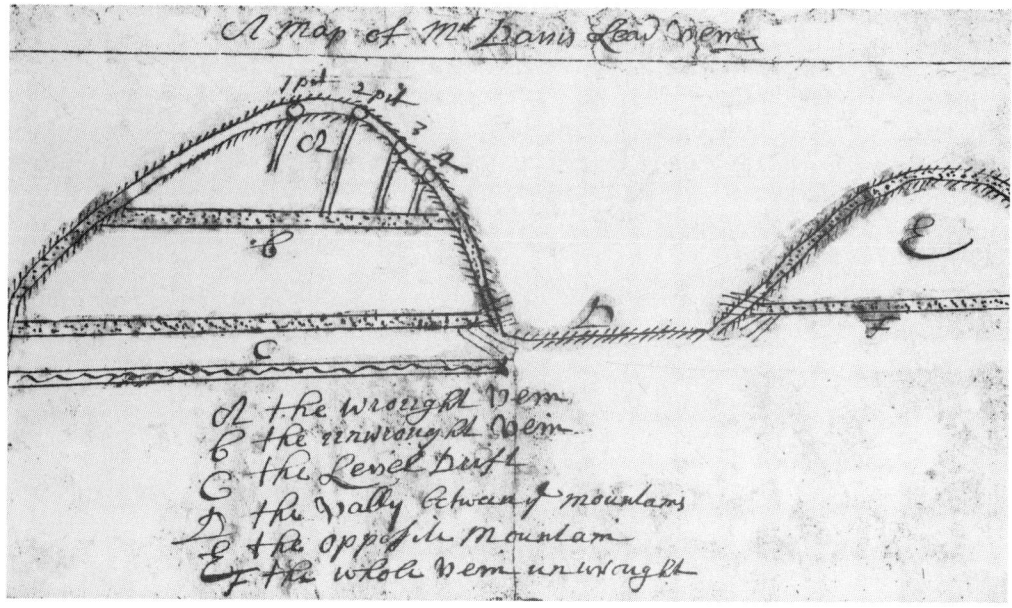

Top: Goldscope Mine and Scope End looking south from mine road. Ian Tyler Collection.
Bottom: Goldscope Mine section 1698 by Thomas Robinson. P.R.O., Carlisle.

Goldscope Mine. Martin Thompson Collection

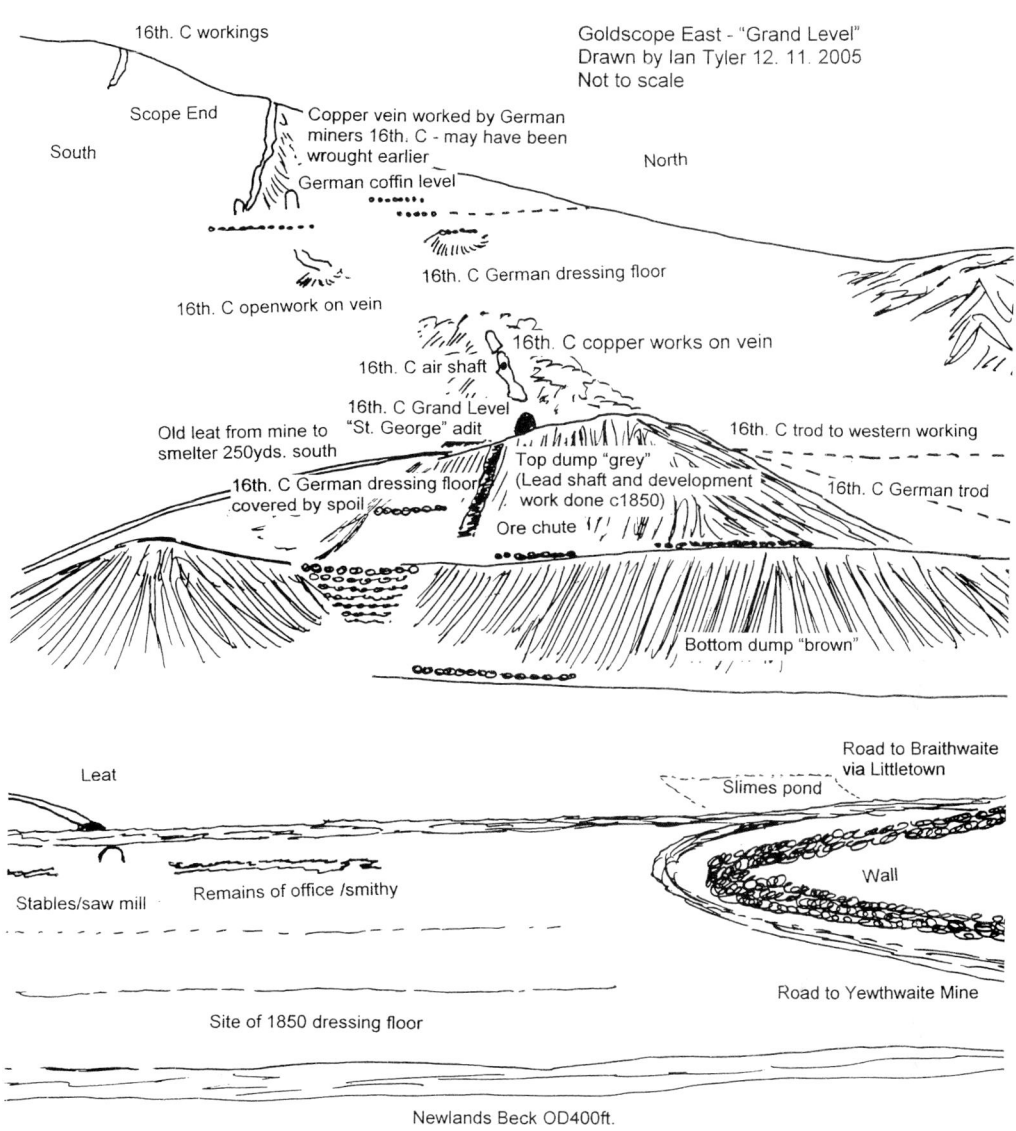

Goldscope East 16th. C. workings and dressing floors. Drawn by Ian Tyler.

Goldscope Mine, 16th. C. St. George Adit (Grand Level) looking west to internal wheelpit. Ian Hebson Collection.

Top: Goldscope Mine, shrine in St. George Level. Ian Tyler Collection.
Bottom: Shrine in St. Clement's Cave, Hastings. Real Cards.

Goldscope Mine, entering copper stope just before wheelpit 200yds. inbye. Ian Hebson Collection.

Goldscope Mine, stope in wheelpit chamber. Ian Tyler Collection.

Goldscope Mine, 16th. C. 25ft. wheelpit hand-chipped out of the solid rock - note timbering above in cistern area. Stuart Clement Collection.

Top: Goldscope Mine, wear on left hand wall of wheelpit by axle. Stuart Clement Collection.
Bottom: Goldscope Mine, wheelpit by-pass level to workings further west. Stuart Clement Collection.

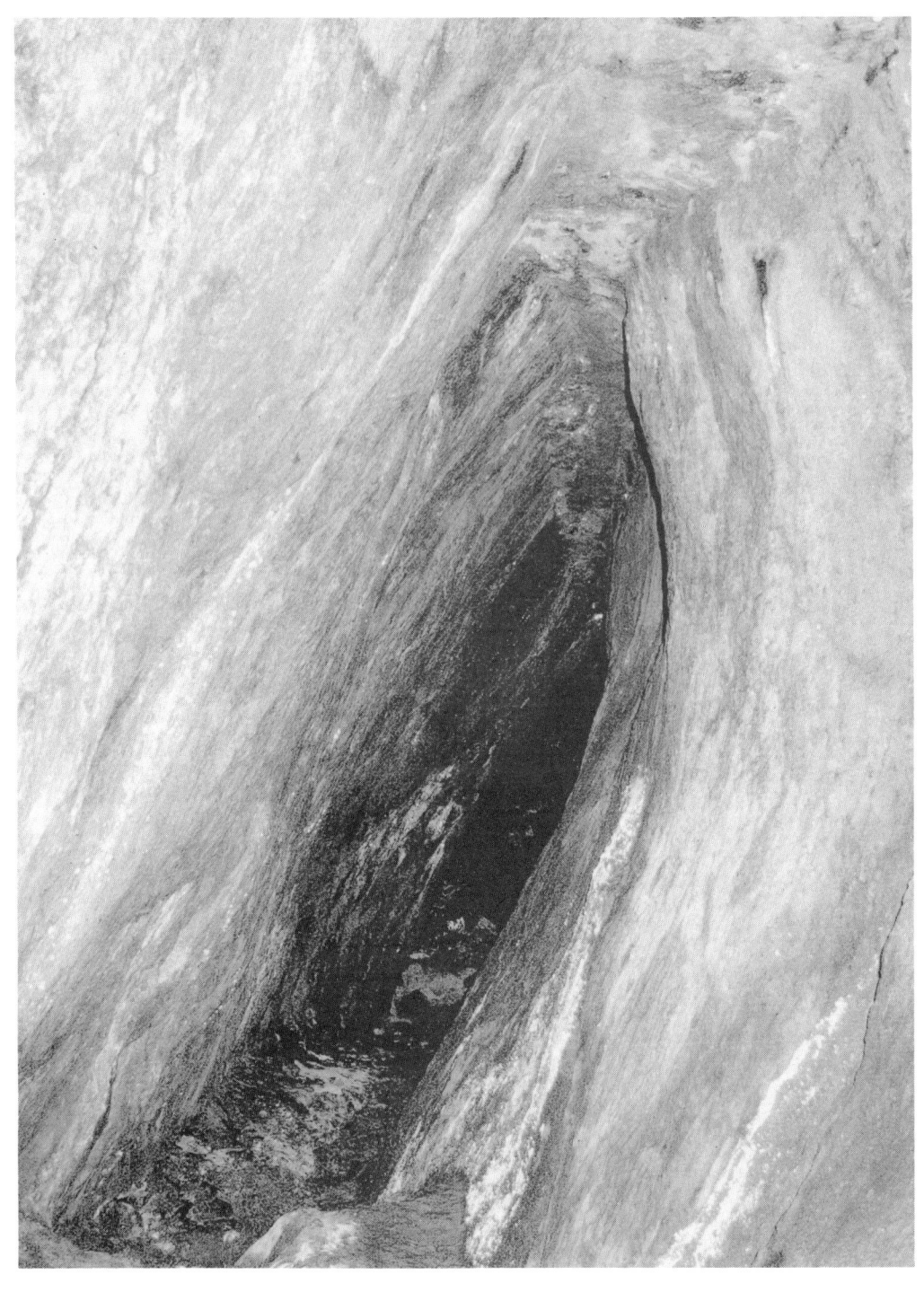

Goldscope Mine, small hand-picked German level above wheel-pit. Ian Hebson Collection.

Goldscope Mine, 16th. C. leat from dam on Scope Beck to power waterwheel on St. George Level. Ian Tyler Collection.

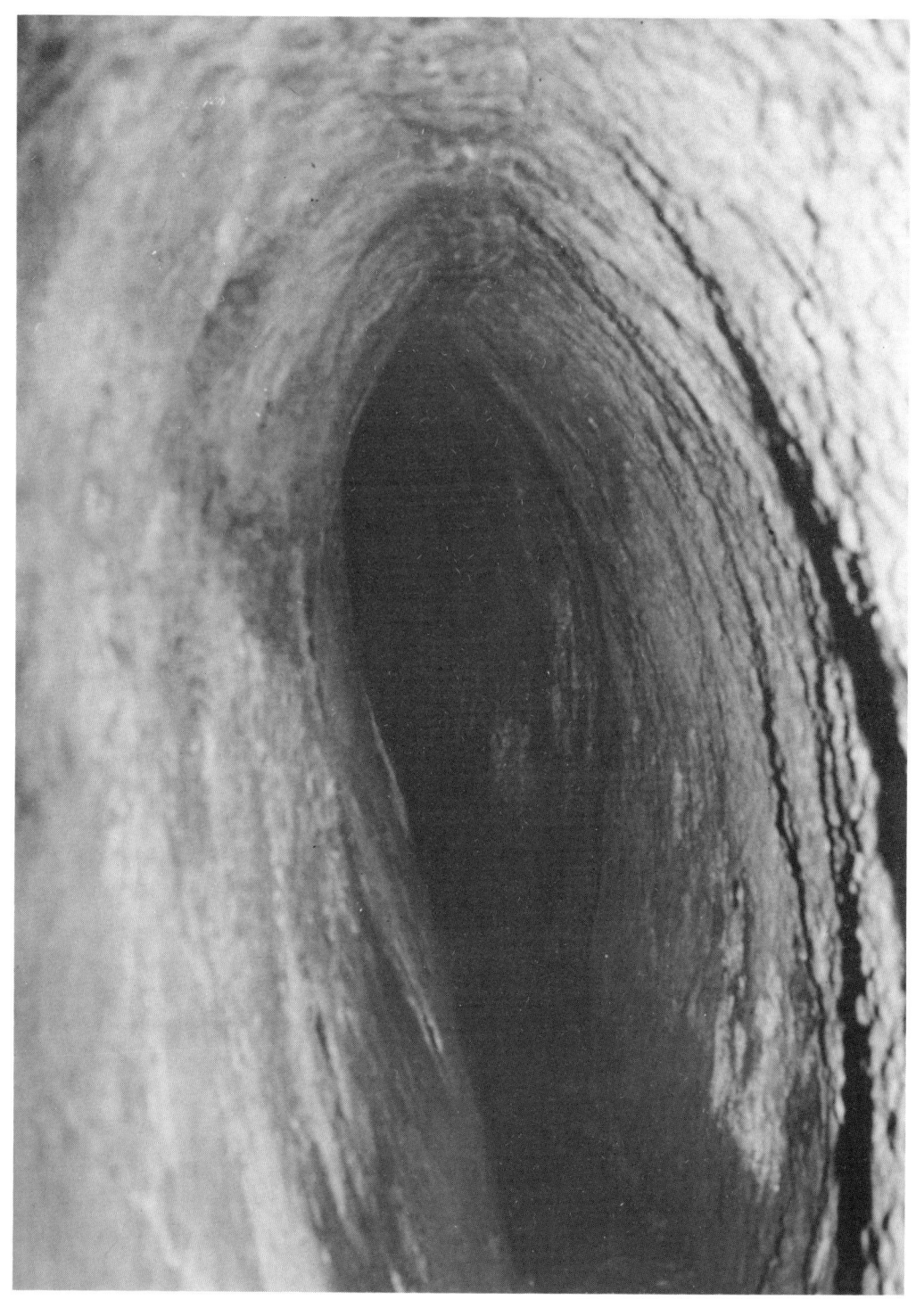

Goldscope Mine, 16th. C. coffin level supplying water to underground waterwheel 180ft. below on St. George Level. Ian Tyler Collection

Goldscope Mine, 16th. C. Furdernuss hauling shaft. Rudy Devries Collection

Goldscope Mine, 16th. C. Furdernuss Shaft at water level horizon. Ian Hebson Collection

Goldscope Mine, 16th. C. copper stopes below Furdernuss Shaft. Ian Tyler Collection

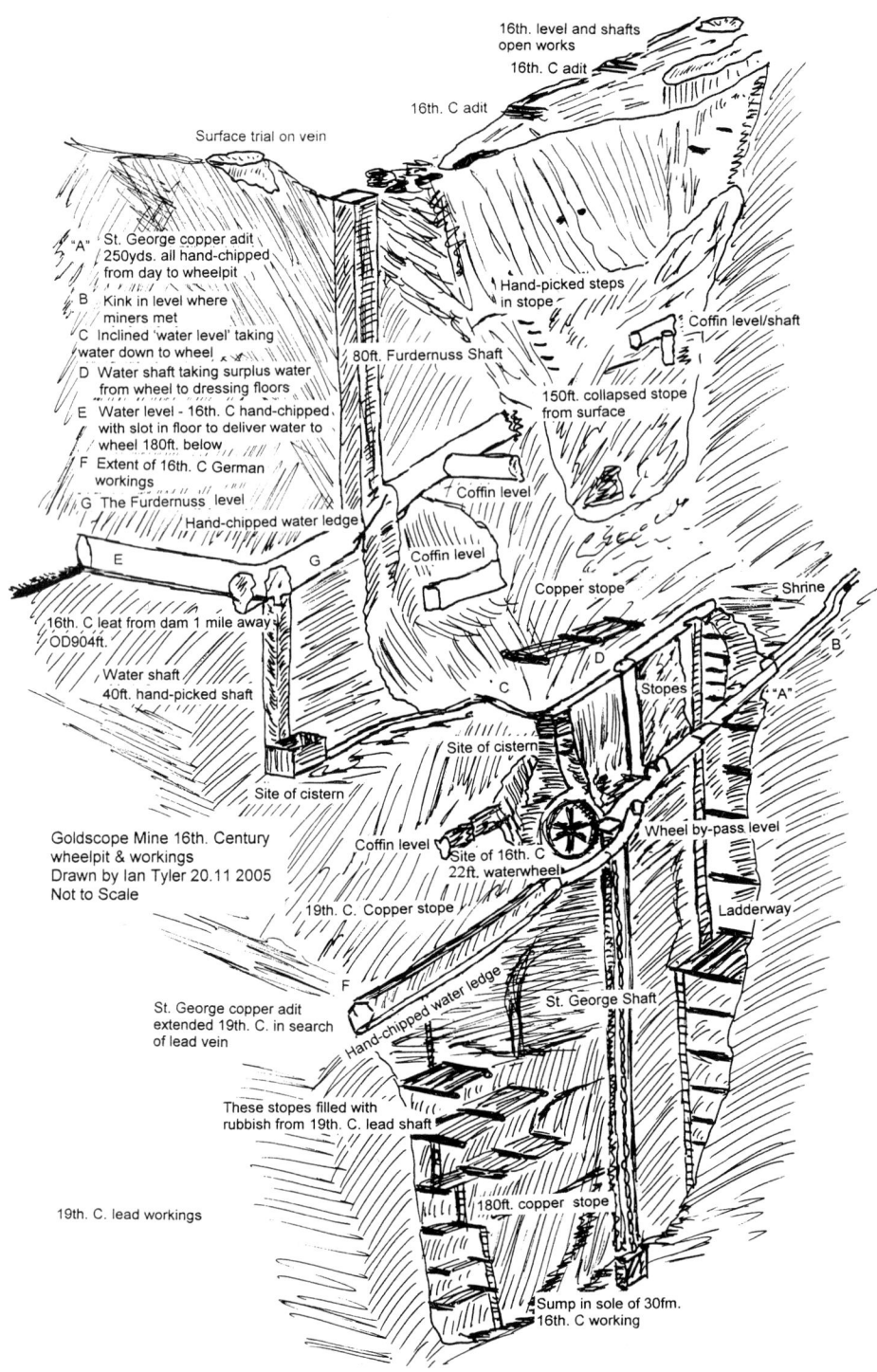

Goldscope Mine, full section of the 16th. C. workings based on underground exploration. Drawn by Ian Tyler.

8 Sudden Death!

Early in 1599 some of the first German miners left to mine and prospect in the Coniston area where the discovery of the great copper lode at Levers Water created much interest and others soon followed. Among those to go were Balthazar, son of Simon Buchberger, who left the family home in Stair for Coniston with four other miners. Discoveries were also made at Tilberthwaite, Greenburn and Wetherlam which would attract even more miners to the area. It was, however, decided that a smelt mill would not be built at Coniston and all the ore would be crushed and graded and brought to Brigham for smelting. Lord Scrope had been asked to do a report on the northern mines and on the 4th. of February, 1600, he sent George Bowes, Christopher Pykering and Edmund Dudley to inspect them. The weather was appalling and the men were greeted by snow, sleet and ice. It was impossible to carry out a thorough investigation and the men hurriedly returned to the comforts of life in London.

They returned to Cumberland on the 23rd April of the same year, in more settled weather and on the morning of the 26th., the men prepared to visit Goldscope Mine. The party consisted of young Daniel Hechstetter, his brother Emanuel, miner Martin Moser, the commissioners Robert Bowes and his younger brother George and George's man, Turn. They made their descent by candlelight deep into the bowels of Goldscope inspecting, as they went, the various ladderways, tunnels and stopes leading off into the darkness. As they were coming up the shaft, there was a fearful cracking sound and cries of alarm rose from the depths followed by an awful clattering. Eventually all was quiet but for moans and groans of pain drifting up from below. Hurriedly, Daniel went back down only to find that the ladder had come away from the rock wall; instinctively he tightened his grip but his body weight was too much and he too found himself tumbling through the stope. His falling body struck the pile of debris, the impact knocking all the wind out of him, and he lay in total darkness, having dropped his candle in the fall. He could hear the others further below but could not get to them, so began calling out to the workmen for help. Eventually some of the miners clambered up with ropes and lights, and fortunately, Daniel, although battered and bruised was not seriously hurt. The others of the party suffered bruises and abrasions to a minor degree apart from Mr. Robert Bowes who was in a bad way, having fallen much further and with heavy timbers falling on top of him; he had sustained internal injuries and he died within the hour. Mr. George Bowes was unable to continue the inspection due to his temporary disablement and also, of course,. the death of his brother. The problems of removing the body from the depths and getting it to Keswick must have been enormous, however, at some point the commission did continue and it was recommended that a great double water engine be installed in Goldscope to de-water the workings: the cost would be £301.

Finally, after a period of vacillation, in 1601 the Company leased the works to the Hechstetters - Emanuel and Daniel, his sons and Joseph, Emanuel's son - and other

"There was a fearful cracking sound..." J. Tyler

partners, for a 21 year term. In 1602, another commission was sent to Cumberland and the recently erected waterwheel was viewed with satisfaction as it creaked and groaned on its axle deep in the heart of the mine. .

In 1603, Queen Elizabeth died and her throne was taken by James VI of Scotland who, in 1604, created a new Charter. Emanuel and Daniel were named in this and virtually the same privileges were allowed as in the previous Charter of 1568.

In August 1605 a new lease was prepared for the Hechstetters of the Company of Mines Royal and then, in October 1607, another 21 year lease was issued by Sir Francis Radcliffe, Earl of Derwentwater, to the Mines Royal for a further 3 acres of land at Brigham, on the northern bank of the Greta down-river from the smelter. Here there was a water race and dam and the site was used for copper beating. It is probable that a smelt hearth was built here also, in order to cope with the extra ore coming from the now thriving mines at Coniston.

Daniel and his brother increased their interests in 1607, when they took a lease on the wad mine in Borrowdale, displaying their expertise there and extending the workings underground by hand-chipped levels.

On the 30th. of October 1610, Radagunda, widow of old Daniel Hechstetter died, like her husband, many hundreds of miles from her homeland. Radagunda had supported her husband through all the early years of the mining enterprise with its difficulties and setbacks, and had brought up a large family. Her sons and daughters had done well in their adopted homeland and her grandchildren were thriving. Radagunda was buried in the choir of Crosthwaite Church beside her husband and members of the Radcliffe family, and she left bequests to the school where her children had been educated. Only four years later, alas, Emanuel died and his son Joseph carried on the business with his Uncle Daniel.

In 1616, Joseph Hechstetter was living near the smelter at Brigham with his wife Joyce, the daughter of Sir John Bankes, the Lord Chief Justice. This was the gentleman who had purchased the land with the graphite mine on it at Seathwaite, and who's family was to hold it for so many generations. He endowed Keswick with a Poor House (on the site of the present Post Office) and apparently, when the smelter was destroyed during the Civil War, the huge beams from it were taken into Keswick for the building of it.

Ore was still being raised in Newlands in 1617, but this was a scant amount and the quality was poor. The rich, copper-laden ore of the early years seemed to have disappeared but there were still 8 men working into the following year and in 1619, they were working above God's Gift and draining water from the mine.

There were still men working in the St. George in 1620 but they were raising just 6 kibbles of ore a week. A huge land-slip in the valley occurred in this year which, due to the terrain, may well have been in Longwork, as this is an open cut working. Although production had slowed down so much, ore was still being raised in 1622 but then, in 1623, there was a second attack of the dreaded plague which must have had some repercussions on labour in general.

Sadly, in April 1623, Daniel's wife Jane died and in the September of that year, he leased out his estate Parkamor near Hawkshead, and took a 5 year lease on a property at the Heads in Keswick, which had 12 acres of land attached. He shared this house with his daughter Radagunda and son Francis.

Over the last 50 years or so, the German smelters had constantly experimented to obtain the best metal possible, but there were still improvements to be made, and in 1632, a further development took place. This had been perfected by Edward Jordan who used pit coal, peat and turf as fuel, and a few years later Sir Phillip Vernatt patented a further method using only coal.

Daniel Hechstetter the Younger died in 1635 leaving his nephew Joseph to continue running the business. At this time, Captain Thomas Whitmore was managing the works and the accounts were being kept by Francis Hechstetter who disbursed the money for him. It was Thomas Whitmore who had claimed to have invented a method of extracting silver from lead using water, but without smelting. Despite Francis lending money to the mine, by 1637 things were not looking good. Over a 2 year period, £2,146 had been paid out, and despite a small contract agreed between Joseph Hechstetter and Thomas Bushell to sell 17cwt. of copper to the Royal Gunfounder, John Brown for ordnance, within a few months they began to sell off the stores at the Smelthouses to pay the workmen. By 1638, money was still owed to various persons but the mining was finished.

The Dutch Huts, built earlier on for the miners, were apparently burnt down in 1641. This was a dismal time for all, many of the German miners had gone to Coniston and to make matters worse, the third outbreak of the plague was now raging through the country. And then, having survived the ravages of the plague, the good people of Cumberland were now to be subjected to the ravages of Oliver Cromwell's troops who, on their rampage through the Lake District's quiet and peaceful land, brought war and brutality. What had taken nearly a hundred years to build was wantonly destroyed, some miners were pressed into service, some fled and others not so fortunate were apparently shot. However, contrary to some reports, not all the works and mines were destroyed and Col. Graham, an ordnance officer who was in charge of the area, realized the importance of some of smelters and mines and ensured that some of the works remained intact. Unfortunately, the huge complex which was Smelthouses beside the river at Brigham was apparently destroyed by troops at about this time, so that another site had to be found for the smelting of copper still being mined, albeit now a much reduced amount. The two possible sites that spring to mind are the Stonycroft smelter and Copperheap Bay where slag has been discovered.

In 1649, Joseph Hechstetter was continuing to mine Newlands on a lease which covered Rowling End and Barrow, and his total of 316 tons of ore raised made a return of £39 10s. 0d. The workings continued until October 1655 and Joseph had also taken a lease to work the mineral veins at Gategill on Blencathra near Threlkeld; as far as we can find, this was the last lease to be taken by a Hechstetter. By 1654 Joseph was a man about town and was now the respected Foreman of the eighteen governors of Great Crosthwaite School in Keswick.

Though the Royal Charter was still in place, the Hechstetters did not carry out any further mining operations themselves, but they were now the lease holders and saw this as a safer way to make money without risk. This state of affairs continued for many years, but unhappily insinuations of blackmail for leases and arrangements were bandied about, and eventually the whole operation foundered. Some miners stayed, others went to the new copper mine at Ecton, but these ventures were beaten by cheaper imports. Unfortunately Joseph did not have many years to dream of his earlier days of success, and he died in 1656.

In the aftermath of the Civil War there was little mining interest, and many of the planned ventures were no more than speculation, but some work went on. Poor old William Monkhouse drowned on his way across the lake in 1657, when his boat load of stone sank; it was said that for years after you could see the stone cairn in the clear blue water.

Some small interest was shown in 1662 when Sir Joseph Berger, a chemist and physician, considered re-working the mine. Nothing seems to have happened however, as a year later, during 1663, the mines were inspected by a Thomas Locke who recorded that the Keswick works were in ruins. Various people made enquiries about the works and the mines, about who owned them and what tools and engines remained but apparently, the Old Men were beyond remembering. Many of the miners and workmen had moved away for work and others had simply died of old age.

The next recorded interest came from Lord Carlisle in 1666 but again this was not pursued. In the following year, a John Bathhurst of London obtained a 21 year lease to work non-ferrous minerals on any of the Duke of Somerset's lands in Cumberland, together with the rights to refine and smelt them. Enquiries surprisingly were still going on, and in 1684, one Lancelot Simpson of Penrith was empowered to investigate the setts. The results of the survey are not known, but in 1685 he discovered that the aforementioned John Bathhurst and a partner were working a mine without right of tenure near Keswick and they also admitted to having done the same at Caldbeck. Around the same period, a Mr. Kirby took up a lease on the Beetham and Arnside Mines but he apparently absconded without paying his dues. It reflects the lack of interest and control at this time when people could jump claims and no one really took much notice.

9 The Breadth of a Sheet

By 1684 things had certainly improved in the area and a gentleman named Sir Robert Reading was anxious to reopen the mines at Keswick and to build a new furnace; at the same time a further enquiry was being made by Messrs. Thomas Goddard, Henry Horgrove and a Major Bret and a 21 year lease was applied for. They were looking for permission to re-smelt the slags, however these applications seem to have been overlooked or simply shelved. During May 1684, Sir Robert Reading was again attempting to re-float the Mines Royal Society in allegiance with a Dr. Martin Lister and certain people in high office such as Sir John Pettus. During 1688, the Mines Royal Act was revoked which in principle meant that copper, tin, lead and iron could now be freely mined, without the interference of the Crown, although it was realized that certain criteria should be met to protect and encourage investment.

In 1689, out of the dust emerged Royal Mines Copper Company, championed by Dr. Edward Wright, a physician and leading Quaker who became the first Chairman, and who also had a private interest in Carrock End copper mine. The inclusion of the word "Royal" in the title was because it was thought that the copper bearing lodes exploited would in fact contain gold, and dues would have to be paid to the Crown. It was actually established that gold was not present and as a result, in 1693, the Royal entitlement was in question. This resulted in the Crown having to accept another Mines Royal agreement with the condition that if no gold was found within 30 days, the operating company would not be held to the agreement.

Five years previously, David Davies, a surveyor and miner, had visited various sites within the area, and then finally, on the 8th. of October 1689, he took over the Bathurst lease and set about the business of mining again. It was Davies who apparently discovered the large heaps of processed ore at Longwork, Manesty and Copperheap Bay and now wanted to know who owned them (they are still lying there today). The one at Copperheap Bay measures around 9ft. wide, 30ft. long and 6ft. high and if one equates the ore to be around 10 tons a cubic yard, this heap would weigh in at roughly 250 tons of dressed copper. This is a large amount of ore which is small sized and has obviously been dressed and sorted as though ready to go to the smelt mill. Records tell us that the Duke of Somerset lost at least 50 tons through the incompetence of the smelters, but this presumably would have been spoilt ore. The brilliance of the original German smelters had been lost through the advent of the Civil War, and severe problems were now arising because of lack of skill. As has been mentioned, there has been a considerable amount of slag found at Copperheap Bay and it may well have been used as a smelt site after the destruction of the Brigham smelter. The heaps in question may have been waiting to be smelted and were simply abandoned at the time of the Civil War.

When David Davies re-opened Goldscope, he found that the mine was in excellent condition and reporting to Prince Charles, Duke of Somerset, he recalled that he had first worked here in Cumberland with 4 old miners who had formerly worked in Goldscope and who told him that the vein was "*the breadth of a sheet*". "*If so*", says David, "*... it was a prodigious thickness or else the sheet was very narrow*". He also investigated a lead vein referred to at that time as the Sand Vein (not to be confused with Barrow Mine) on the western flank of Scope End at Goldscope, but this working is a 16th. C German open work and is waterlogged. David maintained that a short cross cut would de-water this and would cost about £20; this is almost sure to be the one known later as Sealby's Vein. Nearby, at Littledale Brow, David sunk down 12fms. and was able to put twelve men to work here; any water drained away easily in 24 hours presenting no problem, and the ore was worth 50/- a ton. There is another trial, Tinkler's Hole, in the same area of the mountain.

It was possibly during this period that the Newlands smelter was erected. To the south of the St. George Adit, a large complex of buildings was constructed, the approximate overall size being 16ft. wide x 98ft. long within which was a smelt hearth area of around 8ft. x 7ft. Adjacent to this is another area 64ft. long with another building around 16ft. x 14ft. and in between the two buildings is a waterwheel site for an overshot wheel and run off (see plan). The wheel has been supplied with water from Newlands Beck and from the St. George Adit, both of which fed into a small reservoir for the purpose. The building was constructed with substantial foundations throughout and a slated roof over. Nearby, just 60yds. to the north of the Newlands Beck is to be found another building location, possibly a dwelling, measuring approximately 16ft. x 21ft. and nearby, a strong dam has been constructed from which two leats have been taken off, one to supply the nearby smelter.

Another initiative of the time was the formation by 1691 of The English Copper Company, created to ensure the development of the brass and copper industry. It was decreed that only English copper would be used in coinage, and this contract was given to the English Copper Company based on a three year contract in consideration of an annual sum of £2,000. Sadly this venture appears not to have been totally supported, as the Crown imported Swedish copper in 1694 at a price of 18d. per lb. (£8 a ton approx.), although the Company did continue making coins into the next century and there was actually a contract for the production of 700 tons of halfpennies and farthings.

The last record of David Davies who was living at Braithwaite at this time, was in March 1692 when various veins were being worked by 4 men and then, 5 months later on the 17th. August, he surrendered the old lease and took out a new one for a 21 year term on Derwent Fells for lead only. He was of the opinion that the Goldscope venture had been worked out, pumping costs were prohibitive and a new low adit would be the only way forward, but this would be too costly. Although reports were rife that further investigation on the site revealed that the waterwheel by now had been removed and reports say this was dismantled and the wood given to the workers in lieu of wages owed, and that it would be ideal for house construction

Smelting was also another problem as all the old copper smelters had now either died or were too old to remember the process. It seems that David had experimented himself with some of the copper slags in Newlands but that these efforts were abysmal, so he turned all his attention to the lead veins at Stoneycroft and Barrow.

The Reverend Thomas Robinson, the Rector of Ousby, a parish on the western shoulder of the Pennines beneath Cross Fell, was the next real prospector and entrepreneur. He had been educated at a local grammar school and from there attended Christ's College, Cambridge leaving with a BA in 1668. In the same year he became a deacon in Carlisle, was ordained in 1669 and in the same year married Jane Relfe in Addingham Church; three years later, in August 1672, he became the Rector of Ousby. He was a keen amateur geologist and writer who already had penned "The Anatomy of the Earth", dedicating it to "The Gentlemen Miners" and no doubt his local surroundings had over the years created his deep rooted interest.

"Robinson's Anatomy of the Earth.

Licenced January 12th. 1690 Edward Cooke

TO THE GENTLEMEN MINERS

Gentlemen,

I Could not direct this small Treatise, unto a more suitable Patronage, than by devoting it to your Fraternity; the Contents of it, aiming at the more hidden, as well as visible Parts of the EARTH. And the Opportunities I have had, of being sometimes Underground, and the Curiosity of making that dark or occult Region, a Subject of Speculation, will, I hope, plead my Excuse, if I attempt Philosophically to describe those several Metals, Mines and Minerals, with the different Natures and Qualities of their Feeders, or Mineral Waters, which a Mechanik relates only by Rott: It is not out of any great conceit of these Notions, that I have been bold to make them publick, or Dedicate them to you; but out of a strong desire to set some greater Wits on work, to Improve the Subterranean Philosophy; and if these may but contribute to carry on that Design, and have a candid Acceptance, they will encourage me to carry on some further Projects I have in hand, which may be diverting atleast, if not profitable: I am, in the mean time,

GENTLEMEN,

Your hearty Well-wisher
and humble Servant,

THO. ROBINSON"

Surrounded by mines and minerals and the striking geological formations such as High Cup Nick along with the fossilized limestone of the western Pennines area, Thomas Robinson was in his element. However life in the shadow of the Pennines at Ousby was good. By this time his wife had provided him with a large family, eight in total, the first two being boys, Thomas and William. He was apparently well liked by his parishioners, mixing well with them and after most sermons he would join some of his flock in the local ale house, but would warn any man spending more than a penny of the dangers of the demon drink!

Thomas was totally taken up with the subject of geology, minerals and the fascinating proposition of mining, and he decided that with his knowledge he would attempt to reopen the copper mines in the Newlands Valley. Consequently he approached Charles Seymour, the sixth Duke of Somerset, for a lease on Goldscope and the Bolton Coal Mine. His credentials being impeccable he obtained a 21 year lease in 1696, at £60 a year. The Bolton Colliery near Caldbeck was indeed the same colliery that the Hechstetters had used years before, but Thomas, after driving two new levels, was to have no success here. He realized that perhaps coal mining was not his forte and so he turned his attentions to Goldscope and the surrounding valleys. Whilst he was involved in his exploitation of the area at nearby Thomas work in 1698, two new veins were discovered at Goldscope and a total of twelve miners and a smith were working there. Thomas, to give him credit, appears to have been a real hands on person; he had spent months walking the ground and investigated the workings both underground and on the surface, and had made copious notes and observations. Armed with this information, and his belief of the riches which still lay below the sole of the ancient German workings, he provided a section of the workings to the Duke of Somerset in the hope of eliciting the Duke's financial help for the future development of the mine.

To assist the Duke further in his deliberations Thomas laid out a strategic plan of action and costings, and his geological findings which proved he could not be wrong. He recommended the driving of a new low level from the eastern side of the mountain below the St. George. The Duke asked the opinion of David Davies with regard to the scheme planned by Thomas, which was indeed speculative. The driving of a level at least 255yds. long before coming into the old workings would cost at least £1,275 and take ten years to complete. Thomas was quick to point out that the driving would be in the vein, and a considerable amount of ore would be won on the way which would part fund the venture as it advanced, in much the same way as the earlier German adventurers had worked. The prize would be the 24fms. of backs of ore which could be accessible below the existing German works. David Davies had stated in his report of 1698, that he considered that the workings went only 10fms. below the sole, as this was about the most that the engines of that time could draw. Thomas, however, had sight of some of the old German accounts that stated : *"Gods Gift being wrought 30 fathom below level in 1593".*

In March 1698, with Newlands in the grip of winter, the miners were struggling; water had inundated the workings and conditions underground were ghastly. Apart from the wet, the air was foul with the smell and smoke from the tallow candles and besides this, the men were also starting to use gunpowder for blasting in the south side near the old men's wheelpit. Outside the conditions were appalling as the snow and frost prevented the use of any machinery, and copper ore stood frozen solid in the heaps where it had been dumped from the mine. No stamping or washing could be done and consequently smelting was also at a halt... and still the weather persisted.

Realizing his time was being wasted at the mine whilst the weather was being so intolerable, Thomas Robinson attempted to fight his way through the drifts to go to Carlisle, 35 miles away. The journey was epic and he decided that it would be useless to return until the weather had truly abated. Whilst he stayed in the comfort of his abode, he used his time to catch up on correspondence, and ponder the foreign market prices of minerals which at this time were more favourable than ours. The snows melted and he was soon back in the valley, the washing of ore commenced and the stockpiles reduced after a constant twelve day stint, thus ensuring the smelters could once again go about there business.

As we know Thomas was a geologist and he was convinced the lead vein in the far western end of the workings was shaped like a church doorway; in his studies below ground and on surface he had also identified at least one other vein. His miners were still driving forward west and when miner John Bonner and his team intersected a new vein, Thomas was delighted and paid John for finding it; the vein was to become known as the New Goldscope Vein. During this period the work force consisted of eight miners amongst them, Ewart William and Joseph Tickell. Stores were being purchased on a regular basis and on the 28th. of September 1699, gunpowder appears in the accounts when 6lbs. were purchased at 1/- a lb., three dozen tallow candles cost 12/-, all very necessary expenditure.

During October 1699 Lord Lowther who, apart from having extensive land holdings in the Lake District owned most of the coal rights in the west of the county, and at Moresby had built and was experimenting with a coal fired copper smelter. In discussions with the Duke of Somerset it was suggested that copper from Goldscope and Newlands would be welcome. However the Duke of Somerset was already planning to smelt his own ore, and had approached Thomas with some tacit arrangement that if he could produce malleable copper ore he would consider part funding the venture, he had already consulted with John Woodward the Duke's chemist on the subject but they could never really agree on the correct formula. This resulted in Thomas continuing to pursue the refining of copper with the utmost urgency on his own and he engaged the services of a Mr. Baker in 1702; he employed him to prospect for the best copper ore and then attempt to smelt it. Thomas was convinced that the copper veins at surface in Newlands were too sulphurous, and the deeper they tried the richer the ore would become, hence his desire to eventually enter the old German workings below the wheelpit chamber. In the meantime he terminated the contracts of his existing miners who were at that time working two veins south of Goldscope. He then created new contracts which required the men to produce 5 tons of ore per week for the sum of £12 10s. 0d. Mr. Baker in fact left in November of that year after failing to produce malleable copper, so Thomas engaged another smelter by the name of Myddleton Shaw from Staffordshire, to see if he could provide a finished product and so hopefully gain support from the Duke.

Thomas was obsessed with his objective of de-water the old German pumping shaft where he was convinced the copper ore would be rich and pure the deeper the orebody went... surely the Germans had not taken everything. This was an enormous challenge - to de-water the shaft and clear it of any debris would cost at least £130 but Thomas went ahead and instructed his mine foreman Thomas Hanson to proceed with the work. For this he would be paid £2 a ton for ore raised from the shaft bottom, provided this was free of spar. Timber was purchased and brought to the mine so that the work could proceed, and it seemed to his workforce that this could be a good proposition. Results were essential as total of £797 had been spent on the venture over the last year - a vast amount of money for a single adventurer! By the end of 1703 Thomas was worried and frustrated for, despite all his efforts, he was not producing malleable copper. His latest smelter, Myddleton Shaw, was blamed and in fact, Thomas actually classified him as an ignorant operator! In his defense, it must be said that Myddleton was an experienced smelter and that he could command £100 per ton from the Bristol smelt mills. However this was of no consequence as far as Robinson was concerned, for he had again failed to present even 1cwt. of ore to the Duke of Somerset. Consequently, Thomas was seeing his possible benefactor drifting away and his debts rising.

By November 1704, Thomas Robinson's ventures were in a serious state of decline and his plans for the reopening of Goldscope were now at a standstill. The Bolton Colliery was still losing money and in the interim, another wild scheme of Thomas's had been to exploit the iron deposits of Wasdale to raise money, but this was also doomed to failure.

His debt had now spiralled up to £460 and in a final effort to retain his leases, he made overtures to the Duchess whilst on a visit to London; alas his charms did not make the slightest impression on Her Grace ... Thomas had failed. Now an utterly broken man, he despondently returned to his parish for solace, but there was no forgiveness here. His church was rundown, his neglect of his parochial duties was more than evident and the elders were left with no alternative but to request he leave. Robinson's leases were terminated and the mines put under a caretaker by the name of John Scott, who was to remain there for ten years in that post.

Later that year the Duke dispatched John Hutchinson, an experienced mine surveyor and long time retainer of the family, to inspect the mines. He started in the north at Bolton Colliery, then onto Newlands armed with Thomas Robinson's scant drawings. On arrival he discovered the bunning at the entrance to Goldscope collapsed and the mine closed; workmen were brought and the adit cleared, this was entered and the workings explored to the 20fm. Level. It was here they expected to see the orebody reflecting silver and bright yellow copper, a great proposal for a further trial according to Thomas's reports. The riches however were not there and where the lodes were present, they had been greatly exaggerated. Hutchinson's subsequent report was certainly not conducive to the further development of Goldscope or Newlands.

By 1708, Thomas's financial state was critical and he fled to London away from the bailiffs, where he became a Naval chaplain and was seconded to His Majesty's ship "Panther". This was the end of his involvement in mining era, and he turned his hand to writing his second book, entitled "The Natural History of Cumberland and Westmorland". It was published by Freeman's of Fleet Street, London in 1709, and by all accounts sold reasonably well. The following year, in 1710, he was paid off from the Navy and he returned to Cumberland.

As a mining engineer and businessman he failed, perhaps inclined to exaggerate but then, what entrepreneur doesn't? But his sketches and surveys of the area have proved invaluable in establishing the siting of the mines in Newlands Valley at that time.

10 Copper Bottomed

The next lease to be taken up was by Thomas Ackersley in the year of 1713 and was for a 21 year term. His miners entered Goldscope and discovered Robinson's pumps and timber still lying there. However little was done by Ackersley and soon he was in financial difficulties, so in an attempt to stave off the inevitable, he penned a letter directly to Charles, Duke of Somerset asking if his rent could be reduced, or perhaps His Grace would accept a percentage of the profits instead which would alleviate the situation; it appears His Grace however, was unsympathetic.

In May 1719 Thomas Robinson died and was laid to rest in his own church at Ousby. the last years of his life had been a torment of avoiding bailiffs, although he had not been greatly successful as he had been arrested at least six times. His rising debt now stood at £695 which he owed to the Duke of Somerset had been pursued by his bailiffs, they had removed equipment from his Bolton Mine in lieu of the debts owed, Robinson to the end contested that the bailiffs had removed far more equipment than that of the debt. With Ackersley and Robinson now history, the mine fell into complete dereliction and during 1738 it is recorded that much of the remains of the now derelict works in Newlands and Goldscope were sold for scrap in weighted lots. There were stamp heads, grates and plates, pincers, tools and old iron, thus one can imagine nothing of much use would be left. Buildings would be de-roofed, good timbers taken and any stone worth having would be sold. Any odd bits left after that would be stolen by farmers for building, walling etc. The next adventurer was a Mr. Gilpin, who in 1756 took over the mine and spent a considerable amount of money de-watering it, but what he eventually achieved we do not know.

Despite the huge amount of effort which had gone into the brass and copper industry over the past years in this country, it was estimated that by now £45,000 had been invested to stimulate the industry and yet the overall returns had not been enough. It would be another 3 years before British coins would be struck at the mint using all British Copper. Naturally as the years went by and technology grew, other uses for copper apart from pots, pins, buttons, woollen cards, coinage and ordnance sprang up. A major step forward occurred in 1781, when the idea of copper-bottoming ships took shape, particularly the ships of His Majesty's Navy. The initial trials had been a resounding success and the 82 gun frigate 'Alarm' was the first to be encased in a shining copper coat. The Captain announced that trials had been an incredible success. The effect of this crude form of armour-plating was to increase the speed by reducing drag, prevent barnacles and other sea molluscs adhering to the ship's hull and prevented worms attacking the wood. The demand now created for copper caused the price to spiral to around a £100 a ton.

During December 1819, John Tebay of Whitehaven took over the lease of the mine along with others in the area including Brandlehow, where his main interest lay, along with other mines in the sett. In the intervening years all the spare cash for development went into Brandlehow and Yewthwaite, and Goldscope was basically ignored. It was virtually sixteen years before any serious efforts were to be made when, on the 5th. of August 1835, John Tebay made a partnership with one Isaac Sealby an iron monger from Keswick and James Reed, an experienced miner from Loweswater. The new company negotiated a lease for seven years, at a royalty of 1/8th. The venture was short lived, although they did drive a level beneath the old German workings on the western flank of Scope End just south of the Water Level and the trial was called Sealby's after Isaac. The end result was a paltry 20 tons of lead and not the huge returns the men had been anticipating. It is not clear if anything was done in Goldscope, but one can imagine that the mine would have been in poor shape, nothing having been done for upwards of 60 years. The lead vein was to become immortalized as Sealby Vein after the discoverer, but the venture had stretched the resources of the partnership to the limit, both Brandlehow and Yewthwaite had been a particular drain on the cash flow and so the Goldscope mine was once again closed up.

The mine did not stay closed for long and in February 1847 another partnership of men took out a lease, at a royalty 1/15th. These men were mining engineers and businessmen, William Clemence Snr., John Bowden of Hawarden Foundry, W. Clemence Jnr. of Mold and John Floyd also of Mold. It is this group of men who, under the mine captaincy of William Clemence, actually widened the main level at Goldscope and in so doing, partially destroyed the longest German coffin level in the county. They started by clearing the level, then they erected a replacement 16ft. waterwheel at the site of the German shaft and commenced pumping the old working out.

It would have been totally impractical to wheelbarrow ore that distance, and so the level was railed out from the wheelpit to day, a distance of 250yds. The level was also widened from around 3ft. 6ins. to 4ft. 6ins. down to the level floor, leaving the top section just as the Germans had hand-chipped it out nearly 300 years before. As the level widening advanced, iron rails were laid to a gauge of 22ins. on sleepers 30ins. x 5ins. and probably no more than three tubs would be required. The German miners had cut the level to around 7ft. high and so, as the miners widened the tunnel, driving 24in. advances, they packed the floor with waste to a depth of 6ins. for the new rail bed. This meant that some of the debris from the widening would not have to be trammed out, and an 8in. gap was left on the southern side of the adit to provide a drainage culvert. This allowed water to flow freely out of the level, then via a leat, to the new crushing floor 60ft. below on the old spoil heap - just as the German miners had done all those years before. A new era of mining was coming to one of the oldest mines in Cumberland. The development work had been excessive over the past two years, but the reward was a mere 46 tons of copper ore, which was brought up from the sole and the stopes of the wheelpit chamber area. During their tenure, the company is recorded as having erected a furnace and dressing plant, bringing the total development costs to upwards of £5,000. The poor return on all this work had basically bankrupted the company, but fortunately it appears that another group of business men was prepared to purchase the company as a going concern, and they took over in 1849.

The new company was spearheaded by Andrew Richard Clarke who held two shares, Charles Nicholas Patrick Chapman, also with two shares and Thomas Hart and George William Horn who had one share each. The new terms were agreed with Cockermouth Castle and the lease was for a 21 year term at a royalty of 1/15th. and also included Yewthwaite. Mr. Horn remained only two months with the company and then left, his share being divided up between the other partners.

The previous company had paved the way for success, the level now cleared and cut to a suitable size for efficient tramming, and had been well prepared for further development. The mine captain for the new adventurers appears to have been William Jeffrey, who recommended that the way to develop the mine further was to continue the main adit west, which would give 40fms. of backs, and to forget the old German shaft. Eventually they should intersect the lead vein now known as Sealby's which hopefully would provide a valuable strike, The mill constructed by the previous company seemed to be in good order and suitable for all their requirements; the Cockermouth and Penrith railway connection was now well established and the new station at Braithwaite would have been a bonus for the transportation of incoming and outgoing goods.

The manager was a man called Henry Lowden who was by all accounts a miner of some ability, however rumours were rife that he was unreliable, being late for work or simply not turning up, and was also accused of being drunk. Perhaps the fact that he also ran the Mill Dam Inn with his wife Jane could have had something to do with his plight. Further investigation confirmed there had been no letter of appointment as manager, and the embarrassing situation was further inflamed as it was discovered that he could neither read nor write! However, local engineer R. B. Shepherd wrote to the Mining Journal to repudiate these claims which were probably no more than malicious rumours. Under Lowden's management, the work continued at a great pace and the wage bill for the miners and general expenses for the past year mounted up to £1,068.

Clarke's men commenced by preparing the levels and in so doing entered the innermost workings where they discovered an old 16ft. 3in. dia. waterwheel, and some old wooden 4in. square pumps, but it was not clear to which period they belonged. The men now continued driving west, securing the floor over the shaft area; they were not distracted by the old German workings but were committed to driving the level forward as planned. The miners continued the drive, but all they encountered was barren ground and the so called Sealby bonanza lode was not discovered. Some of the investors were becoming impatient and, as the costs mounted, when further calls were made on the shareholders, in some cases enough was enough. Thomas Hart left the board in May 1850, unable to make the necessary financial commitment and his mood was one of bitterness. He left the boardroom threatening that if the mine ever made good he would be back for his money! By the end of the year 32 tons of copper had been raised at a value of £137 10s. 7d.

11 The Great Bunch

During April 1852 Chapman also was disillusioned with the way the things were going and went to find his wealth in the Australian gold fields, however he made an agreement with Clarke, that in the event of the mines becoming profitable, any monies due upon the shares he had relinquished would be paid to himself or his heirs until, the amounts paid should equal the capital he had invested; to this Mr. Clarke agreed. On Chapman's departure in May 1852, Clarke pursued the venture alone, determined to succeed and indeed, so much money had already been spent, he was also at the point of no return. Another four months went by and the miners followed Clarke's instructions, blasting and timbering their way through the mountain, dumping the waste down the old German shaft and workings to save tramming it out to day. Eventually, Clarke's tenacity was rewarded and the miners intersected a lead bunch in September which, after some general excavation, proved the intersecting lode to be 15fms. long and with sparkling silver galena in the north and south faces; it was 3ft. wide with other stringers up to 8ins. thick. If this continued it would be a bonanza strike. Initial inspection revealed that they could expect 6 to 8 tons of ore per fathom with a silver content of around 7oz. per ton.

News of the Goldscope strike was publicized in the local press and Thomas Hart, still smarting from his financial loss, now saw the sole owner Clarke ready to make a killing. As good as his parting words, Hart's course of action was to take Clarke to court and a long and expensive action followed which dragged on for months and into 1853. Eventually a judgment was found in favour of Hart's claim, and thus he regained his share. Clarke then bought Hart's share from him for £4,500 but his health was failing and shortly after the case he passed away.

By now the workforce was quite substantial with about twenty eight men underground and twenty two working the mill and on general surface duties. It seemed that things were looking up and around 201 tons of lead had been produced and sold for £2,749. Anticipating success, it was decided to erect a new mill and processing plant on a site below the spoil heaps at OD550ft., however, the main crusher would remain on top of the old German dump for the time being..

By June 1854 the massive lead strike had become known as the "Great Bunch" and was worked south and above the old copper adit, but later in the year disaster struck when hundreds of tons of ore peeled off the hanging walls and cascaded into the workings below - it was described as "the great crush". Miraculously, as it occurred on a weekend when no-one was working, there were no fatalities which must surely have been the case had it happened during the week. However, a slippage of this magnitude caused massive logistical problems Access was prevented, ground was unstable, and it was anticipated it would take three years to clear the ore and debris. Work started in securing access so that ore could be transported to the mill to keep up production. Despite the problems, by the end of the year 505 tons was produced which realized a return of £7,286 8s. 11d.

It was during this period that the manager of Yewthwaite R. B. Shepherd was asked to come over and take charge, and bring with him most of his best miners; this really was the death knell for Yewthwaite, but Goldscope was where the new investment was going to be.

Naturally further access to the new orebody was required, and it was essential to prove its potential at depth. To do this, in 1855 a level was driven in from the western side of the fell at OD864ft. and this would intersect the lode. The workforce was still being maintained at around fifty men, many of whom were occupied in clearing the crush much of which was part of the rich orebody, while others were engaged in timbering and making the mine safe. The new level was driven forward with all possible speed and was referred to as the Back Level, and at around 60ft. in, it turned south for around 40ft., and at this point it was decided to commence a shaft. This was not put down vertically but inclined at roughly 80 degrees and once they were down 10fms., a heading was started south. By the end of the year, the shaft had arrived at the 20fm. horizon but here they encountered water and this had to be removed. A windlass was being used to haul out the dead work, and a 4in hand pump was installed to clear the water, and was being operated by two men.

The engineer John Taylor Jnr., had with the passing of the final shareholder A. R. Clarke, been appointed trustee whilst the company was involved in its legal problems and the mine was to be run to secure the future of Clarke's children. This must have been a traumatic time for the company, having been run solely by Clarke, now all the future plans would have to be made by a board of Trustees solely for the benefit of his surviving children, therefore no wild and reckless decisions could or should be made which would mean a short fall in the children's wellbeing for the future.

One can only assume that the vein was of sufficient richness at depth and that the Trustees considered that further development of the shaft would not constitute a major risk; it was therefore decided to make a serious commitment and continue below the copper adit horizon. To ensure the ore could be wound from the lower workings, it was planned that a 16ft. waterwheel would be installed underground 20ft. above the Copper Adit, in what was to become known as the Engine Level. Its position was crucial and water was taken from the old leat, diverted through the Back Adit down the shaft into an underground cistern which in turn supplied the 16ft. hauling wheel. The spent water was then diverted into the copper adit and laundered through the adit to day where it was used at the dressing floor. It was soon realized however, that this small wheel had very limited use, and if the mine was to develop, a larger and more efficient wheel would have to be installed for the purpose of pumping. In order to ensure sufficient power for a new wheel, a substantial 35ft. high stone dam was constructed just south of the old German dam which had far greater capacity; the water was brought to the mine via the old German leat. A further new adit would be required, and this was situated 20ft. above the Back Adit. Here, the new pump-rod adit was hewn out of solid rock, along with the installation area and footings for a new 40ft. waterwheel. The spent water again would be channelled underground into a cistern for use by the smaller wheel which would do the hauling, the spent water then being transferred to the copper adit below and out to day via the St. George Level, just as the Germans had done 300 years before.

Naturally the installation of the new waterwheel in 1856 and the new pumping and drawing machinery, created a shortfall in the production of ore and this was also aggravated by the running down of Yewthwaite. Whilst the shaft was being sunk the copper adit was still being driven south, and was now in blue douky ground; it was driven a total of 160fms. but no new ore deposits were encountered. Four men were driving here and air was being supplied by 3in. pipes but at this point little or no ore was to be seen. By the end of the year the shaft was down to the 30fm. Level whilst above this, the 10fm. Level was being developed and had been driven 7fms. north. Meanwhile, the new mill was being constructed below the Grand Level at OD550ft., and an 18ft. waterwheel for a set of 12 head stamps was being erected, along with buddles and other equipment.

The year of 1857 started poorly as, during February, Henry Lowden died after being involved in a blasting accident. Henry had worked many of the local mines and had been the manager at Brandley, but had had a disagreement with Taylor who had sacked him. His position had always been defended by Mr. Clarke and R. B. Shepherd who had taken him on at Goldscope. Sadly he left a wife, eight girls and a boy in arms; he had been generally well liked in the community and upwards of. 300 people attended his funeral in Keswick and a subscription was taken for the family's future.

The production of ore had been aggravated by the installation of all the equipment at the pump-rod shaft and the new dressing plant; 313 tons had been sold in comparison with 440 tons the previous year. The only good news was that by the end of the year the "big crush" had been cleared and work could now hopefully be resumed; the new engine shaft was down a distance of 30fms., and headings 5fms. north and 6fms. south were being struck out and were in good ore. The 30fm. Level had a particular purpose in the northern heading as this was planned to be the pumping adit, and eventually the main tramming level to the mill. A substantial leat would carry the water directly to the new dressing floor, and this would save haulage and pumping over a considerable height.

Over the last 40 years a considerable amount of investment had been made in the construction of a full dressing mill on the east side of the workings at OD550ft. below the mouth of the Grand Level. The first horizon consisted of the usual office and smithy which were sited beside the main haulage road; the second terrace was overshadowed by the 18ft. waterwheel for the crusher and nearby were the jiggs, the mine house, large stables and the ore house. Below this were two buddles which were driven by an 8ft. diameter waterwheel, and nearby was a set of Brunton's slimes frames; below this and just above the river was a set of catch pits for the slimes. All the main buildings were constructed of local stone, some of which were slated. Indeed two different layouts of the dressing floor were drawn up by W. L. Newby on the 16th July 1858; these were slightly different to each other, although both were based on the development of the 30fm. Level. He also drew a plan of the mine, however his ordnance datum for the Goldscope Adit is incorrect as is given as OD500ft. and current OS indicates this as being OD710ft.

Despite what appears to be a successful operation the company was restructured, and on Christmas Day 1859 the lease was transferred to Messrs. George John May and Richard David Holland and was for a 21 year term at a 1/15th. royalty. Clarke's shares were left in the company in trust and the newly formed company had to support his children.

Within the year of 1860, the Goldscope royalty produced 415 tons valued at £5,611 13s. 7d. with cartage costing £415 2s. 0d. There were fifty miners employed at the mine and the N/S lead vein was being worked. A letter confirms that the new 40ft. wheel was now installed and working, and in August 1861, the plan for the 30fm. Level was put into operation. The location for the adit would be on the land of Robert Faulder of Low House farm and so before work could commence, the land purchase had to be negotiated. The sale was concluded by the company solicitors and the amount of £17 7s. 6d. was duly paid and the rights of way through the land secured. Work started on the new venture in September 1862 when a tramway was surveyed, whilst underground the level was pushed north towards day. Another group of miners prepared a timber entrance at OD560ft. and commenced driving forward to meet the underground team; virtually all the spoil created was trammed round to Newlands to the site of the mill. This was now under review for further upgrading: a large carpenters shop was being incorporated into the building next to the stables, the slime pits were re-sited and a further two sets of trunking buddles were to be installed to ensure maximum recovery.

During 1862, the company at Goldscope introduced a sick scheme for the miners who contributed a 1/- a month, and this enabled them to draw 7/- to 8/- a week sick pay. The company at this time was employing thirty three miners working in the mine and twenty two men at the mill. The operation was moving forward successfully, the engine shaft was down to 82fms. and the orebody being worked was 90yds. long with around a 12in. lead rib in both faces and in the sole; so far the venture had produced a profit of £25,000.

Goldscope, despite its dramatic "crush", had fortunately not claimed many lives, and throughout its years appears to have had an excellent safety record. This however was to be tarnished on the 9th. of May 1864 when William Tarleton, aged 38, was killed in fall of rock.

During 1864 it became patently obvious that the 40ft. wheel used for pumping was struggling to raise water from the increasing depth; the shaft bottom was now at the 90fm. Level and the wheel was not capable of lifting the water from such a depth. A larger wheel or steam engine would have to be purchased to ensure that the mine could continue, however the vein was not showing enough promise for further major investment. Consequently, it was considered that it would be prudent to close the mine to ensure the secure future for the Clarke children which the directors and trustees had undertaken. During the period of 12 years 5,000 tons of lead plus 22,000ozs. of silver had been extracted.

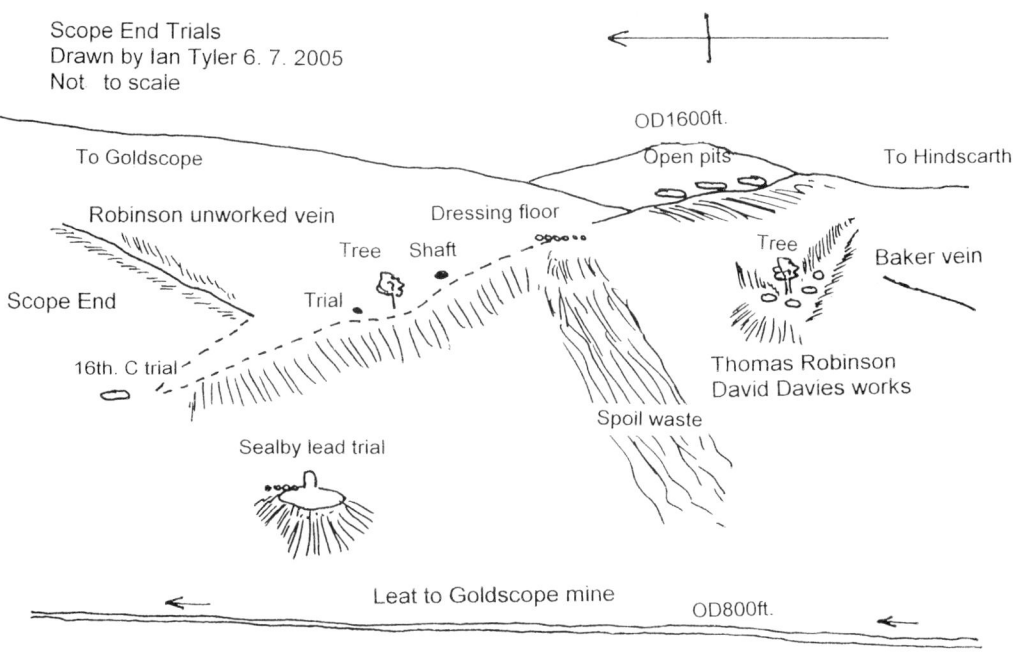

Top: Scope End trials west. Stuart Clement Collection.
Bottom: Plan of Scope End trials west. Drawn by Ian Tyler.

Scope End, hand-picked working Scope End West near Baker Vein - possibly Tinkler's Hole. Stuart Clement Collection.

Scope End, hand-picked working Scope End West near Baker Vein. Stuart Clement Collection.

David Davies lead trial c1690, 100 yds. south of Great Lead Crush. Stuart Clement Collection

Trial on Sealby Lead lode - note wooden railway lines with metal strip on top c1840. Stuart Clement Collection

Stoped area on Sealby lead vein near internal shaft. Ian Tyler Collection.

High Snab ridge - ancient opencut on back of vein. 17th. C. workings continue down to valley bottom. Ian Tyler Collection.

High Snab workings, 17th. C. looking south to site of Goldscope dams and Scope Beck. Ian Tyler Collection.

Goldscope West, 40ft. waterwheel - pump-rod adit c1850. Stuart Clement Collection.

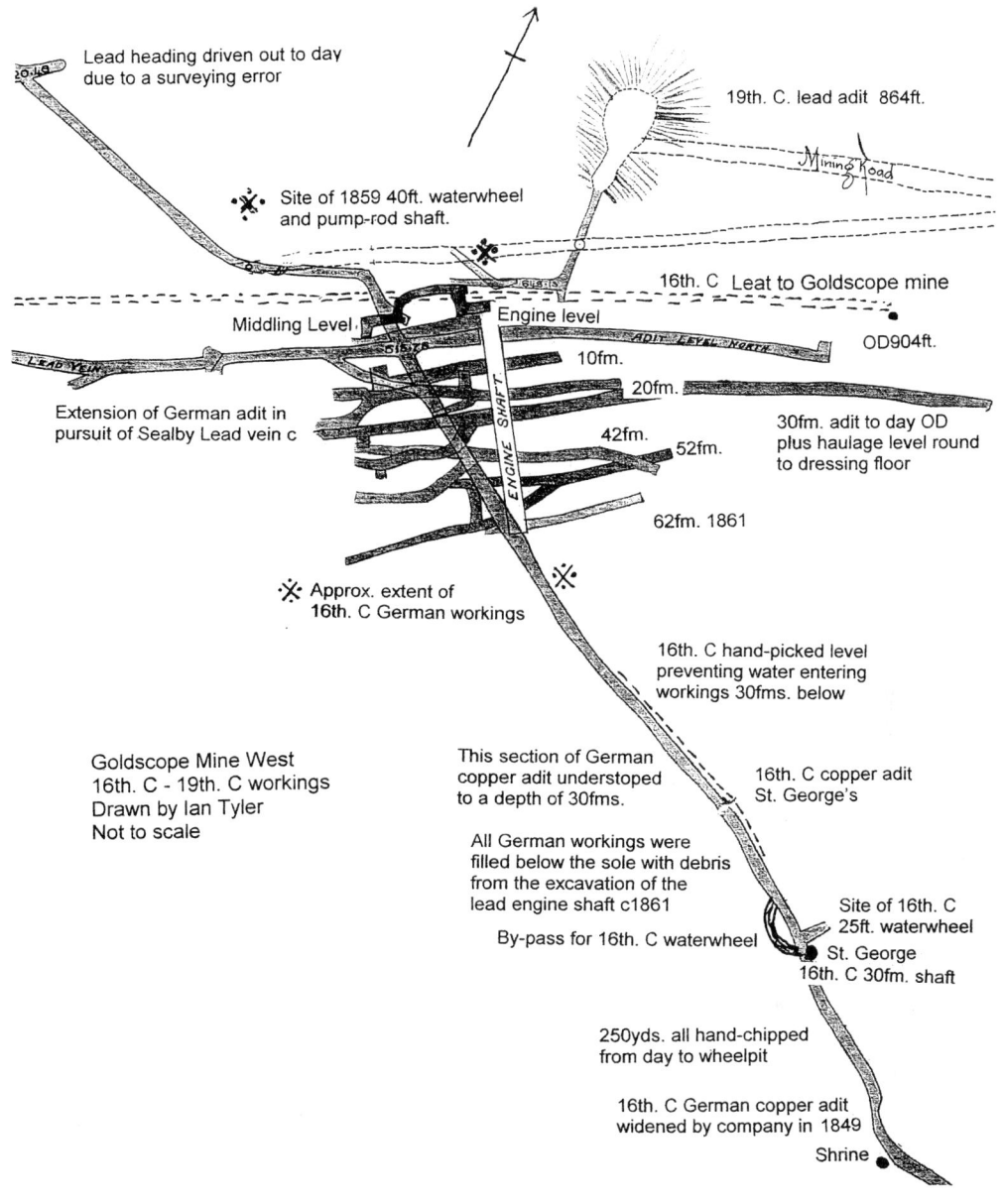

Goldscope West - plan of back lead workings before external 40ft. waterwheel. Re-drawn by Ian Tyler.

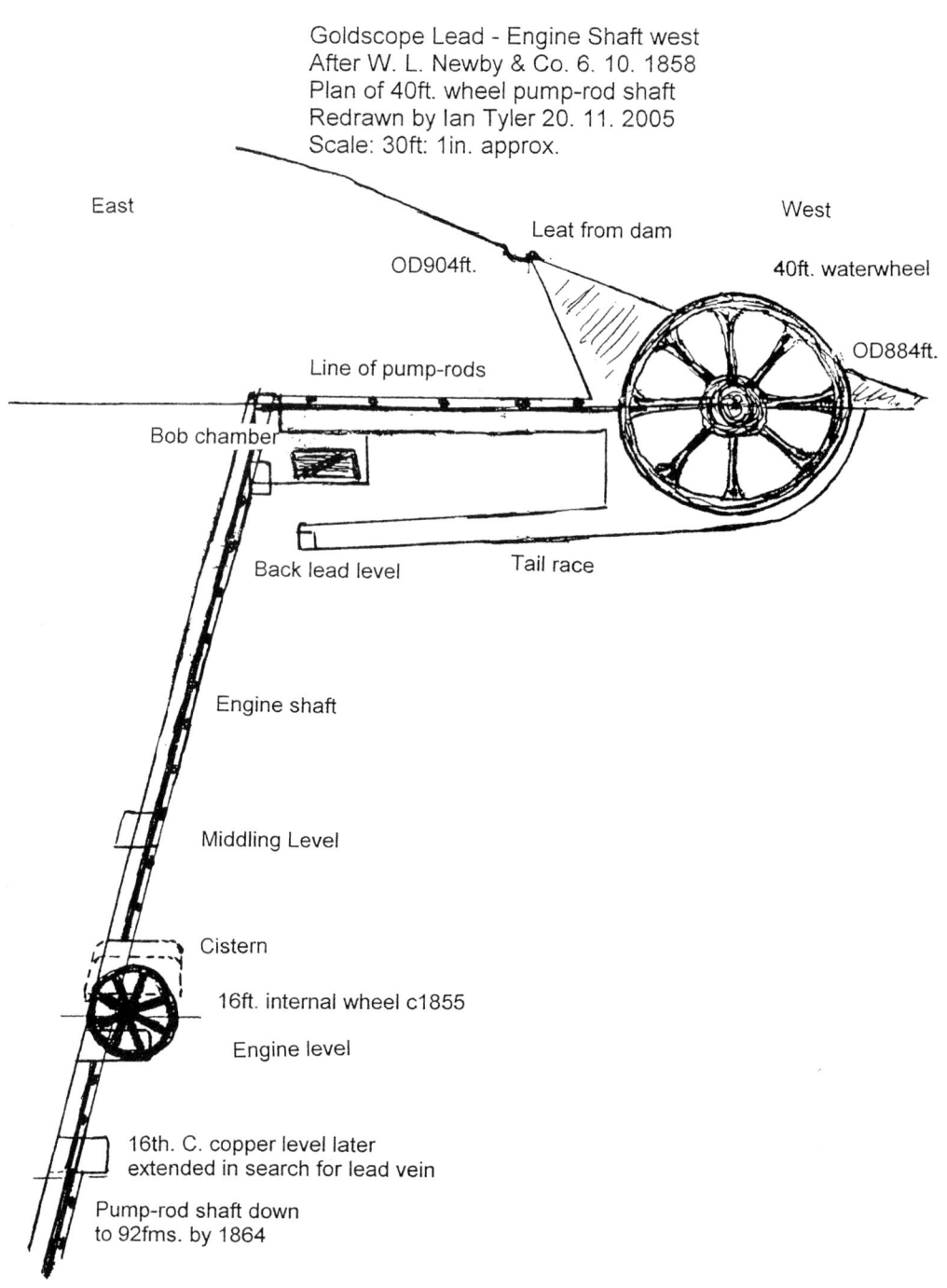

Goldscope West Lead Shaft, Plan of 40ft. wheel and pump-rod shaft. Re-drawn by Ian Tyler 20. 11. 2005. Scale 30ft: 1in

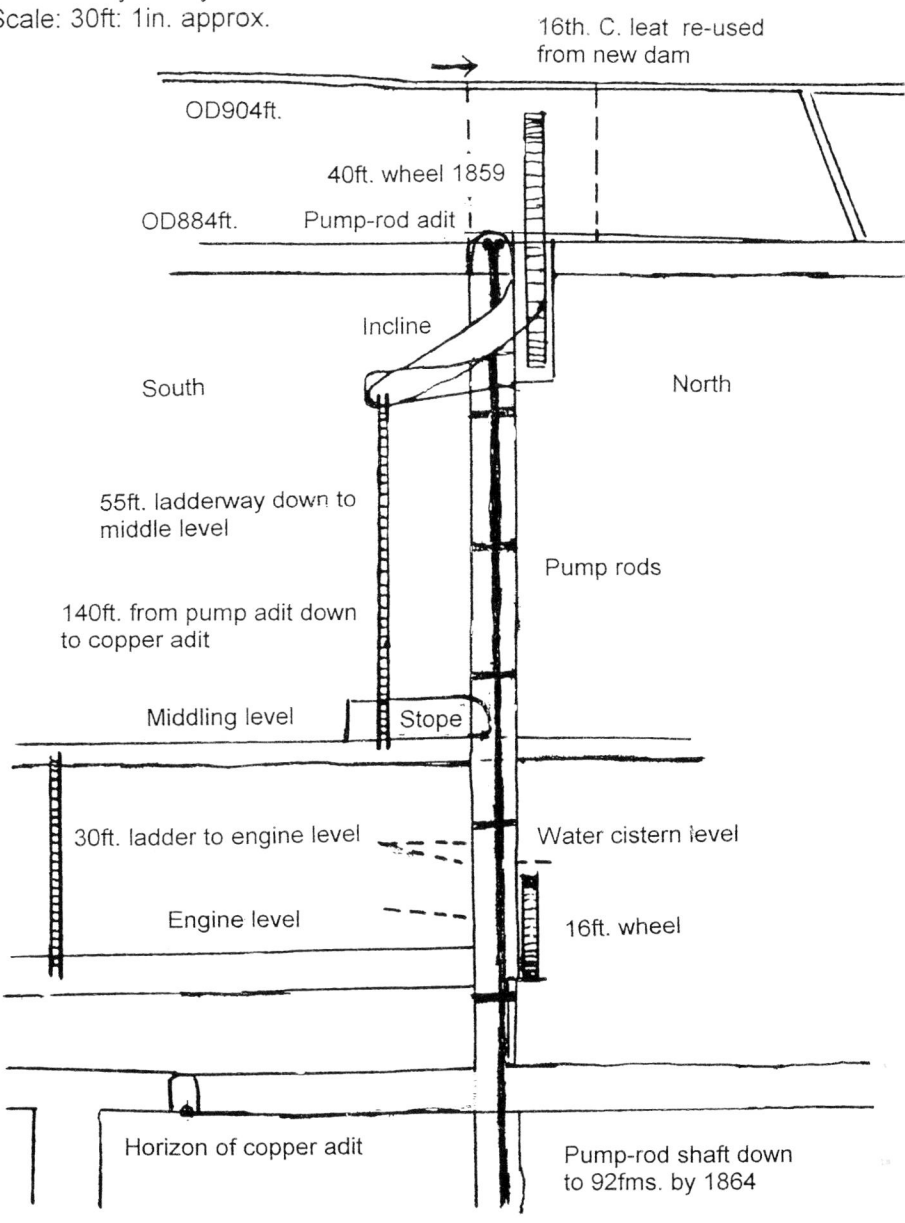

Goldscope West Lead Shaft section. Re-drawn by I. Tyler 20. 11. 2005. Scale: 30ft: 1in.

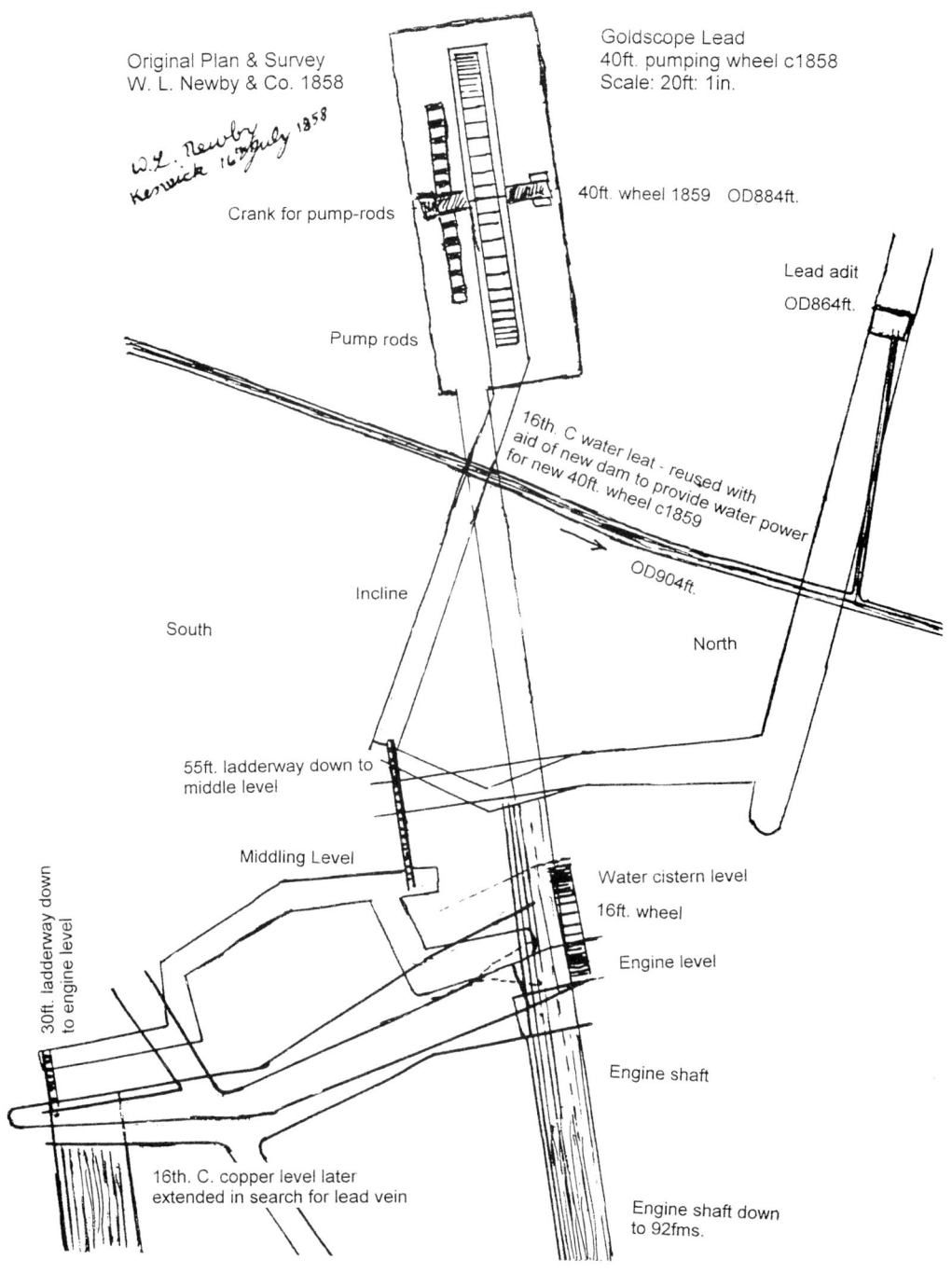

Goldscope West Lead Shaft plan. Re-drawn by Ian Tyler 20.11.2005. Scale: 30ft: 1in.

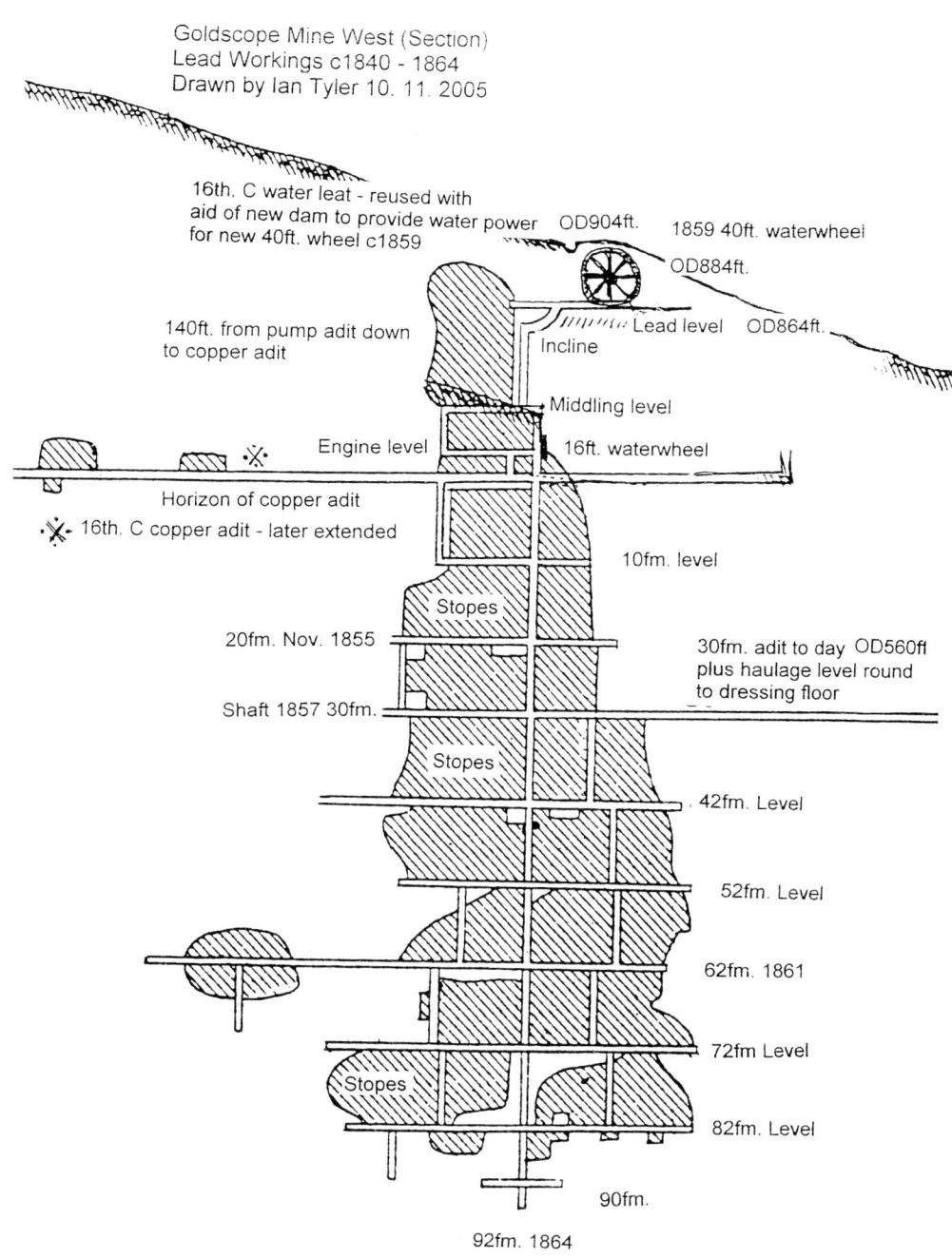

Goldscope West lead workings, shaft section 1840 - 1864, 92fms. in depth. Drawn by Ian Tyler

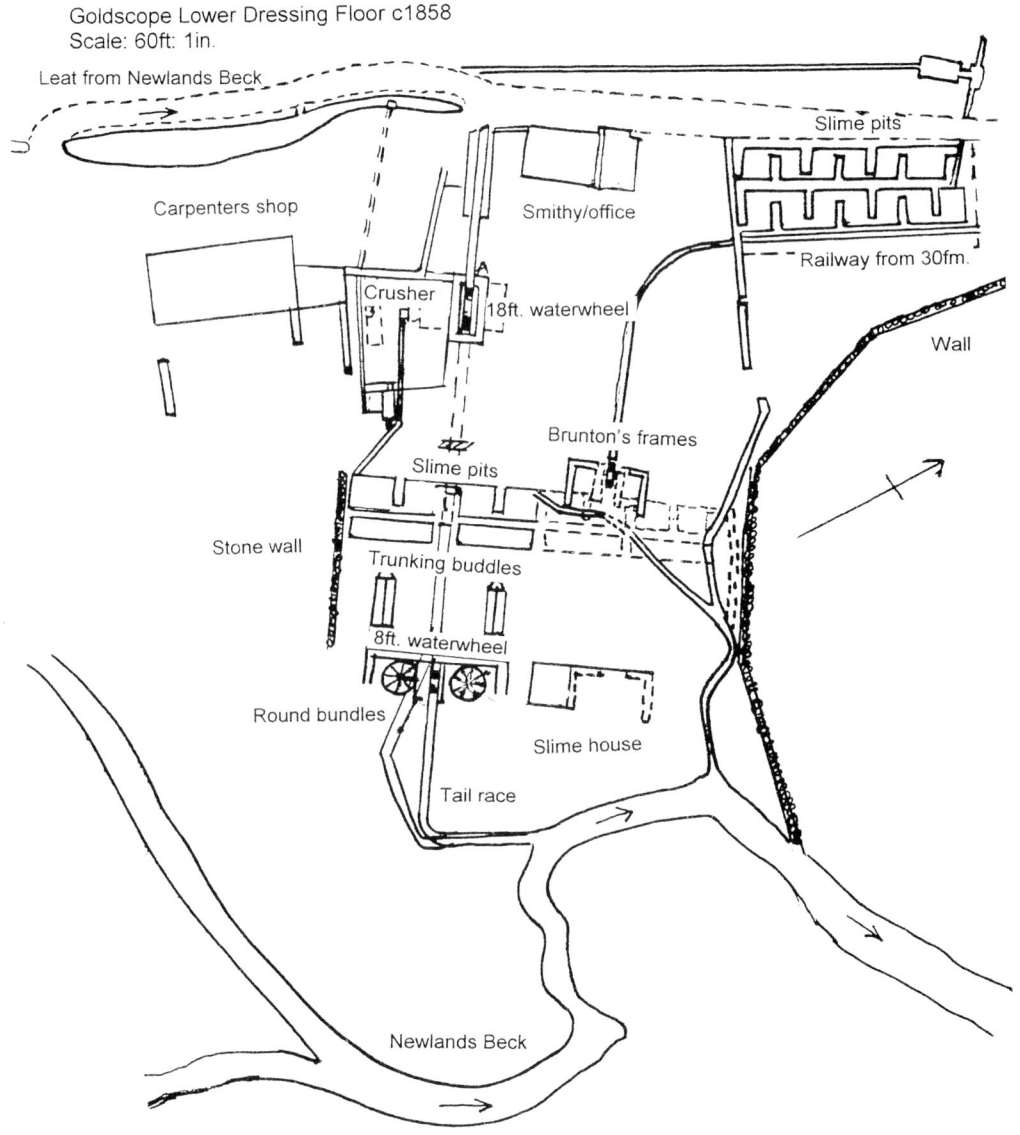

Goldscope Mine, plan of dressing floor beneath St. George Adit for lead working 1858. Drawn by Ian Tyler.

Goldscope Adit - Grand Level, with tubs outside c1920. Courtesy of Tullie House Museum.

12 Goldscope - Goodbye

By 1866, almost 16 years since the discovery of the lead bunch, the orebody, which had been worked down to a depth of 90fms., had been totally removed. The Great Bunch certainly lived up to its name producing 50cu. yds. of solid galena. At the southern end of the mine, the 60fm. Level intersected the Borrowdale String Vein which revealed only a 9in. vein of lead, and here the miners rarely needed explosive but were able to remove the lead with crow bars. By 1867, the Engine Shaft was down to 92fms. below the copper adit, a total vertical depth overall of 700ft., and this was not pursued any further.

February 1869 saw the Goldscope Mining Company before the Petty Sessions at Keswick, which was duly presided over by T. S. Spedding, S. Z. Langton, William Oxley and J. J. Spedding, answering a charge of pollution, brought by the Derwent Angling Association. Samuel Gordon, along with schoolmaster Mr. Peter Harrison, John Bowe of Stair and Thomas Faulder, a local inn keeper, declared they had known the quality of the Newlands Beck for many years, that it was a fine trout spawning river, and trout could be caught from Bassenthwaite to Goldscope, but now the mining company at Goldscope had destroyed this. Benjamin Plummer, the mine manager. naturally refuted all the claims, declaring that they had in place no less than eleven catch pits, and he displayed his plans of the plant. Two miners, Charles Lowden and Joseph Pooley, said that they did not see how things could be improved and this was further endorsed by C. A. Haywood, a chemist and analyst who had taken samples from the stream and had not found anything which would harm any fish!

Around 1870, H. K. Spark of Darlington, took on board the lease of Goldscope amongst others in the area. He was a speculative adventurer and by 1873, he was driving a trial level into the western flank of Maiden Moor at Near Broad Gill, and at the same time, with a team of twenty six men, he began working the 90fm. Level at Goldscope, but gradually, things were literally grinding to a halt. A brief report on the 17th. of November 1877, indicates that four lodes were being worked, two of lead and two of copper, however these are not individually identified. The final year of the venture appears to have been 1878, when a total of 38 tons of ore was raised, and then Henry K Spark died. His estate was wound up and the Goldscope mill was auctioned off along with some plant from Yewthwaite, for £57. The auctioneer, Mr. Mumberson, completed the sale of the plant with the remnants of the 40ft. Goldscope wheel which fetched £3 7s .0d.

It was almost 30 years before any further work was done when new interest was shown in 1908, and one can imagine what state the mine was in after being derelict for twenty years, and at the mercy of the local weather. The Cumbrian Mining Co. obtained a Take-note at a rent of £50 and 1/20th. royalty, and which had a strict covenant with regard to any stream pollution. By 1911 the company was in serious financial difficult, owing rent and dues to the total of £220 16s. 8d. Another change in the lease came during 1912 when a Mr. Dennison took a 1 year Take-note at a royalty of 1/20th., but this was a short lived affair and the Take-note was not renewed. However, in 1913, another group of adventurers made up of local men took up the challenge. The new venture was called the Coledale Syndicate and the partners were Bennett Johns of Keswick and W. H Heywood from Huddersfield, the initial Take note was for one year, at a rent of £25 and a royalty of 1/20th. During their tenure the men pushed the copper adit forward and also inspected the workings at Castlenook and Longwork. During 1917 changes were made to the lease which required four miners to be engaged in full employment, the following year the company raised 16 tons of ore.

It was decided in 1919 that further development work would be done, however the lower lead shaft workings were, of course, totally flooded and inaccessible and with no means of pumping available. Later in the year, lead ore was being obtained from a stringer of the Goldscope lead vein near the old lead shaft where the workings were very unstable. Meanwhile further development in the Copper Adit saw the level being driven forward in the hope of coming into the Sealby lead vein which it was thought lay westward. By the 22nd. of September 1919 the heading was now in a total of 305yds. and had still not intersected the elusive Sealby lode. The miners were driving the new westerly heading under the direction of Bennett Johns but the ground was deteriorating and becoming shaley and loose. The miners continued their routine of drilling, charging the holes, retreating and firing until the day when the charge blew and they walked down the level to inspect their work. And there, instead of the forehead of rock, a gaping hole appeared through the smoke and dust revealing a clear sky and fresh air - they had come out to day ... who was going to tell the boss?

The drive had come to day in private land at OD720ft., well below the main workings and Bennett Johns was furious. He blamed Mr. W. L. Newby by whose plans he had been basing his headings, which had resulted in them being at least 400yds. from their supposed position. It is difficult to see on looking at Newby's plans how he could be blamed for the error; his northing compass on the plan is correct, he even locates and identifies the N/S Sealby lode in the trial some distance to the south, and he only refers to one other lode, the Goldscope lead vein which runs SW/NE. This was worked with success by the previous companies and was the vein on which the engine shaft had been sunk. As the plans had been obtained from the Cockermouth Castle Estates office, Bennett Johns appealed for some recompense for the error, claiming it was not his fault! He had had no real financial gain after spending thousands of pounds on the works and it appears that after careful consideration, his rent was reduced by £10 a year. The drive had been an unmitigated disaster and all they could salvage was 18 tons of low grade ore picked from anywhere, whilst a further 25 tons was raised from the Copper Adit.

Despite the mediocrity of the results, the miners continued to raise ore and during 1920, four miners raised 26 tons which resulted in sales of £473, but the development was going nowhere. The other company trials at Glenderaterra Mine were also floundering and so the decision was made, in 1923, by Messrs. Heywood and Johns to abandon their failing mining empire of Longwork and Goldscope.

So ended mining in Newlands Valley from the early, crude workings of Mediaeval times to the 20th. Century, and we have found a colourful picture of life during those eras.

Today

Newlands Valley was the cradle of Cumberland mining and here, buried deep beneath the surface, is one of the most complex mysteries of our mining heritage. We know the workings here predate the coming of the German miners in the 1560's and we have in the previous chapters tried to unravel some of the secrets, the complications, the conflicting information and hopefully, we have succeeded in elucidating the facts for the reader. Much of our information is borne out by the level of underground access we have had over many years, so that we have been privy to the physical situation of those men so long ago - the dark, the wet, the hard rock - but never to the sheer, tough, rough, strength-sapping labour involved.

Goldscope today, for the mines historian and industrial archaeologist, is a brilliant location - the whole spectrum of mining is all here to see, from the earliest open workings hidden in the crags, to the final dressing floors of the latest entrepreneurs; for the newcomer to the subject it is a revelation. The contention of whether Sealby's Vein is also the Goldscope Lead Vein or another will be argued for ever. Underground, the longest coffin level in Cumberland is still accessible, although one side of it has been altered by contemporary mining, and leads to the hand-chipped waterwheel pit in the heart of Scope End, the finest and most stunning example of German mining in the country. The Water Level, whereby the water, brought down from the dam, supplied the underground wheel, is the most superb example of a hand-chipped German level in the county. Also to be seen are the dam and the 1,200yd. leat which brought the water from beneath Robinson Mountain to the German workings, and the later dam which still functions and supplies water to the local farmer. Over the years a considerable amount of spoil has been removed for local road infill, and larger waste has also been put to good use in the local dry stone walls. On the way to Littletown Church one crosses a very ancient pack horse bridge and a little bit farther on along the way to Goldscope and the valley is a tree where three different species have grown together - oak, rowan and silver birch- can you spot it?

The Newlands smelter has long been a mystery but perhaps we have now solved this; the site at OD600ft. and 250yds. south of the Grand Level, now obscured by undergrowth and gorse, has been under consideration for a long time but where were the remains of the building and the usual big give away - the slag? Actually, it is there on site - in the adjacent wall - slag, building stone and slate - yes, the local farmer, hundreds of years ago, conveniently moved it... just a few yards!

The conundrum of the two spoil heaps beneath the St. George adit, has puzzled mining circles and local historians for years, and the usual suggestion has been that there is a lower level hidden behind the top spoil. The answer is no, there is not, for David Davies, in a letter to the Duke of Somerset 1698, proposes this idea, but it was never executed. The lower dump is originally from the German working and the brown coloured copper spoil can still be seen, although later the waste from the lead crusher was dumped on top of it; the top dump is predominantly grey and is from the widening of the adit and the sinking of the engine shaft by the lead entrepreneurs in c1870.

Perhaps, using our imaginations, we can conjure up a picture of Newlands Valley in those early times. Those small, tough, industrious men applying their wonderful expertise in this beautiful but harsh environment, so similar to the mountains of their own homeland. We can see the pony trains, laden with panniers of ore, making a long line around the fells to Fawe Park and Copperheap Bay, the boatmen loading the bags and baskets onto the "big boat" to row over to the Middingstett, and then the onward journey through Keswick to the smelter, the men chatting amongst themselves in their own native tongue. Back in the valley, the crash of the stamps crushing the ore, the smoke rising from the smithy, the men pushing the "rowle" wagons about laden with ore, the women in aprons and linen caps, sorting and washing it and the children picking on the spoil heaps. The great wheel turning in the heart of Goldscope, creaking and groaning on its huge axle and a single miner hurrying up by the leat to Littledale to open the sluice at the dam in the morning, and another going back in the evening to close it. And deep underground, at Goldscope, Longwork, St. Thomas, St. Richard, St. George, Franckenstein, Birdsong... the men, chipping and picking, shovelling rock into baskets and buckets, tending the great wheel, toiling up and down the ladders and always, always winning the precious copper.

But still... in spite of all the information we have turned up in old and dusty documents, all the deciphering of Elizabethan English written in many different hands and faded on the parchment pages, despite hour after long hour spent in those dark and deep tunnels and workings, Goldscope keeps its past hidden away from us and perhaps this is as it should be... the enigma remains... a mystery for us all to think on.

Yewthwaite Mine

1 Home of the Wild Cats

Catbells is perhaps the most visited mountain in the Lake District, its craggy little summit dominating the start of the Newlands Round, and those who tread its path not only have stunning views of some of our finest Lakeland scenery, they have already walked over some of the most important sites of German mining history, namely Minersputt on Skellgill Bank and Old Brandley. The view down from the summit towards Derwentwater reveals the site of Copperheap Bay, Derwent Isle and the ancient town of Keswick, whilst just below, on the north east flank is the old Brandley Mine. To the west is the mountain of Barrow and directly SW lies the yawning valley of Newlands where is to be found the famous Goldscope mine. On the summit of this small mountain, one has Cumbria's mining quite literally at one's feet. and deep down, in the dark recesses of the ancient rock lie two huge mineralized veins, one hadeing NW/SE known as the Yewthwaite lead vein and the other the NE/SW Goldscope copper lode. These have been worked both from the surface and the heart of the mountain in what is now known as the Yewthwaite Mine.

The first recorded workings on the Yewthwaite lode were on the western flank after the German miners had been alerted, in 1577, to the location of the lead vein by local farmer Mr. C. Boner, who was paid the sum of 2/6d. for his information. Miners G. Hegler, T. Flettshur and S. Kalcher opened up the working and over the next year or so raised 226 kibbles of ore (15 tons approx.). The working was named St. Reichhart, but for some reason, after that first year, there was no further development. The German adventurers had bigger fish to fry... the Newlands Valley, Buttermere and Grasmere, and the huge lead veins of the Caldbeck Fells. It would be many years before other adventurers would come to discover its riches.

Certainly in the coming years the mine had several serious attempts working directly on the back of the vein, prior to the use of gunpowder and this is most evident if the old, narrow, high trod is followed south from Skellgill along the outcrop of the vein. Here there are numerous early workings; first is a small surface trial, followed by a short, hand-chipped underground level and a few yards further on is rock cutting where the vein has been removed by the ancients (on the left hand wall is an example of the Old Men's work). About 50yds. further on is the main working, originally hand-chipped, leading to a shaft. The path on its way has been chipped through the rock for free and easy passage to ferry ore and gain access to the higher workings. It is thought the sheepfold at Yewthwaite Combe could well have been an old bothy converted later by shepherds. Numerous small hand dressing floors are evident near the workings along the length of the vein.

From this point the main Yewthwaite lode can be seen from the northern shoulder of Maiden Moor and can be followed along the western flank of Catbells for a distance of about 1,000yds. and the early miners have attacked every exposure. By the saddle, Yewthwaite Combe at OD800ft., the old miners have built a hand dressing floor next to the previously mentioned sheepfold and nearby are three main drawing shaft workings. The most important of these, at OD798ft., has been sunk to a depth of 44ft. and appears have been worked by horse gin. A second one at OD810ft. was sunk to 27ft. and a few yards further north at OD818ft. the third shaft was sunk to a depth of 22ft. These would have been operated by simple jack rolls. All these workings, and others, were sunk directly on the back of the vein and would have provided a considerable amount of lead ore over the period they were worked. No proper dressing floor with waterwheel etc. was ever established here, all the ore being roughly hand-cobbed and almost surely taken to either Brandlehow or Goldscope for final processing if required.

These workings were not given up because of lack of a rich ore deposit but more likely it was due to the frustration and difficulty of constantly trying to keep surface water out. In an effort to prevent constant inundation, just above these workings, to the east, the old miners have dug a trench to divert the surface water from entering the shafts and the open works. These are not to be confused with the leats which are also in evidence. The diverted water was channelled to the dressing floors sited below the sheepfold. Hidden in the crags just west of the vein are the remains of two small stone dwellings, one of which appears to contain the remains of a small smithy. The smithy provided a much needed service during this period of working, for quick replacement of steels and wedges which would be blunted easily on the hard rock.

A further working from this pre-gunpowder period is where the vein cuts into the northern shoulder of Maiden Moor, and here, at OD904ft. the miners commenced a hand-chipped level, however its success seems to have been very limited and they obviously gave up after a few yards, there being little ore. However, from 1577 through to 1600, the German miners had made a substantial mark on the back of the vein.

Due to lack of documentary evidence, it is not until 1791 that we can take up our story; 34 tons of ore were raised in this year and in 1793, a further 6 tons were produced. Also recorded in 1793 is a payment of £21 5s. 0d. made to a W. Bell, and another brief reference is made during 1795. A further problem with the Yewthwaite Mine is the fact that when the leases were drawn up, the sett would normally include Newlands Valley and Goldscope, Brandlehow, Barrow and maybe Thornthwaite. Unfortunately the ore production figures were, over many years, amalgamated with the other mines and so accurate individual output figures have been lost.

Up to this period all the underground exploration and advancement of the levels would have been done without the aid of gunpowder, winding was virtually all by hand and access into the workings would have been down precarious ladders and by the wavering light from tallow candles.

2 A Grand Level

A new lease was taken up for Brandlehow Mine in 1819 by John Tebay and this apparently also included the rights to Yewthwaite. Tebay was a mining man of some reputation and he would realize the problems encountered by the old men and that it would be useless to try and pursue the open works, indeed with no lower point of access these workings would already be brimming to the shaft collars. More time would be wasted trying to de-water the mine than extracting the ore as the old men had discovered to their cost. A lower adit would have to be driven to intersect the vein at depth, but here the terrain is steep and would be unsuitable for an adequate dressing floor which would be essential to the success of any new venture.

The nearest suitable location was some way below the old workings; general mining practice usually creates levels 60ft. vertically apart, but here this was not feasible and the new level would have to be sited at OD574ft. a distance of 140ft. below. This would mean a 120yd. crosscut drive to the vein, and then a vertical connection made to de-water the old workings which would take time and money. On the plus side the workings would be slightly protected from the weather and water for the dressing would not be a problem as this could be contained in a series of dams in a shallow plateau above and also taken off Yewthwaite Beck which ran conveniently close. To service the mine, a new and well graded mine road was commenced north of the site at OD600ft. at the same point the original adventurers had started to trace the vein.

Work started on the series of dams and the construction of a huge catch pit, fronted with large boulders, to maintain the height of the beck in order that it could be diverted into the leat to supply the waterwheel and the new dressing floor. Fortunately, the new crosscut had only a few yards to drive through the overburden before encountering solid rock and the level was then driven straight towards the vein; all this preparation work would have taken the miners a good 18 months. In order to defray development costs, lead ore would be taken from the Old Men's workings and over the hill to Brandlehow for dressing, whilst the construction and development of the site was completed.

Over the next fourteen years, the crosscut was completed and the level was driven south in the vein; a rise/ore pass was put up 60ft., from the top of which an intermediate level was driven south for over 200yds. and became known as Tebay's Level. From this level the vein was stoped out another 100ft. towards the sole of the Old Men's workings. This must have been a joyous day for the men when the final few feet of rock came crashing down followed, unfortunately, by a few hundred gallons of icy water gushing through the hole and drenching the men to the skin. The discomfort of this would soon be forgotten as the inevitable blast of air followed - the vital connection had been made. How that clean, fresh air must have felt after the reek of tallow, stifling bad air and sweating bodies that the men had known for years. Between the years of 1819 and 1835, a total of £4,827 had been spent on Yewthwaite and Brandlehow Mines and around 135 tons of ore had been raised. The development work however, had created a serious cash flow problem and it was decided to relinquish the lease on Yewthwaite.

Over the next fourteen years the mine appears to have been worked by tributers, who benefited from the development done by Tebay's efforts, but the production recorded is no more than a few tons a year. During this time little or no real maintenance had been done, and the tributers were only interested in producing what little ore they could find working their own individual stopes. Naturally this state of affairs could not continue and eventually the mine was taken up by a more serious group of gentlemen, in 1849. Indeed they were the company working the nearby Goldscope Mine, Messrs. Clarke, Chapman, Horn and Hart and they were convinced that Yewthwaite had potential. Under the direction of Richard B. Shepherd, the new mine captain, the miners commenced the reopening of the Low Adit No. 3 driven by Tebay years before, and this was renamed Clarke's Level after the senior director. The level was tried to the north first of all, but little was found so they turned their attentions to the southern heading in the footsteps of the old men, and here they intersected some good ore in the middle ground of the Old Men's workings.

Outside, the now derelict dressing floor was refurbished, a 16ft. waterwheel, new ore bins, a smithy and an up to date washing plant were constructed. To ensure an increased and steady flow of water a further two reservoirs were built, just below the others.

The mine progressed and was enjoying a relatively steady run of ore, however a major strike at the company's Goldscope workings in 1853 saw all but of eight of the work force transferred there and in consequence, Yewthwaite became the poor relation and was virtually neglected. Despite this setback, by the end of the year the men had produced 64 tons 12cwt. of lead ore selling at £860 2s. 0d.

Around 1854/55, the management of the Goldscope Mine had some serious disagreements; Captain Shepherd apparently was required at Goldscope and young John Taylor Jnr. was put in charge of the operations at Yewthwaite. John was full of great ideas however he did not have a completely free remit and was told to forget shaft sinking and opening up any new ground. Consequently he had to content himself with removing what ore was readily available from the Old Men's stopes. However the robbing of existing workings without development would soon bring a mine to a halt, and new known reserves must be available. Consequently permission was given to explore, the High Level on Maiden Moor, the Old Men's level was extended and a few tons of ore removed from the sole; during this period a short crosscut trial was driven at OD700ft. and just north of the No. 3 Clarke's Level; this was called Goose Adit. This intersected the old lead vein at around 30yds. inbye and would give around 60ft. of backs, but what production was achieved from these ventures are unknown. The operation here was once again short lived, production was falling and the previous year's results were more than halved to a meagre 18 tons. These results could not sustain the running costs and by 1856 the mine was closed and along with it John Taylor's dreams of deep workings and waterwheels were over.

On Christmas Day 1859, Andrew Clarke, the last and most senior of the original partners died and his majority share of the company holdings passed into the care of the Trustees, who would ensure the financial well being of his surviving children. This resulted, happily, in the company being managed efficiently and it appears that all decisions on capital expenditure had to be fully justified. This, in turn, would make for an assured future for Andrew Clarke's widow and children.

Speculation was rife about the wealth left under Catbells for the mine had hundreds of feet of backs, let alone what could lay in the sole, and it was therefore decided in 1863 to drive a new crosscut low level at OD458ft., to be known as the Trustee Level. Once the vein had been intersected, the level would be continued south and it was planned to sink an engine shaft from it down to a depth of 20fms. to prove the lode at depth. The shaft would be de-watered and ore brought up by a steam engine which would be situated underground.

Six miners were put to work straight away on the preparation of the level, the overburden was cleared to the bedrock in less than a week, and the work of mining commenced. The drive forward was assisted east as the miners were following a clay vein to intersect the main lode after a distance of 149yds. In anticipation of its success, the level was railed out to a 22in. standard Cornish gauge and was cut to a good size of 6ft. 4ins. high and over 5ft. wide... indeed this was to be a grand level.

Whilst the work underground continued, surface preparation commenced on widening and improving the old farm road which comes in from Portinscale and runs along the foot of Catbells. The road, at the 600ft. contour, was extended through to a levelled area in front of the new adit from which all the spoil was spread out to make a considerable plateau. Here, beside the entrance to the new Trustee Level, a large single storey building was constructed with local stone and slate roof, the overall dimensions being 126ft. long by 24ft. wide and divided into seven separate rooms. The central one was open fronted and contained the smithy, and rest comprised an office, a small lodging house for the miners, stores, carpenters shop etc.

Rail tracks from the mine were laid so the development rock and (later) the ore could be dispatched straight from the level into the three 12ft. high stone-lined ore bins, and then to the newly cobbled dressing floor. Here on the first bench, the ore would be sorted and dispatched by wheelbarrow or small wheeled tubs to the lower dressing floor where the 40ft. waterwheel powered the newly installed crusher; its supply of water came from a new reservoir situated just to the south at OD600ft. Some of the water was transported in stone covered culverts, some by leats to other parts of the dressing floor and water was also delivered to the mine for the new steam engine. The third level of the dressing floor was the area where the crushed ore was separated in jiggs ready for eventual dispatch to the smelt mill.

During February 1865, the Old Men's High Level on Maiden Moor was again pushed forward to see what further reserves could be found, and the old sump in the floor revealed a small bunch of lead, but the vein in the level above was poor. No further work was done, the level was dialled and it was recorded that it measured 140yds. to the forehead.

It was realized that water shortage could be a major problem, particularly during the inevitable summer drought; with a steam engine to run and a large waterwheel to power it was essential that there would be no shortage which would of course stop production. The solution was to divert the water make from Clarke's Level, the Old No. 3 Adit; this was rebuilt and the stone entrance was curved and paved so that water could be carried by leat to the new reservoir a few feet below, very simple but effective.

The Trustee Crosscut, on intersecting the vein, was driven south with all possible speed and once the total drivage had arrived at around 380yds. it was considered that this should be the site of the engine shaft. Work commenced sinking the shaft and creating a chamber for the steam engine and winder. The expectancy of the mine was great, good ore had been encountered along the drive and early indications in the sole were already proving the quality of the lode. It was anticipated that at least 300 tons a year would be more than a break even; things were looking well. Under the supervision of Mr. Benjamin Plummer, the mine agent and the mine captain John P. Walton, the advancement of the level was continued. A rise commenced to connect with the old No. 3 Clarke's Level so that any engine smoke or vapour could be released using the old adit as a large flue. It must be assumed that the steam engine with its 10in. cylinder had now been manhandled into position and was securely bolted down. The 6in. pumps had the capacity to pump the workings dry within five hours. Naturally the engine had to have an engine man and the responsibility for this fell on the shoulders of Matthew Barnes who lived at Tower Cottage in Portinscale, a distance of just over 2 miles away. In principle, an installation of this nature sounds fine, but a chugging steam engine underground using coal as a fuel, leaves one wondering what state the mine was actually in when this was working. As to the idea of using the No. 3 Level as a flue .... would this actually work in practice? The idea had apparently been used at Roughten Gill mine on the Caldbeck Fells with disastrous results, however the ventilation flue here was working over a much shorter distance to day. Clinker and ash were disposed of on a regular basis and, once cold, this was trammed out in the mine cars and simply dumped on the southern side of the waste heaps, just opposite the ore bouse teams.

By February 1869, the engine shaft was down to the 10fm. Level, which had been driven 80yds. north and 140yds. south; the Trustee Level had been pushed on a staggering 260yds. beyond the location of the engine shaft and was now well beyond the No. 3 and beneath the Old Men's workings, proving a vast new area of ground. The speed of development continued and by January 1870, the engine shaft was down to the 30fm. Level. On the way, the 20fm. Level was blasted out 80yds. north and 140yds. south, the same distance as the 10fm. above, in preparation for stoping. During the last four years, over 1,200 tons of lead had been sold which must be considered a reasonable return. During this period the engine shaft was ready and operating and down to a depth of 30fms. which was in fact the final planned target depth. Upwards of 1,060yds. of development ground had been driven over seven years and this was a fine record when 100yds. a year was considered to be good progress. When figures like this are analyzed in the cold light of day, it becomes obvious how hard the miners had been working.

Unfortunately, by the end of the year, it was revealed that despite all the new development, only a small amount of ore had been raised. Consequently, the company was in serious financial difficulties and the development work came to a halt.

3 *A New Partnership*

The mine was sold to Messrs. Henry King Spark of Darlington and Benjamin Plummer of Little Braithwaite, but it appears little was done under their management. The year of 1871 was a disaster - Benjamin Plummer, who lived less than a mile down the road, woke to find his house ablaze and although he escaped along with the rest of the household, he was badly burnt. The next few months saw the new the partnership's business affairs totally collapsed and what had promised to be a new venture was in ruins. King and Plummer were bankrupt to the value of £14,000, the company was wound up and the mine closed down and by 1873 was once again on the open market.

This was a mine with so much potential but a sorry state of affairs was confirmed when the mine was visited by Mr. Thomas Davidson, the Goldscope Mine Captain. He commenced inspection of the underground workings and saw that the new engine shaft was flooded to the collar and so he decided to bring in some men (possibly from Goldscope) and start to put the mine into working order. Under his guidance, the miners commenced de-watering the shaft down to the 20fm. level. It was estimated that the engine would take a few days to pump the water clear and would require 10 tons of coal. This would cost £6, the engine man's wages would be £4 11s. 0d. and it would be £12 to repair the pumps. He also recommended that the engine shaft should be increased in depth by 30fms. to 60fms. and headings put out 30fms. north and south to prove the vein. These appear to be very ambitious plans, and obviously the recent development work had certainly not been exploited to potential. It is more than likely it was this company who were responsible for the attempted trial on the Goldscope Vein which cuts over from Littletown, and which intersects the Yewthwaite Lode just north of the Trustee Level. These short trials proved the vein, and a fair sampling of mineralized ore was brought to day.

During 1874 it is recorded that a total of fourteen miners were employed at the mine, however the workings below the 20fm. were all still flooded, so their attentions would have been curtailed to those workings still accessible and the Old Men's working. By this time, this had been connected by a major ore-pass of around 130ft. from the Trustee up to Clarke's Level and nearby to the north was the connecting ore pass of 60ft. up to Tebay's Level which by now had been railed out to the head of the ore pass. With these connections complete, it allowed the miners to literally rob the ancient workings efficiently and any ore raised was sent on the newly engineered road, which had been constructed for just this purpose, to Goldscope for dressing. However this was to be a short lived reprieve as by July 1876 the pumps were shut down. completely, and the operation ended.

With the mine closed, W. Hind an old Thornthwaite miner who lived in nearby Braithwaite applied for permission to work the dumps and he got a two year Take-note on the 29th. of January 1878 at a royalty of 1/5th. and no fixed rent. During this period he sold a total of 25 tons which fetched a price of £284 12s. 4d.

and this was bought by Joshua Dinning, lead merchant. Shortly after this enterprise, in June 1879 some of the plant and machinery was apparently sold.

During September 1883, Henry Burrow Vercoe of Portinscale took over the mine and formed the Newlands United Mining Company, which also operated Barrow and Brandlehow Mines. His associate partner was Mrs. E. C. Bradley and on the 17th. of December in the same year, they appear to have sublet or transferred their holdings to a newly formed company by the name of the Yewthwaite Proprietary Syndicate Ltd. This was registered in London and its share based capital was £6,000 in £1 shares. The directors of the newly formed company all hailed from Liverpool; these were Edward Hale, Robert T. Currie, William Bright Fairfield, William Currie and Walter Bradley. Naturally the head office and bankers all would be based in the same location. The 21 year lease with Lord Leconfield required a dead rent of £50 for the 100 acres and a royalty payment of 1/16th. Over and above this, the price for the transfer of the concession to the Syndicate was a payment of £1,000 cash, £1,000 in debentures and two thousand shares to Henry Burrow Vercoe which equated to a value of £4,000 - nice work if you can get it!

The prospectus wrote in glowing terms of the potential of the 100 acre sett which was situated upon the "Champion Lead Bearing Lode in the District" and indeed one mine within the sett had "worked continuously for 2,000 years" and another had made regular profits of £30,000 to £36,000 per annum! In actual fact, only 2 of the 100 acres of ground had been opened up.

Reports were obtained from eminent mining engineers like Captain Francis of Ladstock House in Thornthwaite, who recommended the deepening of the engine shaft and the development of the mine south to come up under the old workings. Here, an abundance of ore was waiting to be mined and so far had been totally neglected. Captain David Douglas of Llanidoles, after his inspection, could see no reason why 800 tons per month was not achievable and with a 20hp. engine for pumping and winding, large ore reserves were there for the taking. By September the following year, a team of miners was re-timbering the portal of the Trustee Level and by the beginning of December, the men had cleared the Trustee Level to the engine shaft and work was being continued to the end of the level. It appears though, that on completion of this work The Yewthwaite Proprietary Syndicate foundered and no further work was done.

4 Vercoe the Villain

Another company took up the lease on the 12th. of December 1885, its new title, the Yewthwaite & Newlands United Mines Ltd. of 120 Chancery Lane, London. Capital was to come from £20,000 in £1 shares and the directors were Mr. Richard Jordan, Edward Timewell, architect of Liverpool, John J. Huddlestone, a farmer from Walton, Liverpool, Edgar Callwood, a merchant of Rockfield House, Liverpool, Sydney Kirk, a merchant of 80 Lord St., Liverpool, John Kilgom, a merchant of Soho St., Liverpool. J. T. Greenwood, Auctioneer of Richmond Road, Liverpool and W. Morgan, an Insurance Broker also of Liverpool. T area of the sett had now increased to a total of 233 acres and was leased for 22 years at a base rent of £50 and a royalty of 1/16th.

Henry Vercoe did not enjoy a happy relationship with his men and his treatment of them was harsh and peremptory. On the 29th April 1886, a disgruntled miner at Brandlehow, Robert Bear, took the law his own hands and threatened to shoot him. He told the mine foreman in front of John Reed, another miner, "I'll shoot Vercoe dead before Saturday night"! The foreman, knowing that Bear had firearms, told the police in Keswick and subsequently Bear was arrested; he did not go quietly and, in front of the police and further witnesses, continued to threaten to kill Vercoe. He was charged and at his trial was bound over for six months with a surety on him of £20. Mr. Vercoe had been a very lucky man but what the actual details of the problem were, we shall never know.

A general stores list for the period reveals the amount of material required to keep ongoing work in progress:

Carpenters store - 393ft. of log timber 5in., 9in. and 10in. diameter.
Side boards 1,121ft. of 2in. to 3in. pitch pine plus a further 84ft. of general timber. Axe and saw.
Smithy - 2 x Pavis smith's bellows, anvil, 48ft. of 1 ¼in. steel bar, 28ft. 1" ft, 72ft. of ½ in. bar, 4 x smith's hammers, 9 Pavis smith's tongs, 24 x new steel drills, 2 x augers, 3 x shovels, 8 hammers.
General Store - 2 wheelbarrows, 1 hand barrow.
Magazine - 1,500 detonators, 41 fuses, 8lbs. of dynamite.
Mining - 75 hammer shafts, 1 bogie wagon, 1 white painted bogie wagon, 234yds. of rails, 120ft. of hauling rope.
The office furniture consisted of 4 chairs, fender, office table.

Work had continued steadily over the last couple of years and the 6 miners who were employed in April 1887, had recently been put to work and had cleared the Trustee Level to the working faces and made the mine ready. No sooner had the work been done, than disaster struck. A fierce overnight storm descended on the mountain of Catbells and the rain lashed down with uncontrollable fury. The steep hillside above the level was soon awash with torrents of water sweeping down waves of rubbish and loosened debris, which completely enveloped the mine entrance. The workmen coming down the road realized the storm had been a bad one, but were not prepared for the maelstrom with which they were greeted on their arrival. After their weeks of endeavour they found the whole of the entrance of the Trustee Level was completely run in, the timbers were down and there were tons of rubble covering the entrance.

As we have seen, materials were required on site to cover every eventuality, but lack of funding in the mercurial business of mining was even more instantaneous, and like the other previous companies this one again collapsed through lack of cash.

Yet another company was formed on the 26th. of April 1888, the Mid Cumberland Silver-Lead and Blende Mines. Ltd., and the share capital to commence the venture was £25,000 in £1 shares, no doubt the low price of the shares was to entice a greater catchment of speculators. The prospective board was headed by the Marquess of Donegal, London, Lt. Col. Inge of Scarborough, Joseph Cunliffe of Chorley, Jacob Salter of Manchester and Messrs. T. Charlesworth, Engineers of Manchester. It was intimated as before that with suitable investment, a steady return of £6,000 profit per year could be achieved. The Company offices would be in Manchester along with their bankers. The costings of this new development were as follows:

Yewthwaite Mine Development Costs Jan. 12th. 1889

A	16 hp. winding engine	£300
B	Pumping engine/crusher	£800
C	30hp. portable steam boiler	£400
D	13in. Reliance air compressor	£350
E	16ft. x 4ft. steel air receiver	£ 80
F	3 x 3in. Eclipse air rock drills	£180
G	4 x 2 ½ " Eclipse air rock drills with legs	£240
H	2 Tripods	£ 21
I	6 lengths of hose couplings	£ 50
J	18 Dozen drill bits	£113 8s. 0d.
K	2 sets of swages	£ 2 2s. 0d.
L	300 fathoms of air pipes	£ 79 4s. 0d.
M	Water wheels and crushing plant	£300
N	Buildings	£200
O	Carriage Fixings	£140
P	Timber	£600
Q	General	£292
R	Sinking Shaft	£620
S	Driving new level	£100

£4,917 14s. 0d.

Their prospectus appears to have been based on the economics of the mine's potential: the cost of producing the lead from the mine was around £4, market price was around £10 a ton and it was expected that the lodes would produce 10 tons a fathom! Based on a production it was obvious that many people still had Yewthwaite earmarked as a winner and what was needed was investment by a committed group of men. This company had the mine inspected in July 1889 by Mr. D. N. Dalglish who's idea was quite simple: new ground had to be proved and the vein worked along its already proven length; a new drainage level had to be driven to intersect the engine shaft at a much lower horizon and the engine shaft would have to be deepened to 40fms. Many of these company portfolios make glowing statements of untold wealth just lying there for the asking - or at any rate for a modest investment. Some of them certainly make speculative reading and under the scrupulous eyes of today's various watchdogs, would almost certainly be considered fraudulent. :

These findings and the speculated potential of the mine were endorsed by Captain Douglas and Captain Vercoe who pointed out that Thornthwaite worked the same lode and that he, Vercoe, had himself recently worked the Barrow mine with great success.

Director Joseph Cunliffe however was not really a mining man and his efforts to exploit his "lucrative" new asset were fast failing. He had employed Mr. Dalglish to present his plan for the future development of the mine to endeavour to ensure its success for himself and the shareholders. But all the speculative reports and high blown ideas on paper are fine especially when its not your equity disappearing down the hole.

Joseph did open up a new level 100ft. below the early trials on the Goldscope copper lode in 1891, and at that time he was employing seven miners to drive the trial into the fell directly from the mine road just north of the Trustee Level and at the same horizon. After a distance of 22yds. the vein revealed some copper ore, and short trials were put out north and south in the hope that its eventual intersection with the lead vein would produce a great ore bunch, but it was not to be and this company folded. Perhaps the glowing report which would no doubt appear in the next company prospectus would entice would be speculators to take up the lease... it was taken up within months!

5 Into the Scrap Man's Hands

Obviously undaunted by the failure of the previous five attempts, a further company was formed and floated in November 1891 and in order to stimulate the wavering interest, there were several enthusiastic reports on the sett and the mine revealing its recent successes and the fact that shareholders that year had been paid 110% on their investment! Talk about gilding the lily! The share offer was £50,000 in £1 shares and the directors of the newly formed Derwentwater Copper, Lead and Zinc Ore Company were Lt. Col. Hubert Slater of Burnley, Thomas Turner of Dewsbury, William Gregson of Southport, Samuel Furniss, William Bratby and Samuel Hinchcliffe of Hale. There was a report by Professor W. Boyd Dawkins MA. FRS. FGS who wrote in buoyant terms that a steady return would produce £5,880 and that a regular production of 420 tons of ore had been achieved by previous companies. Indeed at the time, the mine was being tried on the Goldscope copper lode which bisects the sett and into which a level was being driven; this was showing a 4ft. rib of copper pyrites. It was anticipated that the mine would produce a tonnage of 500 tons of lead, copper and zinc which would realize a return of £4,500 a month. This could be achieved with a work force of 55 miners at 22/6d. a week, 20 boys at 6/- a week and two ponies.

A further report produced in the same month by Captain John Woolcock ME, reiterated the value of the Goldscope Lode which had been virtually ignored by the previous adventurers and stated that ore taken from the lode had already been assayed by Messrs. Charles Roberts, Smelters of Manchester. Messrs. Vivian of Swansea also reported the potential and richness of the orebody. Ore was also assayed by Messrs. Walker Parker of Newcastle who confirmed an 82% lead content. Finally, the report stated, for a small cost the engine shaft could be pumped dry to expose the lodes below.

The month of June 1892 saw just four miners in the Trustee Level working in and around the area of the pumping engine, this evidently being just general maintenance in the expectancy of a buyer but as yet, there was no real mining taking place

It seems the previous company had now collapsed, as the 24th. of February 1893 saw yet another attempt to raise capital by the Lake Mines Company by floating £20,000 £1 shares. The company directors were Samuel Furness, Joseph Cunliffe, St. Anne's on Sea, Joseph P. Riley of Salford, and the Mine Captain would be John Woolcock. The lease with Lord Leconfield would be for 60 years, at a dead rent of £50 per annum and a Royalty of 1/16th. and the area of the sett was 500 acres. The prospectus again revealed all the promises of success and fortunes waiting to be collected, and endorsed this by the fact that 200 tons of copper ore were now at surface produced from the Goldscope Copper Lode. Further development along the 170fms. of proven lode, which was known to extend over two miles in length and 1,000fms. in depth would ensure the future of the company... according to the prospectus!

Obviously not many people were encouraged by these fine words and by the end of 1893 the share capital had not been reached and the site became derelict. Without the usual signs of activity being present, the local farmers moved in, slates and roof trusses disappeared along with anything that was useful, ironwork which was not actually bolted down also vanished into the scrap man's hand. All this was made all too easy by the two well made hard-core roads leading to the site.

After two years of neglect only two miners were on site, and in March 1895 of the following year they were in the copper level which had now advanced by a distance of 36yds. This venture was nothing more than a token offering to keep up the status quo in the event of a buyer being found. Unhappily, during this diminished level of work, it was reported that a miner was killed on the 22nd of December 1898.

These were the last reported workings and without capital and commitment, the mine once again shut down and was to remain closed for eleven years.

During this closed period, a Mr. Harrison from the Estate Office of Cockermouth Castle was on site at Yewthwaite when a horse and cart trundled along the road loaded with timber. The driver, by the name of Carr, commenced unloading it and putting it into the old office buildings and, thinking this was odd, Mr. Harrison asked the man by whose authority he was doing this. Carr said he had been sent by a Mr. Dawson, and the timber was to board over the old shafts. He had been instructed to secure the one up by the old sheep fold at Hause Gate, and the old trials above, which were protected only by a couple of rails.

A new adventurer in the shape of a Mr. Dennison took a Take-note in 1912 for one year at a Royalty of 1/20th. and a dead rent of £25 but this was really a one man band with little or no capital; the dumps were hand-picked through but no actual mining took place. The Take-note was renewed for another year under the company name of the Coledale Syndicate but after the second year, the interest fizzled out and once more the mine became derelict.

Cockermouth Castle granted what was to be the final Take-note in 1913 to Messrs. W. H. Heywood of Huddersfield and Mr. Bennett Johns of Keswick at a rent of £20 per annum with a covenant of four men to be kept at work. It appears that though other mines on the sett were worked, nothing took place at Yewthwaite. and in 1923 the license to operate terminated and Yewthwaite was finally closed for ever.

Yewthwaite was in the right place but always at the wrong time, overshadowed time and again by its nearby rivals, Goldscope, Brandlehow and even Thornthwaite; the big money men never seemed to be around.

Unhappily, the mine featured in the news of the 30th. of March 1962, when the body of a man was found hanging in one of the old lead vein shafts and recovered by Keswick Mountain Rescue team. Shortly after this, the shaft, which was very close to a path, was filled in.

Today

In 1988, just after a heavy snowfall, one of the old lead shafts opened up and we descended though this into the Old Mens' workings and eventually found our way down into Tebay's Level which was still railed out; much of the middle ground had been worked out for a vertical height of 130ft. Our objective was the ore pass which we knew would take us down to Clarke's Level, but this was completely fallen and despite a valiant dig by another group, a way through could not be achieved. However there was maybe a chink of light at the end of the tunnel when, during 2003, Mines of Lakeland Exploration Society negotiated with the National Trust to reopen the Trustee Level, one of the last mysteries of our Lake District mining heritage. MOLES gained entry in the same year and found that the rails were still down with the remains of an old tub sitting on them, but after 80yds. a fall was encountered. During 2004, a dig commenced on this to come into the N/S lode and to the main level where, it was said, the old steam engine would still be in situ! The dig had to be temporarily suspended but is to be resumed, and maybe, just maybe, we will be able to unlock another one of the Lake District's underground mysteries.

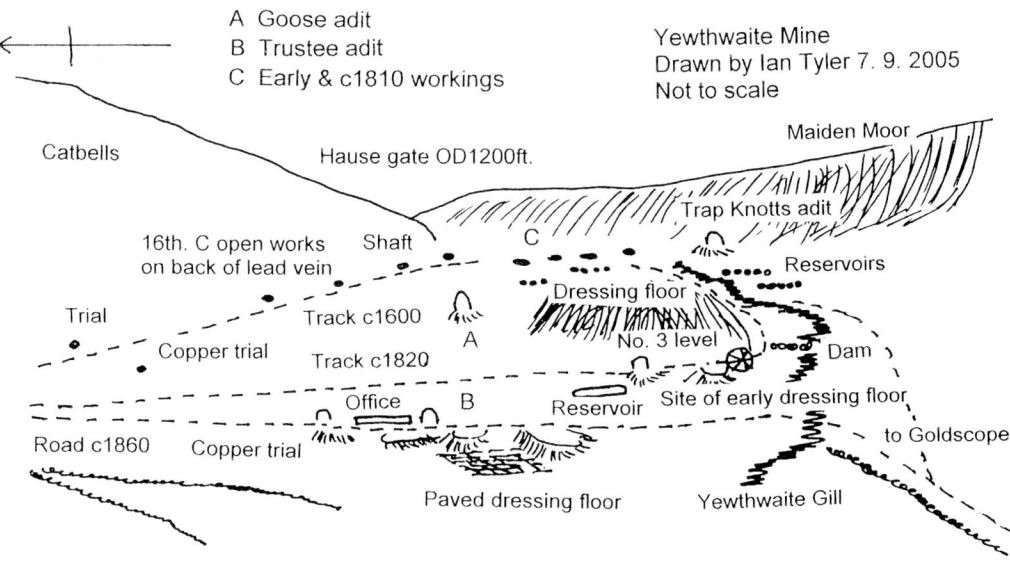

Top: Yewthwaite Mine site. Stuart Clement Collection.
Bottom: Plan of Yewthwaite Mine site. Drawn by Ian Tyler.

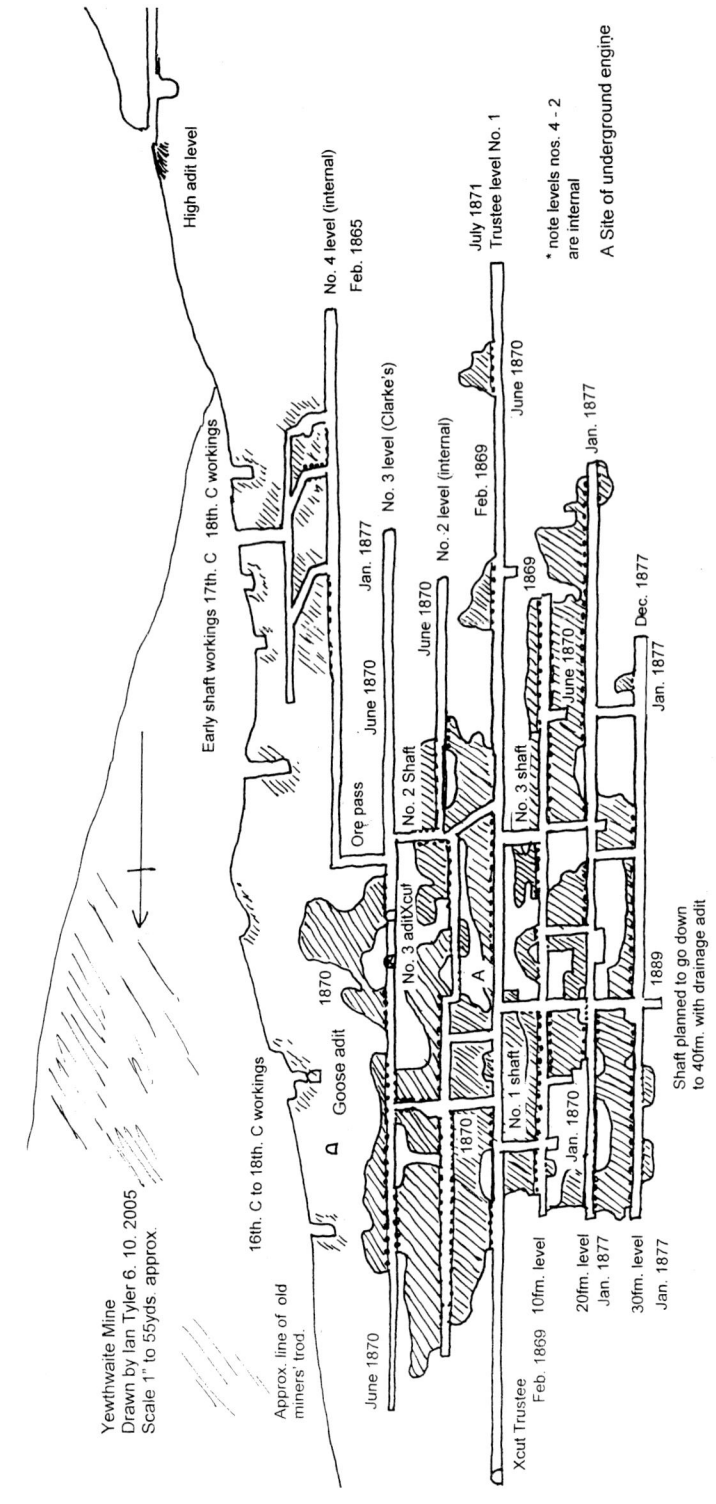

Yewthwaite Mine. Drawn by Ian Tyler.

Yewthwaite Mine, Trap Knotts, high adit driven on vein. Ian Tyler Collection.

Yewthwaite Mine, looking south towards Trap Knotts, openworks and shafts. Ian Tyler Collection.

Top: Yewthwaite Mine, looking north from Trap Knotts, openworks and early dressing floor. Ian Tyler Collection.
Bottom: Yewthwaite Mine, old shaft on vein above Goose Adit. Ian Tyler Collection.

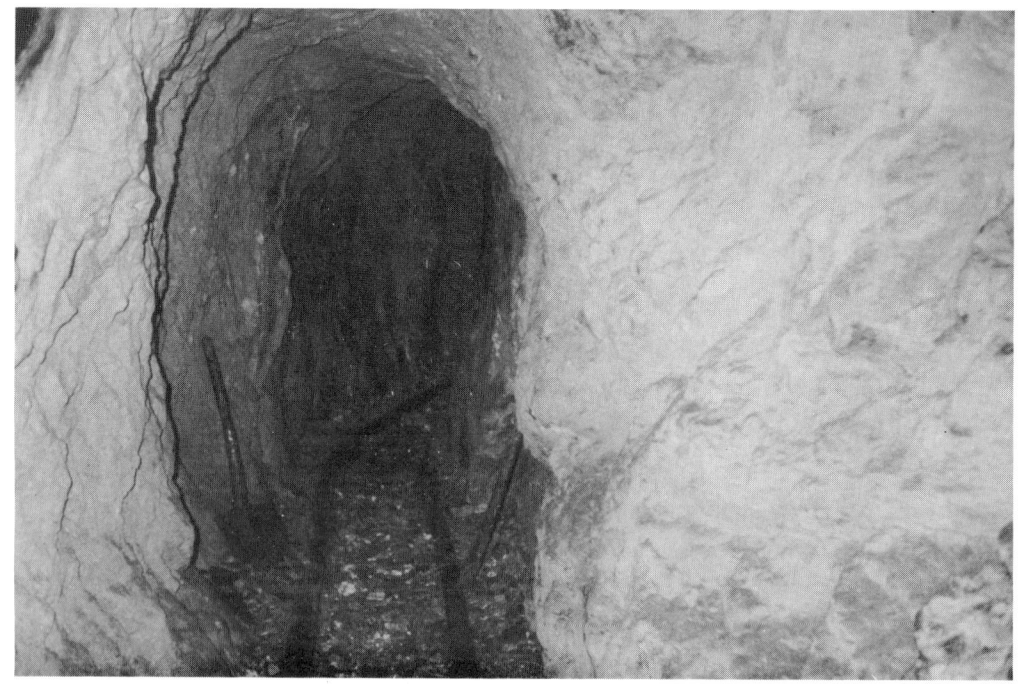

Top: Yewthwaite Mine, No. 4 Level internal - note early wooden rail. Ian Tyler Collection.
Bottom: Yewthwaite Mine, rise from No. 4 to sub-level 60ft. above through stopes. Ian Tyler Collection.

Top: Yewthwaite Mine, site of No. 3 Level and dressing floor. Stuart Clement Collection.
Bottom: Yewthwaite mine, Trustee Level and cobbled dressing floor. Ian Tyler Collection.

Yewthwaite Mine, collapsed entrance to No. 3 Level later used to supply water to Trustee and vent hole for steam engine. Ian Hebson Collection.

Yewthwaite mine, Trustee Level c1870 - old collapsed tub in situ. Ian Tyler Collection.

Yewthwaite mine, Trustee Level crosscut to main lead vein. Ian Tyler Collection.

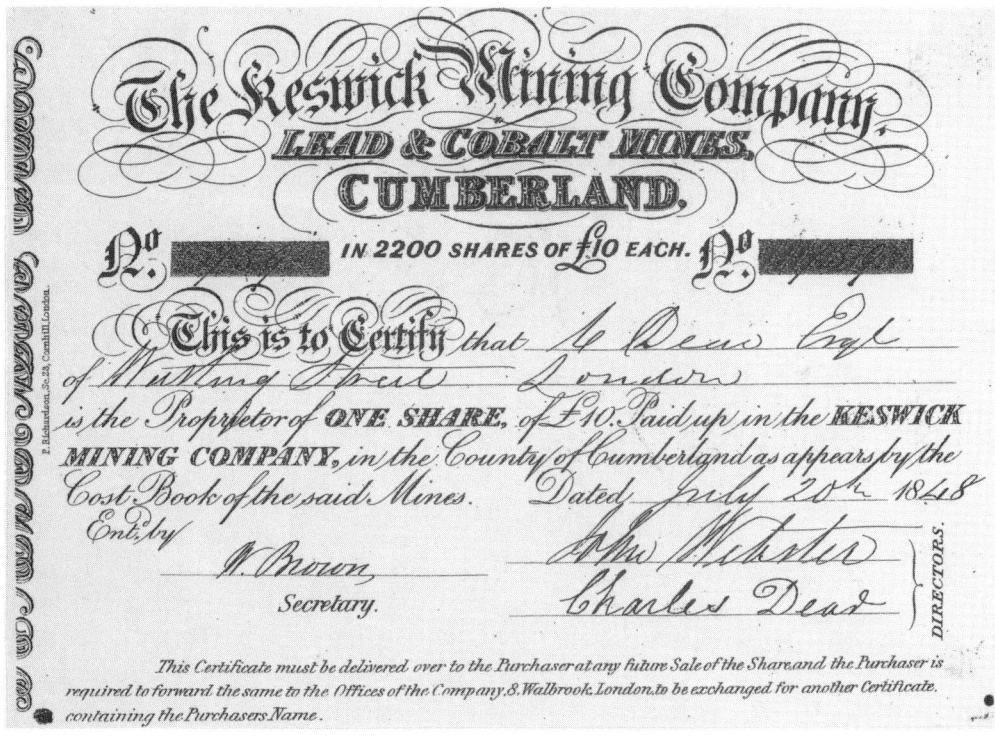

Top: Bothy at Colbalt Mine, Sale Pass. Mine in crags. Ian Tyler Collection.
Bottom: Keswick Mining Company Lead Cobalt Mine £10 share certificate c1848. Keswick Mining Museum.

Cobalt Mine, No. 5 Level and stope area - No. 4 is just behind and below. Ian Tyler Collection.

Cobalt Mine, No. 3 Level cut through sound rock connects through to No. 4. Ian Tyler Collection.

Cobalt Mine, looking down remains of incline from No. 4 Level to bothy. Ian Tyler Collection.

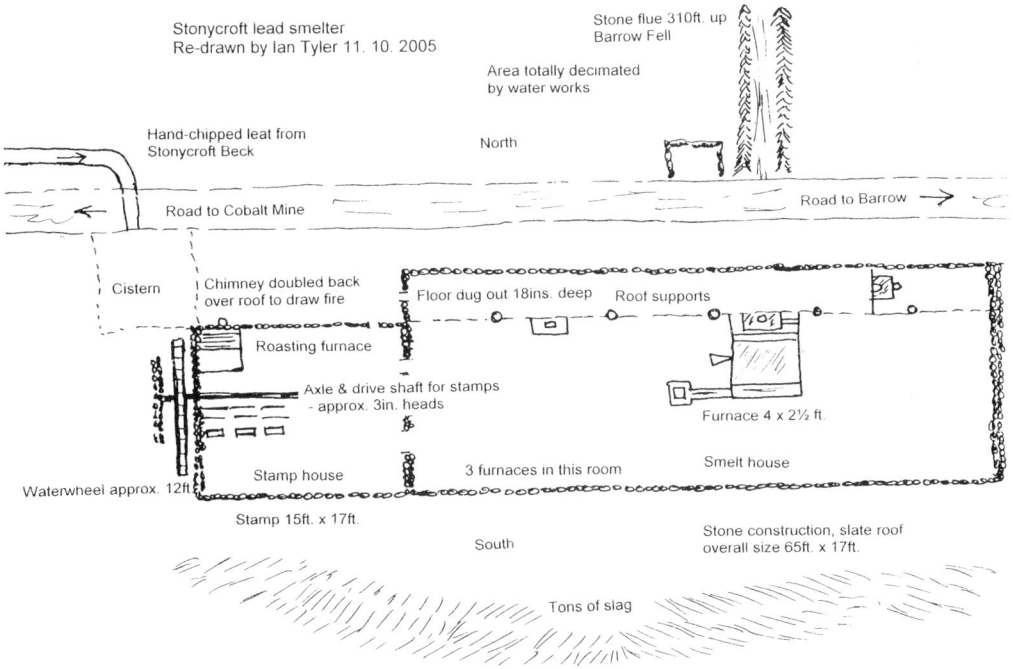

Top: Looking down Stonycroft smelt mill flue. Ian Tyler Collection
Bottom: Plan of Stonycroft Smelter, destroyed by 19th.C. waterworks. Drawn by Ian Tyler.

Top: Remains of Stonycroft Lead Smelter - note flue running up fellside. Ian Tyler Collection.
Bottom: The site of the Cobalt Smelt Mill beside Stoneycroft Gill, 250yds. west of Stonycroft Lead Smelter. Ian Tyler Collection.

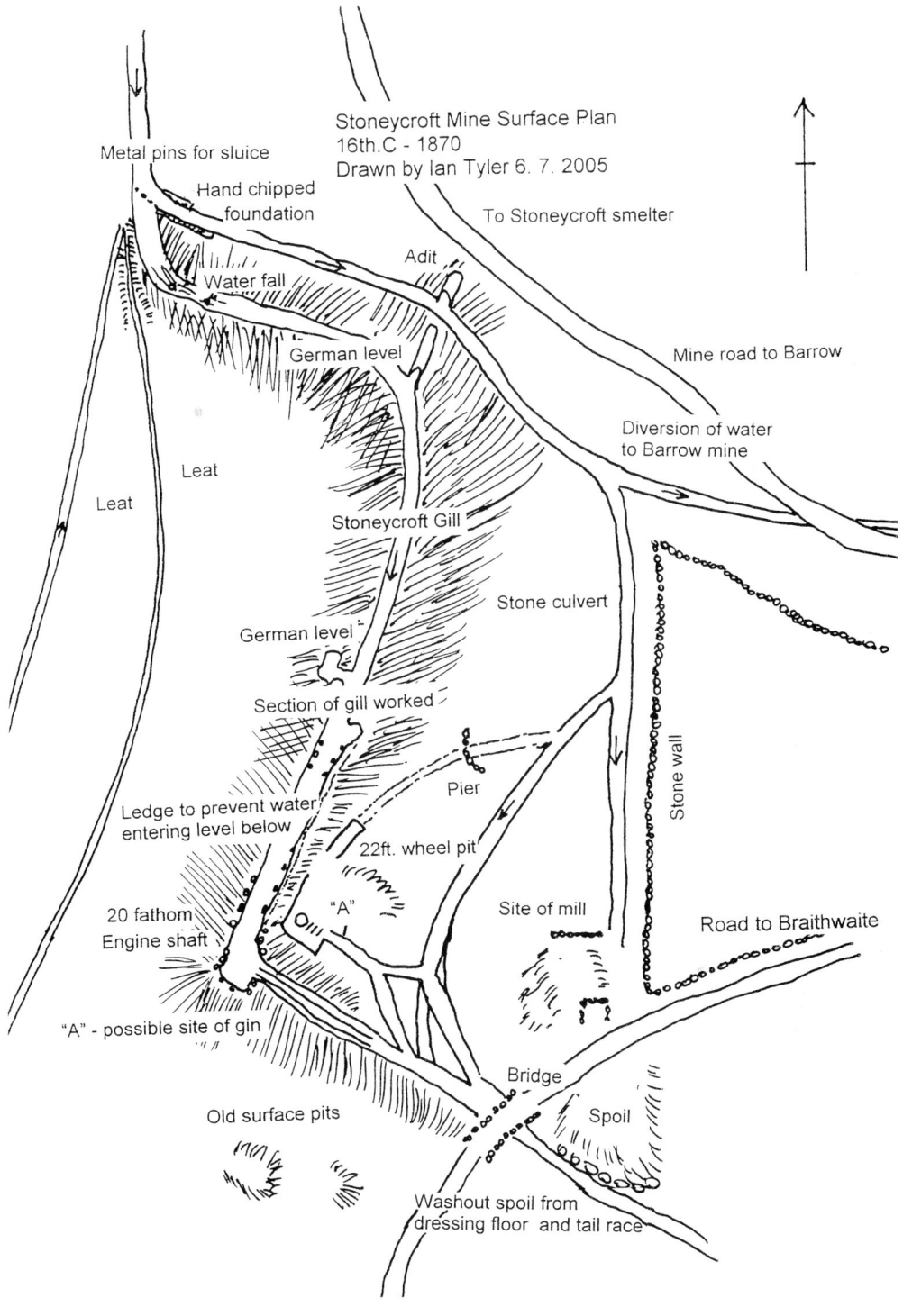

Plan of Stonycroft working. Drawn by Ian Tyler.

Top: Site of Stonycroft Mill area 17th C. Ian Tyler Collection.
Bottom: 16th. C .German adit in gill driven in the vein - note hand-chipped area to prevent water entering working. Ian Tyler Collection.

Stoneycroft Mine, original 16th. C German working in Stoneycroft Gill bottom - note groove in wall to prevent surface water entering workings below. Ian Tyler Collection.

Stonycroft Mine, the ill-fated shaft where miners were drowned in the late 17th. C. Ian Tyler Collection.

Stonycroft Mine, site of 22ft. wheelpit - site of shaft is directly opposite by large tree in gill. Ian Tyler Collection.

Rowling End Trials

This mining area is to be found on the steep slopes on the eastern breast of Causey Pike where the rock is bisected by at least two NW/SE veins and these have been worked by pits and surface trenches. The earliest mining records for these reveal that in October 1651, Joseph Hechstetter and Hugh Potter were working the sett, and a Royalty of 1/8th. was paid. These were very small superficial workings on the back of the vein. During November 1770, Messrs. John Gilbert and another leased the sett from Earl Egremont and in May 1771, raised 6cwt. of ore; for this they paid a Royalty f 1/14th. which amounted to 2/7d. They apparently carried on working sporadically until May 1778.

The Stonycroft Smelters

It is possible that there are at least three different smelter sites beside the gill at Stonycroft, the most obvious being at OD680ft. and situated on the northern bank of Stonycroft Gill. The site is reported as working by 1613 and roads were cut leading from the local Barrow Mine a mile to the north. A further road was constructed from Newlands Valley and Goldscope Mine around two miles away and presumably at great expense. It fords Keskadale Beck at Mill Dam near to the old Sportsmen's Inn and from there follows a steady contour around the breast of Rowling End on Causey Pike, which is on the southern side of Stonycroft Gill. The road, once at the same horizon as the smelter, bridges Stonycroft Gill allowing the pack mules or small carts access to the site.

The smelter was constructed of local stone from a quarry just west of the site, and its flue can be traced up the southern flank of Barrow Mountain. Water for waterwheels to operate the bellows, crushing and processing plants required at the site were supplied with water from numerous leats, some up to a mile long. Holding dams to ensure a regular supply are to be seen higher up the gill at OD750ft., and another is located directly above the smelter at OD1000ft. From this, a leat, some of which is hand chipped, contours round to the eastern side of Barrow, to supply water to the ancient workings at Barrow Mine. It is not clear who built the smelter but it appears that it worked until c1650 from when it seems it lay unused. Reports indicate that it was re-designed and a lead smelter was possibly erected on the site c1690 and was used to smelt lead ore from Lord Wharton's mines at Caldbeck. It is possible that the reason for the re-opening was the fact that the local forests had now re-grown allowing a ready source of fuel and this is thought to have continued until 1715. The site is reported to have worked after this date in particular accepting lead ore from Greenside mine; this policy would certainly have stopped by c1826 when Greenside constructed their own smelt mill.

Unfortunately, the site was vandalized during the early 20th. Century when a water scheme was planned for the site and a huge underground tank was installed. This thoughtless action has ruined the area for any future accurate archaeological interpretation. Due to the importance of the site in our local history we have made the following, rather basic, assessment: the site is situated just below the track leading to the Cobalt Mine. The flue is at the far eastern end of the building and extends 310ft. up the fell and the rock for its construction was quarried from an area roughly halfway up and also near its termination. At its base is a small building, possibly a condenser. The hearth area is directly below the road level at this point, and the northern side of the building foundations have been hewn out of the local rock. The overall size of the building is 58ft. long by 15ft. wide and at the western end an area 15ft. wide and 17ft. long has been recessed. This was possibly the area for a cistern to retain water for the wheel, which could have been used for the bellows or a crusher of some type. The leat supplying this is cut through the local stone and carries water from Barrow Door and Stonycroft Gill, just above the road. Numerous shapes and types of furnace brick abound, along with a whole variety of slags in an abundance of colours.

A suspected site is just below the main Stonycroft Bridge at OD420ft., however it is possible that this site and its attendant slags are washouts, brought down over many years via the bypass leat.

Another rumoured site is just to the south of here at Stair Bridge where, opposite the flour mill is a very ancient house with a date stone F F 1647. The house at this time was the home of Thomas Fairfax, a Yorkshireman, who was a soldier of some merit. He later became a General and acquitted himself with distinction during the Civil War. Apparently the house was used for many clandestine meetings during his tenure. Regarding this residence and the neighbouring land, is a suggestion that it could have been the site of a smelter. During 1709, Nehemiah Champion was operating this smelter, receiving ores from Tilberthwaite and Cockley Beck. Apparently the smelter had some success and continued producing metal until 1717. From 1717 until 1740 all smelters appear to have been shut down and were under a caretaker situation. The next working appears to have been in 1755 when 27 tons of copper ore were treated at a smelter for Messrs. John Gilbert and there is a further record of smelting in c1789.

Unfortunately, all these three sites have been altered and subjected to the rigours of time and to add to the puzzle of locating which sites belonged to whom, much of the evidence is contradictory and inconclusive. The documentation available does not positively identify the individual sites with any accuracy.

Stonycroft Mine

The Stonycroft Mine sett is to be found under the N/E flank of Causey Pike and the southern shoulder of Barrow mountain. The vein which is the Brandlehow Lode courses NW/SE lies literally in the bed of the ravine of Stonycroft Gill, which is the main water shed of the Oughterside basin, the valley formed by Scar Crags and Oughterside is deceptive in its size, the length of the valley being nearly three miles long and virtually ¾ mile wide.

Various trials have been made in the area but the main vein, as already mentioned, is literally in the bed of the gill at OD500ft. and in the steepest part of it. The earliest workings were started by the German miners in 1566, when they expended a total of £35 on the mine. The ore they were raising was lead and revealed a very high silver content of around 22ozs. to the ton. In a letter to George Lamplugh in November 1567, the miners refer to problems with water in the workings. Despite this obvious problem, the working was not abandoned and a further report confirms that in 1568, £22. 7s. 10d. worth of ore was raised. This ore was removed by the early German adventurers from the vein in the bottom of the gill, no doubt confining their operation to the summer and drought conditions. The working is around 6ft. wide and 35yds. long and on the right hand wall of the ravine, a ledge has been cut into the bedrock to prevent any surface water pouring into the workings below; this same type of engineering is visible at Longwork and Goldscope. Halfway along the working on the north side is a hand-chipped ledge area which could have been a hauling point for the ore. The Germans pursued the vein to the west into a near vertical rock wall of the ravine, where the gorge turns virtually due south. Here a coffin level was driven for a 30yds.; this was cut 8ft. high and 2ft. wide but has proved unproductive. A further trial has been made into the southern bank on a stringer, but again this appears to have been unproductive. About a 100yds. further up the gill, on the southern side, another trial has been made on a NW/SE vein and could be attributed to this period.

Naturally the stream flow was a great inconvenience to the early miners, and so the whole of the beck had to be diverted so that the miners could carry out their work unhindered. The initial diversion was at OD550ft. and at the sluice point here, all the work is by hand-chipped excavations. It is not clear when the German miners left this working but with Goldscope, Longwork, and Barrow etc. nearby there were plenty of places to go.

It was to be over a hundred years before new adventurers returned to the workings when, in 1680, David Davies obtained a lease from Charles, Duke of Somerset. David Davies was a man of much mining skill, and very soon realized the value of the vein; he quickly made substantial process by deepening the old German working, calling it "Mines Gill". Here the whole of the vein was taken out and stemples were placed across the ravine for supporting the ladders as the open work became deeper. The orebody here was rich indeed and based on this, David decided to sink a full working shaft directly on the vein in the bed of the stream, just east of the workings and where the stream turns virtually due north.

To ensure maximum safety and retain the water supply for washing and crushing, the beck was diverted via a sluice gate at OD550ft. and here, the water was channeled in a generous culvert system through solid rock, which intersected the vein directly above the original German trial 50ft. below. The new adventurers drove a short level but the vein here was poor and not ore bearing. The culvert was continued (see diagram for explanation) to circumnavigate the workings below in the ravine. Once the culvert, which is around 3ft. wide and 3ft. deep, arrived at a convenient rock plateau, a dressing floor and wheelpit were hewn out of the solid rock by hand. Once this work was completed the beck could then be fully diverted to its new course, and the sinking of the shaft could commence in complete safety.

To ensure a controlled water supply at least two substantial dams were constructed some way up stream to ensure a steady supply of water to the dressing floor in drought periods. The fall of the Stonycroft beck is considerable and without reservoirs a reliable water supply here would be extremely erratic.

The shaft was sunk in good solid rock directly on the vein to a depth of 7fms., where the miners drove a level off and were working a 12in. rich lead vein, while other miners were continuing to sink the shaft. The mine had enjoyed rich beginnings but fate was to deal a cruel blow on a day when the miners were pursuing their daily routine of winning the ore, bringing it to shaft bottom so it could then be hauled the 42ft. up to surface. They were completely unaware that a fearsome storm was gathering some miles to the west, the sky blackened and the rain hammered down the huge catchment of Oughterside allowing torrents of water to pour down the steep fellside into the waiting Stonycroft Gill... the only way the water could descend through the valley. The sheer power of the raging torrent spewed down the valley and the immense volume could not be contained by the first dam - it was demolished, its soil and rubble construction just carried away under the tremendous force. The second dam was swamped, the brown peat stained water carrying boulders and anything else before and it now cascaded down its course to the flimsy sluice gate which was to divert water away from the shaft. Alas, the workings were engulfed and the full force of the torrent surged, unabated, down into the beck's original course and swept through the old German surface workings and into the open, unprotected shaft. The miners never stood a chance... those poor men were drowned in the sea of boulders, mud and filth which poured down on them with terrifying force. So finite was the disaster that the mine was closed and it was not until seven years had passed, that the shaft was re-opened and the remains of the poor souls were then released from their entombment and given a Christian burial.

It was to be nearly 150 years before further interest in the sett was shown, when, in 1846, the Keswick Mining Company which was run by Messrs. Peter Langton, Samuel Merryweather and Richardson, took up the lease. The quality of lead/silver was the obvious attraction, but before work could commence, it was essential to once again divert the stream by re-instating the sluice gates at their original points. Once this work was done the difficult job of clearing the shaft started which over the intervening years was now once again completely choked with debris. The new shaft was cut to a good size approximately 5ft. x 6ft. and in the process of sinking and widening the shaft, the miners found in amongst the rubbish and debris, the old 50ft. shaft hauling chain made of 2½in. links along with some old hand wedges. Once cleared, the shaft was sunk to a depth of 10fms. and headings were driven off east and west. On the surface, meantime, in preparation for the ore, two waterwheels were erected; the largest was 22ft.x 4ft. and would operate 6in. pumps for de-watering the mine while a smaller wheel was erected to operate a set of stamps and a horse whim was also employed for hauling. The dressing floor was sited just a few feet below the main waterwheel and was supplied with water from the by-pass leat, as was the water for the crusher (see surface plan). Due to the fact the shaft was situated in a ravine the working area was restricted consequently the area to the east of the shaft was boarded over, and the shaft boards were taken up the 15ft. or so to the collar and working platform, which is in line with the waterwheel on the opposite bank. This development work took 2 years and the first ore, weighing in at 21 tons 10cwt., was not raised until 1848; the following year, a further 22 tons 2cwts. was raised. Then, just when things seemed to be going well, the workforce was conscripted to the company's new venture at the cobalt mine and no further work was done at Stonycroft at that time.

During March 1853, work recommenced and the shaft was sunk a further 6fms. to expose a good vein, and 3 tons of ore were raised with a further 3 tons stockpiled. It was even rumoured that. a solid rib of ore, at least a 10ins. thick, was visible in the working face and would weigh in at least 60 tons. By this time the shaft was down to the 20fm. Level and in Richardson's Stope, ore had been assayed by John Mitchell who verified the silver content at 22oz. per ton. Nevertheless, the company was again in severe financial difficulties, mainly due to the commitment to the cobalt venture.

Some parts of the mine had now fallen into disrepair, timbers had collapsed and bad ground was encountered, thus hindering further development and, to make matters worse, the waterwheel had developed a problem and until this was repaired pumping would not be possible. Presumably because of these problems, the company decided to bring the venture to a close, despite good ore being left.

The action of closure mystified some of the local miners who were willing to work for £5 a ton on tribute, they no doubt, realizing the full potential, but despite their offers the mine was still closed. This caused much speculation and rumours were rife as to why the mine abandoned. Apparently 3 tons of good ore were left on site and there were at least 60 tons underground. It was being said that Captain Jeffery of Driggeth Mine at Caldbeck was of the opinion that certain directors allowed the mine to close, knowing its true potential, and would then possibly lease it themselves at a later date. Jeffery refuted this idea as absolute rubbish and stated quite categorically that he had never seen any 10in. leader of lead! No legal action was brought and the gossip disappeared along with the miners' jobs.

The new year of 1854 saw a new mine captain, R. B. Shepherd, in charge of the mine but although the damaged wheel had at last been repaired, the frost had now come and thus prevented its use. It would be the month of May before the grips of winter released sufficient water from the frozen ground, so that work could recommence and the shaft could be pumped out. During this time, the short trial on the leat had been reworked, but nothing of value was found. Once the shaft was clear of water, work restarted in the Richardson's Stope in the 20fms. on the west heading, and some ore was won and valued at 1 ton per fathom. By August, the 20fm. Level was still being driven but was now in poor ground. The shaft continued to be sunk and was now down to a depth of 26fms., and here the once rich orebody had petered out. Indeed it was here the miners had expected great things but the ground was breaking up and proved to be totally barren. By December 1854, the Company could see no financial future in the mine and as a consequence it was closed.

Today

Looking from Stonycroft bridge to the west one can see the whole of the mine site; below in the bedrock hidden amongst the gorse bushes are the culverts, leats and the wheelpit. Hidden in the stream bed is the shaft, and the ancient German workings where the ravine is at its most vertical. (do not attempt to locate these workings if the gill is in spate). Nearby on the grassy bank are the surface trials from the 1700 and also, cutting the breast of Rowling End, is the leat structure bringing water a mile from Keskadale Beck; this was used to supplement the water supply for Stonycroft and Barrow mine.

The Cobalt Mine

"Early smelting operations in the old mines of the Hartz Mountains in Germany often revealed an impurity that spoiled the desired copper metal. This was due to another ore that occurred with the copper ore and the German miners called it 'kobold' meaning goblin.

The famous Cobalt Blue Glaze was prepared from cobalt oxide discovered in Saxony in 1545. The zaffre (oxide) and finer smalt was used by the potters of English tin-enamelled earthenware as their chief source of decoration and on all kinds of 'china' From 1796 it was used on bone china. It was called 'Bristol Blue' because a wholesale druggist in Bristol was the sole importer. This supply was interrupted during the 1756-1763 Prussian war with Saxony and at this time, the Cornish deposits were worked, and again in the 19th. Century.

Cookworthy, as a chemist, is credited with the extraction of pure 'cobalt blue' from Cornish zaffre.

The ore is reduced to the simple oxide (zaffre) by roasting. The zaffre of commerce contains about one-fifth of the oxide and the rest is powdered flint. When this is melted it forms a glass which is ground to form smalt. The pure oxide of cobalt, when mixed with fusible matter, is used in painting the blue on Delft and other imitations of porcelain"

This mining adventure must perhaps rank as the most unusual in the Lake District; in these early days the ore of cobalt was in its infancy, technology was just breaking through into this new area of steel manufacture and indeed, its discovery in the heart of the Lake District would create more than a stir on the prospecting scene. Not only was this a difficult mineral to find and identify, to refine and smelt it would prove very hard indeed.

The vein was located at 2,000ft. on Long Crag on the western face of Scar Crags, where the ground is steep and the vein well hidden. Whoever it was who first discovered and identified the mineral here is unknown, but one can assume it would have been around 1820. The vein hades NE/SW and cuts diagonally across the face of the crag; this is a remote and bleak spot, the ground is steep and rough and the nearest road is at Stonycroft just over three miles away.

The first adventurers arrived during September 1822, having first agreed terms with Cockermouth Castle, and the company of men was led by one of the finest local mining engineers, Mr. John Tebay. Within the next few weeks the vein had been tried in various places, and the first ton and half of ore was raised by November of 1823, a royalty of 1/8th. was paid as agreed, and by the end of 1825, 5 tons 9cwts. of ore had been raised. This is a small amount when compared with lead or copper mining, but the prize here, if the ore was discovered in quantity, would be huge. From their lofty eyrie, the miners could peer down at the Force Crag miners, a thousand feet below, and from their perch in these hard, cold crags perhaps they sometimes envied their fellow men down in the valley bottom. Despite their tenacity, this was becoming an ill fated venture, and the trials made on the back of the exposed vein proved that the mineral existed but not in the quantities anticipated to commence mining. Because of its remote location, and harsh terrain, a more considerable investment would be required than these adventurers were able to commit to.

Nearly twenty five years later, in June 1845, further interest was being shown and Mr. Samuel Merryweather, a local mining engineer, was in negotiations with John Bragg, the mineral agent at Cockermouth Castle. This was as a result of his partner, Jeffrey Richardson, sending a parcel of ore samples; on examining the ore, Samuel felt that opening up a mine was indeed a possibility. Before he committed to anything, however, he first went to London for two weeks to seek out reliable backers and people prepared to invest in the new venture. The trip was successful and as a result, plans were laid down and by June 1847, the company and board were in place. The directors were Messrs. Jeffrey Richardson, Samuel Merryweather, Alderman Carter of Cornhill. Henry Compton, Fenchurch St., London, Alex Graham of New Bridge, Blackfriars, London and secretary John Watson. The company would be known as The Keswick Mining Company Lead & Cobalt Mines, and one thousand shares at £2 10s. 0d. were offered to float the company, which would realize £3,000 if all were taken up.

The Mining Journal produced an article in 1848 which one can only say was enough to raise eyebrows, stating that "there was enough cobalt at Keswick to pay off the National Debt" - the Bank of England was subsequently informed! Cobalt was a relatively new mineral and would be used in the steel industry, and if the company was successful, a substantial amount of money could be made.

Investment was absolutely essential to the success of the venture, and it would cost a fortune in time and manpower just to set up the necessary infrastructure, let alone running the risk of driving yards of barren levels; the miners had to make a good strike early on and prove the lode.

To begin with, a suitable road (one report suggests that it was to be a railway) had to be engineered which, when completed, would be just over three miles long. They had a slight head start here as a road of sorts was already in place to the Stonycroft Smelter, but this had not been used for years and was in a poor state of repair. The higher reaches would also have to be carefully engineered and laid down and pitched properly; good drainage also would be essential to prevent the road being washed out during inclement weather. A few hundred yards above the site of the derelict lead smelter, a suitable site at OD820ft. was found for a small mill and new smelter. Leats were dug to bring water to power the overshot waterwheel which, in turn, would run a set of stamps and operate the bellows for the furnace; all this however, would take a considerable time to achieve.

The first project was to establish a base at the mine itself, and a substantial stone bothy and smithy were constructed at OD1750ft., and a sled road was put down into the Coledale Valley whilst their own company road was under construction. The Force Crag mine road was of course by now well established, and no doubt some local agreement was struck for its use. This wide, perfectly angled road from Coledale still provides a steady trod up to Sale Pass and the mine bothy.

Whilst all this activity was going on, mining had commenced, levels were now being driven into the hillside and ore was being brought out. The lower trials were proving poor but the higher workings at OD2200ft. were proving more successful and around 48 tons of ore had already been brought out. Mine captain Mr. Jeffery was certainly pulling things together and during August 1848, the mine was really starting to take shape. On the 11th. of the month, the following equipment was transferred from Goldscope Mine at Newlands five miles away, a round trip which would take a day for a good horse!

Equipment from Goldscope Mine

67ft. timber	
78ft. timber	
43ft. timber at 1s. 6d. per foot	£14. 3s. 0d.
wire rope drum and brake	£20. 0s. 0d.
2 wagons	£ 3. 0s. 0d.
33 larch and Scotch firs	£ 1. 9s. 0d.
2 sheets iron plate*	
box of nails*	
12 plates grates for stamps	9s. 0d.
6*	
levers for crushing mill*	
wire rope*	
planks and boards	8s. 0d.
2 barrows and spare wheel	5s. 6d.
2 ropes*	
2 sieves and tool chest	9s. 0d.
wood for roofing	10s. 0d.
scales	£ 1.10s. 0d.
6 x 5lb. weights	£ 1. 8s. 0d.
gunpowder*	

*all these items to be weighed and invoiced later.

The production of the ore from the higher workings was a simple enough job, but to transfer it down the narrow, exposed trod was a feat requiring strong nerves and resolution. It was therefore planned to construct a small winding drum incline from the highest level at OD2000ft. down to the bothy at OD1750ft. During the height of this activity, the Mining Journal produced a further glowing report and estimated that the value of the cobalt mine at Keswick would exceed the value of the Californian Mines! The reality was that in 1849, the mine actually produced a further 58 tons. The hype had created further interest on the stock market, and a new issue of 2,200 £10 shares was offered; it was reported that around 1,000 of these were snapped up immediately. The price of cobalt in Europe at the time was around 22/- per lb. which works out at around £2,464 a ton. and the company was soon claiming reserves of 150,000 tons; in mining and financial circles rumours and speculation were rife. Soon a figure of £3 per lb. was being bandied about and to add to all the speculation, in 1849, a Captain Paul claimed that the No. 3 Level alone would produce at least 2,000 tons.

On site, the investors' money was being used to bring the mine up to full production and the road was now completed. The mill was located a considerable way down from the mine, in a sheltered area at OD820ft., and everything was working. The wheel was in situ, and the mill, grinding house and drying room were operational; the ore was first crushed and processed through mesh at 16 holes per square inch. Two furnaces had been erected and 100 tons of ore was ready to be processed; Mr. Langton was at the works and Mr. Bancraft was smelting ore.

However, as quickly as the company ascended into the limelight, by 1850 the venture foundered; the last adventurers had produced just over 104 tons of cobalt ore and spent a total of £7,000 on building a road, smelter and dressing floor and had driven at least five levels. The highest of the workings, No. 5 at OD2000ft. was the most developed and extended a distance of around 70yds.; it has been stoped in the roof and understoped, connecting through to the No. 4 Level, 30ft. below. The No. 3 Level, 30ft. lower is cut in solid rock and extends beneath the higher workings; here the level has been blasted out in solid ground and at 70 yds. inbye the level splits. The left branch is blind while the right hand branch connects through to the higher workings. This was developed to become the main drawing level, however the demise of the company stopped any further development. Below these workings, hidden in the lower crags, is the No. 2 Level, a small crosscut around 12yds. long and entirely barren. On Sail Pass trod is another level at the same horizon as the bothy, this however is totally run in.

Today

The Cobalt Mine is still there but is as elusive as the cobalt ore it was worked for; it is hidden in the steep face of Long Crag above Sale Pass and all but three of the levels are now completely run. The incline foundations have now collapsed and become part of the natural landscape. The old bothy at the foot of the incline is barely recognizable and doubtless the many walkers passing by would think it a sheepfold. Yet this place is where the early pioneers of this venture huddled for warmth a hundred years or more ago. The smelt site can still be located below the company road, just above the Stonycroft smelter, and the leats supplying water for the wheel are still clearly evident.

Barrow Mine

1 The Golden Mountain

On the eastern side of Barrow Mountain, from which the mine takes its name, are what appear to be hundreds of feet of shimmering scree, the golden yellow and brown rock reflecting the sun's rays. Tourists and walkers can be forgiven for thinking this to be natural erosion, but the mine explorer knows that in the eastern bulk of the mountain lies Barrow Mine, and that most of this sand coloured rock is the hundreds of tons of quartz and mineralized waste brought up from the bowels of the earth. Referred to as 'the shivering mountain', the spoil is ever in motion and the endless whispering can be heard even on the road below.

The Yewthwaite Lode divides into two veins around 15-20 fathoms apart and the northerly one, known as the Barrow Lode or Main Vein, was of a relatively solid nature but suffered badly from water penetration. The southern vein, known by the miners as the "Sandy Vein", was friable, unsupportive and to say the least unstable. This vein was also referred to as the Sugar Vein or the Sun Vein, "sun" being an old word for "south". Yet in this friable ground the ancient miners pursued their craft from the earliest of times, creating a veritable labyrinth of workings with much timbering but suffering many roof falls. Interestingly, the vein here is not one solid mass but a series of stringers, maybe eight or more, until they meet, creating an exceptionally rich orebody which could produce a solid rib of lead ore 18ins. to 24ins. wide and as long as 30yds. The vein is not without other mineral content and in the friable quartz, baryte, gossan, galena, cerussite and aragonite have been identified

The main two veins bisect the mountain NW/SE and have been worked over a total distance of 1,400yds. by hushing, bellpits, openworks, adits and shafts. The mine certainly predates any gunpowder working and was worked for lead by the Germans in 1567, but we can only wonder by what name the German adventurers knew it.

High up in Barrow Door, at OD1300ft., are two ancient hand-chipped levels which date from this period, and 400yds. away, in Barrow Gill, at OD700ft., is the site of an ancient dressing floor. This would have been operated by the early adventurers working this site because this was one of the few natural sources of water. Indeed Barrow was a very active and industrious operation and seems to have been overshadowed over the years by its many neighbours, however records are very scant which has no doubt contributed to the fact that a bigger picture has never been revealed.

The mine was being leased from the Duke of Northumberland at a royalty of 1/8th., in December 1649, and the mine is recorded as working and raising 124 tons 15cwt. of lead ore over the next three years. A further lease was ratified in the year of 1652 with the same royalty of 1/8th. when Joseph Hechstetter, a direct descendant of the original Hechstetter dynasty, and partner Hugh Potter commenced work and raised 21 tons 4 cwt. 2qts. of ore in the first year. In the following year the output had increased to 23 tons 2cwt. 3qts. and the mine was worked by the same partnership until April 1655 when it appears new blood was brought into the company. These were experienced miners by the names of Richard Tickell, Col. W. Beale, John Fisher and William Tickell By October 1657, Messrs. William. Beale, Hugh Potter and Thomas Tickell held the lease on the mine paying a royalty of 1/8th. as had been agreed years before. The development of the mine continued and in the first year they had raised 26 tons of ore. The partnership was still operating in 1659 but how long they worked after this date is unknown.

It is considered that all these workings took place around the crown of the hill at OD1000ft., an area which had already been investigated by the early German adventurers. The various partnerships had created a series of terraced dressing floors on the western shoulder and they also built small dams in series to collect water essential for the hand dressing process. This water, once used, was channelled towards the back of the vein to create the makings of a hush, the water eventually running into Barrow Gill hundreds of feet below on the western flank of the mountain.

The bedrock on the western side was much harder to work and it was the vein on the eastern side where the early miners commenced, excavating a great deal of ground directly on the back of the vein, the debris being allowed to fan out across the front of the barren fell. In these deep surface workings, the men soon experienced flooding, necessitating removal by jackroll; this would have been an arduous task, the workings being 40/50ft. deep. The old men, now realizing the back of the vein had been laid bare at depth, had only one course of action and that was to commence an underground working. This was level No. 5 and would eventually undercut the open works; a rise was put up to de-water the open cuts and allow them to open up new ground.

In 1690, the following report by mining engineer, David Davies now residing in Braithwaite, to the Duke of Somerset confirms the vast amount of work already completed by previous adventurers:

"At a hill called Barrow we first sett on, after the lease was taken, where ye old men had wrought before, but he was outed with too much water and too little air. When we got on we gave it air and pumped out ye water and when we came to ye sole of ye old men's work we found no ore. Then we sunk 10fms. deeper and found none. Then we drove north and south upon a level 20fms. each way, but none or very little ore. Then we did drive into ye east side and found a good quantity of ore lying soft in sand which sunk down into ye hill from which we pumped water 40fms. to ye day and brought down the air in wooden pipes 40fms., but a wet season came on at Michaelmas that the water was too strong for us. We concluded to bring up a level to clear ye water. We set upon a level 28fms. deeper in ye hill than the sole of our work, and on a perpendicular from ye top of ye hill 70fms. and we had to drive before we came under the sole of ye work 300fms. we wrought this level night and day for seven years. It cost upwards of £900 and when we came to clear ye work of ye water ye ore did not continue 2fms. deeper, but we found ore on our way which

did help us on. In this level as we went we found ore in our sole, but we could not work it for water. Then we got on another level 26fms. beneath that and we have driven on it 140fms. where our main work is now, in which we have ore in diverse places betwixt us and the first level which is all the ore of any consequence we get at present.

We find ore in the bottom of this present work which we call ye Middle Drift and we have set on another drift 6 fms. deeper than that and have driven 50fms. and together in it had ore for 20fms., and ore sunk down deeper than our level but watered. We tried to clear it with pumps but the water was too strong so we left that off and set up on another level as low as we could get which is 12fms. deeper than any of ye former. This level is out of ye vein and we have driven it 70fms. and have sunk two shafts upon it and are sinking of ye third. We have been working it for two years and hope to get to ye vein in less than a year. This hath cost us already £350 and when this is up, ye whole hill will be cleared of water and may be aired from one drift to another, so that if ye ore prove good it may last a good work for 40 years without the charge of any other levels and may constantly be aired at easy charge from the drift above".

Indeed the total drivings for this period at one mine seem incredible, but one must bear in mind the vein material here was extremely friable and advancement was faster than driving in hard rock. Barrow was already a mine of great antiquity and David Davies had been working here for at least 9 years continuously, his men working night and day to prove the lode, and at a minimum cost of £1,250 for two levels alone. If the driveages are equated out then the minimum for the venture would have been at least £1,940 and the yardages driven forward work out at around 85yds. a year.

During the last quarter of 1699, from July through to October, the mine was being operated by the following partnership: Rolfe Easton, John Fisher, Daniel Fisher, John Boner, William Boon and Thomas Boon. Thomas Boner was the smith and general labourer and Thomas Tickell was the local carter. During the period, eight dozen candles were delivered by William Mason at a cost of £1 8s. 0d. and 2 new steel jumpers were supplied by John Sharp at a cost of 2/- . During the 3 month period, the 6 miners worked between 72 and 79 shifts and most of the underground advancement was by plug and feather or straight forward pick work.

2 East, West, which is Best?

The turn of the century saw the mine still being worked with great vigour and in March 1702, a new five year lease was granted by the Duke of Somerset to John Scott of Braithwaite, Thomas Henry Inman and William Osmond also of Braithwaite. The new agreement carried a covenant of 8 men employed who were to be paid £6 5s. 0d. for every 23cwt. of ore raised, plus they were to be allowed time off from their work every 6 weeks. The continuity of the mine proves its viability and at the end of the term, a renewal of the lease was agreed on the 26th. of May 1707 by two of the previous company, Henry Inman and W. Osmond and a gentleman by the name of J. Pratt. This time however, the covenant stated that they had to retain eight miners in full employment; four of these were John Scott, Daniel Fisher, J. Rawlin and John Thwaite who started work in the stopes above Wilkinson's Drift in the No. 3 Level. Below this were four other miners, Robert Burfield, Gawen Bow, John Brough and Thomas Fletcher and again they were to be paid £6 5s. 0d. for every 23cwt of ore raised. As one can imagine to have to retain the employment of eight men would require a heavy commitment to the working of the mine, and enough ore raised to ensure a living could be made by all. By November of the same year, new workings were being opened up on the western flank. Interestingly, the lease also gave further dispensation for the workers to smelt the ore at the nearby Stonycroft smelter and that they could also use the smithy there for sharpening and the forging of new jumpers, hammers etc. Unfortunately we are unaware of how long this partnership continued.

The years went by and during 1726 a new lease was ratified, this time for 3 years at a reduced royalty of 1/12th. The man in charge was John Scott, one of the previous partners and the mine worked for just three years with only a few tons of ore raised and after 1729, no further revenues appear. In fact it was to be 26 years before there was any further serious work done and during this time the mine fell into a very poor state of repair.

A new lease was drawn up in July 1755 and the royalty payable on lead ore was now 1/14th., however the covenant of eight miners to be gainfully employed was still included; the lessees were Robert Peile, Robert Potter, Isabella Potter and William Gale, all well known local miners. This was to be a spirited trial and the driving of a new level commenced virtually straight away; they hoped to be into the vein within four months; this level, in all probability was the No. 5 Level. According to the records the same company was still working four years later and had been employing as many as ten men. Since taking over the mine, their biggest annual production up to 1767 was 18½ tons, which netted them around £111. Then, during November 1770, a new agreement was taken up by Mr. Potter, William Gale and Robert Peile but we can not say how long this partnership lasted.

Certainly at sometime in the next few years, the tenure did change when the two Barren brothers from Braithwaite started to work the mine. The Sandy Vein was very unstable and certain areas of the mine had to be well timbered, but despite the dangers, ore could be good here and the miners knew the risks. By 1788, the Barren family had been working here for a number of years, but on the 7th. of June 1788 Edward Barren was trapped and killed by a roof fall in the mine. The inquest was held at the miner's home in Braithwaite and presided over by the Coroner Thomas Benson, who recorded a verdict of Accidental Death.

These were still early days and the mine had in fact been considerably opened up over the previous 200 years. Some of the old partnerships had tunnelled deep into the heart of Barrow Mountain, creating a creditable underground mine. Not all the work was on the eastern side and a considerable number of trials have been excavated on the western flank also. Water was actually more readily available from Barrow Gill and was supplemented by water brought by an elevated leat at OD700ft. from beyond Barrow Door. This was being used to feed a large hush to expose the back of the vein, however the overburden here was up to 6ft. deep. In places the vein was exposed and tried but these were no more than surface trials and a few yards to the east, a series of small shafts was sunk in an effort to find the vein, but these appear to have been unsuccessful. Further up the slope, another hush was created complete with dam but again, this did not succeed in providing an exposure. These workings and trenches, some up to 6ft. deep, cover the whole of this side of the fell with very little sign of the vein being opened up despite the tremendous effort that had been put in.

Below, in Barrow Gill, at OD700ft., the old men had set up a dressing area no doubt in anticipation of ore being raised on this side, and two substantial cart tracks were made, one to Braithwaite and Keswick, the other, which contours round the mountain, from the dressing floor to Uzzicar. In contrast, on the eastern flank the whole face is devoid of any source of water and it had to be brought by a half mile leat from beyond Barrow Door, across the front of the fell, eventually arriving at the hand-dressing floors at the mine entrances. As the workings had developed down the eastern face and were now 400ft. or so below the ridge, it would be impractical to carry the ore back up to the summit ridge area for dressing.

During 1818, two adventurers by the name of J. Barrow and E. Barrow took over the mine at an increased royalty of 1/7th. but this venture seems to have faltered within the year. Over the next two years a few tons of ore were recorded as being sold, but it is thought that this was as a result of the dumps being re-worked rather than underground development and their last records are in January 1820.

Around 1830, mining engineer John Tebay, along with others, held the lease for Barrow which included other mines in the area, and it seems that he became involved with the development of the mine around this time. Certainly the production figures for the next few years increased quite dramatically and in fact, 101 tons of lead were produced in 1835 alone which was a considerable figure. A steady level of production continued until 1838, when there was a definite decline in output. The total tonnage during this period was in excess of 300 tons and to generate this volume of saleable ore would certainly have required a considerable amount of underground development and stoping. Some consideration would have to have been given to the processing of such large amounts of ore, and hand-cobbing at the level entrances would be totally impractical. It could have been John Tebay who laid out the first proper dressing floor just below the No. 1 Level at OD388ft. at the foot of the eastern flank of Barrow. This had been driven years before but was now sporting a rebuilt stone arched entrance and indeed, if Tebay's plans were successful, the No. 1 would become the main drawing adit for all the above workings; no effort appears to have been made to reopen the old Davies level at Uzzicar. But for now, the miners would use the benefits of gravity and all the ore would be simply chuted down the front of the mountain to the bottom; any water brought round in the old leat would no doubt accelerate the passage of the ore down to the mill.

The mill site was 10ft. below the No. 1 Level and was a basic affair with a small waterwheel for crushing rollers, hand jiggs and settling pond. The water for this was supplied direct from Stonycroft Gill via the old bypass leat at Stonycroft Mine; from here a substantial leat was brought the 400yds. to arrive above the new mill at OD378ft. It is interesting to note that the whole of the mill and its surroundings were contained in a small, walled area to prevent any of the live stock from the nearby Uzzicar Farm encroaching on the company's land.

3 Candles & a Good, Stout Rope

During September 1847, the Keswick Mining Company was formed under the directorship of Messrs. Langton, Merryweather and Richardson and the lease was for 21 years, at a royalty of 1/15th., however the mine was not to be energetically operated by this company. Work started in clearing levels No. 2 and No. 4 but it appears the operation was run on a hand to mouth basis and during 1851, only a small amount of ore was raised by a few miners, on tribute. One miner, clearing and digging his way through the old, collapsed levels came across a cache of ore; the lead, in sacks, had been neatly stacked in a remote heading, a rich prize indeed. The tributers of the old days would store ore in the mine for safety, until they were ready to sell - it was like money in the bank. It was safe underground, and by hoarding could ensure a steady income and also not arouse the attention of other miners.

The company soon realized that the old men had done their work well, and virtually all the higher workings had been totally worked out and robbed although, in October 1852, a few pockets of ore were found in The No. 3 in Wilkinson's stope. Some men were clearing the No. 2 Level and reached the forehead which was standing with good ore in the face. The men were in good spirits as this area was not worked out, as the locals had told them it was. They were also in the process of crosscutting west to the Sandy Vein which the men were nearing, but they had struck much water. By March 1853, six miners working on tribute in one pitch had struck ore worth £8 a fathom, and nearby was another worth £10 a fathom. All the work was above No. 1 Adit and because there was no power to pump out the water in the sole, a rise was put up for ventilation and to de-water the workings in the sole.

The development continued into 1854, and in May tributing was continuing in Wilkinson's stope on Level No. 3, a crosscut to intersect the Sandy Vein which had been proven in the No. 2. It was decided that the No. 2 Level should be re-timbered over a distance of 90fms. and likewise, the No. 3 Level was also secured with 80fms. of re-timbering. This type of development revealed a serious investment in both time and money, and this certainly was a year of considerable activity; by September a connection had been made between Middle Level and the No. 3 Level. The tribute pitch, Parker's, was let at £6 10s. 0d. a fathom, and was producing lead. In November 1854, ore was still being raised but the vein was pinching out, and further development would be essential to maintain production.

Despite all this recent expenditure however, the company was now concentrating all its efforts on Brandley Mine and over the next few years, the workforce at Barrow mine was gradually depleted, and by 1857 there were only two men working. It was becoming obvious that the workings were nearing exhaustion, and over the past few years, 300 tons of lead and 1,700ozs. of silver had been sold.

Work restarted after a lay off of seven years when, in 1864, a team of miners was working the No. 1 Level and clearing other levels, when they intersected an old shaft working. Looking up they could see, many feet above, two huge blocks wedged across the shaft while below them it plunged into the darkness. Obtaining spare candles and a good stout rope, one of the miners was lowered down and there, in a working, he found a considerable parcel of ore ready for market. It was retrieved and sold fetching £35 and although a tributer's hoard is usually safe, it may have been that a serious collapse prevented him being able to retrieve it... or perhaps he had passed away taking his secret with him.

During 1869, the old Barrow Mine was re-surveyed by Benjamin Plummer and Coultas Dodsworth or, more correctly, those areas which could be entered. The mine was now in a state of crumbling decay, and the pair relied heavily on hearsay by the old men. All they could glean for sure was that the mine had been worked by no less than four levels on the eastern side of Barrow Mountain and numerous trial pits on the western side of the fell. Certainly some, if not all were worked on two veins, the Sandy Vein to the south and the Main Vein to the north which divided around 160yds. in. Efforts were made to access the levels but No. 4 and above were totally run in and No. 2 was accessible for only a short distance.

Regardless of the poor state of the mine, in 1870, Benjamin Plummer joined forces with Henry King Spark to reopen Barrow. They drove the No. 3 Level forward to undercut the old workings into new ground, but this was not a venture which was to sustain any further development.

During 1874, two men re-entered No. 3 Level and removed small amounts of ore, but by 1876 they had left and the mine was again derelict. Two years later, in 1878, a new company was formed and was to be known as the Co-operative Mining Company, of which two interested parties were William Porter of the Threlkeld Mine and Mr. John Postlethwaite, but what became of this venture is unknown. Barrow had been worked for over 300 years and by now the best was gone; certainly richer mines like Thornthwaite, Threlkeld or the nearby Force Crag would be a safer bet.... or of course if one had the money... perhaps an engine shaft could be sunk to explore the vein at depth!

4 Across the Road to Uzzicar

The Yewthwaite lode cuts beneath the green fields between Stair and Stonycroft Beck on a NW/SE heading before it reveals its presence in the face of Barrow Mountain. Just west of the ancient farm of Uzzicar, a series of bellpits has been put down on the back of the vein; these, by the small amount of spoil surrounding them, are shallow but these early trials date from around the 17th. Century and were the first on the Barrow Sandy Vein. It is not known who was actually responsible for the work, although it is known that David Davies sunk at least three of them whilst driving his Low Adit level in 1690.

During 1883, the notorious and flamboyant Henry Burrow Vercoe, the son of a Scottish mining engineer, leased the mine sett and formed a new company in August of this year. This was to be known as the Barrow Mining Company Ltd., and the capital for the venture was £25,000 in £1 shares. The partners were R. W. Williams of Kirkdale who was the Agent, J. B. G. Petere, Jeweller of Liverpool, J. S. Elmslie of Liverpool who would be the Mine Manager, E R Hartwright of Liverpool who was the accountant, W. Hillmew, Tailor of Liverpool, C. Pearson, Printer of Bootle and W. S. Cook, Engraver of Liverpool. A can be seen, the cross section of trades is completely varied and none were from the local area.

Vercoe, by all accounts, was a man of tremendous vision, a notorious speculator and adventurer who always saw an incredible future in all his mining ventures. Here at Barrow, he realized the success of the mine would be in the sole of the valley at Uzzicar and not in burrowing in the worn out holes in Barrow Mountain.

He and his newly formed company wasted no time in getting the operation underway and in December 1883, a substantial pit head gear was being erected in preparation for the engine shaft at Barrow Bottom near Uzzicar Farm, from which the mine later took its name. An office was built of local stone with a slated roof measuring 36ft. x 12ft. and this was sited to the north of the shaft. Included in this building were the miners' changing room and store, and a smithy and store were sited opposite on the other side of the engine shaft. The engine house was constructed to house a 20hp. Robey steam engine of Lincoln for the purpose of winding. The new shaft was timber lined at the collar and was in three compartments: hauling, climbing way and pumping, foundations and walling were already being laid for a 60ft. waterwheel and dressing floors, water for the power would be leated from Stonycroft Gill to the south. This wheel was one of the biggest to be used in the Lake District.

February 1884 saw the new shaft being sunk and already down to a depth of 14fms. and the speed of advancement was aided by the use of dynamite, of which 50lbs. in 2½ lb. units plus 5 coils of fuse had just been delivered at a cost of £3 18s. 9d. All the explosives were stored in the newly built powder store in a shallow dip just below the smithy. Within a month there was great rejoicing at the mine, the engine shaft now being down 17fms. and a wonderful bunch of lead ore having been cut. Indeed, the lode now proved, Mr. H. B. Vercoe wanted to let the whole of the world to know of his success, including his rivals and would be investors, and instructed his foreman to raise a huge Union Jack above the engine house to let everyone know who was top dog in the Newlands area!.

The pace of development continued and by December 1884, the engine shaft was down 20fms. and in the 17fm. Level, the previously exposed lode was driven upon for a distance of 70fms. but the ore did not continue. The shaft sinking, under the direction of Mr. Vercoe, was being pursued with great vigour with nine miners sinking; the target was to be down to the 30fms. horizon as quickly as possible. By February 1885 the men were achieving a rate of 20ft. a month! The 20hp. engine was winding all the ore and dead material from the shaft bottom and also de-watering the mine. In preparation for pumping from the workings, a 60ft. diameter wheel with a 2ft. breast was now being erected which would develop 75hp., and this energy would drive crushing machinery and jiggs, and also pump water from the mine.

By August 1885 the new company was still sinking the shaft, and a quantity of ore was already standing in the bouse teams, however the intended water supply from Stonycroft Gill to propel the giant wheel was not forthcoming. It appears the summer drought had reduced the supply to a mere trickle. However they still had the Robey engine, but Vercoe had underestimated the cost of running such a hungry beast and not only did it consume coal at a vast rate, but men had to be in constant attendance; this was now becoming a problem, but the pumping had to continue despite the costs. As the ore was raised and the bouse teams filled there was wide optimism about the potential of the mine, and rumours soon spread saying that it could be as grand as Greenside, Threlkeld or Brandlehow.

A full year later, stoping had begun in earnest and the men had been setting underground tramroads, indeed four new men had been engaged as trammers and were to be paid 2d a tub for their labours. Underground however, the air was foul, no real ventilation existed and of the few rises which had been put up, none were through to surface; the only source of ventilation and way out was up the shaft! To ease the situation, Mr. Vercoe approved the installation of ventilation pipes at the level headings. The Robey engine was working flat out due to further drought conditions, but the company was anxious to use the waterwheel for their needs where ever possible, as this was obviously a more economical.

The end of September 1886 saw the engine shaft down to the 30fm. horizon, and also at this time, the old adit level driven years before by David Davies was being cleared out, this had been driven 140yds. from the east and had now been intersected by the new adventurers and was to become the 8fm. Level; this would create much needed ventilation and a secondary way out.

During this period at least twenty-four men were actually mining with four men tramming, plus a team of men working the dressing floor, and wages for stoping varied between 25/- and 30/- a fathom. An important angled rise was being driven up from the 30fm. north to the 17fm. above, and in the north face, good ore was also encountered. Meanwhile, in the 30fm. south a rise was being put up to the 17fm., where the joiners were placing ventilation doors to ensure good ventilation once the connections were made. The 8fm. Level was now being driven south to open up new ground; the drive north now followed the David Davies working in the vein. They intersected the old Davies shaft which was cleared and laddered the 48ft. to surface and was to become known as the Footway Shaft. Once these connections were made they greatly improved the ventilation of the mine. This working by David Davies had cost him upwards of £350 in the 1690s, but this is not acknowledged by Vercoe in any of his plans or papers.

Not all the activity was underground and on the surface the carpenters were working flat out at the mill site which was just west of the shaft on elevated ground. They were making wooden launders and setting stout wooden posts for roofing of the buildings for the crusher house and jiggs. Indeed the pace of work was so frantic that the mill men complained that the joiners were simply getting in the way, when all they were doing was making the place weather proof.... fortunately two days of torrential rain allowed the mill men to see the carpenters in a new light and the work proceeded in a more amicable manner.

In the 30fm. south the miners were working flat out, indeed a new team of men had been engaged to complete this work at 90/- a fathom. Mr. Vercoe's new prize was the Stonycroft lode which was an already rich and proven lode and lay just 200yds. to the south, and at this horizon they would intersect it 10fms. deeper than the Old men had. To accommodate all this activity, the Robey was now working night and day. Above, in the 17fm. Level south, a good bunch of ore had been encountered and the men were rising up; this, in fact, was continued to surface and became the South Air Shaft.

The mine was now producing a steady run of ore, and 7 tons was in the bouse teams with more lying underground and ready to be brought out. The lead, once processed, was taken by cart to Braithwaite railway station, 2 miles away. By November, further work was done at the dressing floor by the installation of buddles to improve the recovery of the ore, and a smaller waterwheel erected to power these. Then, just when things seemed to be moving forward, the miners in the 17fm. north cut into a strong leader of water. Immediately, the men had to start on building a stopping to contain it, and failure to prevent the deluge would result in masses of water plunging straight into the angled rise now connected up from the 30fm. Fortunately, the team, working in dreadful conditions, managed to stem the flow with a timber dam. By December, the run of ore varied between 1 and 4 tons a fathom and the vein was showing 9ft. wide in some of the headings.

The engine shaft was still being sunk and was down a total of 35fms. by the early part of 1887, but Vercoe's target had now been increased and required the shaft continuing to 45fms. For some reason, the pumps driven by the wheel were now only working sporadically and the lower reaches of the mine were continually flooding; at shaft bottom conditions for the men were dreadful, whilst above, the ten miners in the 30fm.. fared little better. The year dragged on and the company had a board reshuffle, which resulted in the company name being changed by the new partnership, to The Braithwaite Mining Co.; this company put the shaft down to the 42fm. horizon. By the new year of 1888, crosscuts north and south off the 42fm. horizon had been driven, but the pumps were still only working erratically, and if this continued the mine would flood.

By 1889, the mine was on its knees and H. B. Vercoe, who had been the driving force, was not a well man. Production over the past three years had been a meagre 210 tons of lead and 21 tons of blende and the company went into liquidation. By December the incessant rain had flooded the mine, as the pumps had remained idle. We conclude that the mine closed due to the death of H. B. Vercoe in 1890, from which time it appears the mine just literally fell into dereliction, and in 1896 the board decided to close it down. The machinery and plant went up for auction on Wednesday the 2nd. of September 1896 at the mine but was a disaster and the unsold machinery was left on site and was still there in October 1899. During this year, an enquiry was made by Captain Borlase to the Estate Office with a view to taking over the mine and he was offered the sett at a rent of £25 pa.. at a royalty of 1/16th. Captain Borlase tried to negotiate for 1/18th. and a £20 rent, but this was not accepted and so the mine fell into further disrepair.

During 1905, the South Air Shaft on the 17fm., which was in the middle of a local farmer's field, was filled in and made safe and the following year, in December 1906, T. Dennison and J. F. Lobb acquired the lease for 21 years at £25pa. rent and a royalty of 1/20th. No mining actually took place but in 1910, 25 loads of spoil were removed by the company. The following year however, the company folded and reemerged as the Coledale Syndicate although nothing is recorded of their activities. In 1929, the last enquiry was made by a Mr. Martin and Mr. W. T. Donovan who had various Take-notes in the area, but these were mostly to rework the tips rather than to undertake any serious work underground.

Today

The story of Barrow is as elusive as are accurate and detailed plans and accounts of the workings, but our story is not finished yet. Down in the bottom of Barrow Gill below the ancients' dressing floor and lead working, deep in the ravine at OD500ft., a strong quartz vein is to be seen in the gill bed and just below this exposure, on the northern bank, are more ancient pits. On the opposite bank is an ancient hand chipped trial and below is an open level. Here the old men have bridged the gill, and have deposited a substantial amount of spoil much of which has, over the last few hundred years, been washed away.... was this one of David Davies' trials to open up the lode and de-water the workings of Barrow from the west perhaps? No records have come to light about this level, but its remaining spoil would indicate a substantial underground working; indeed a considerable time would have been spent here. An air/waterblast shaft is to be found on the hillside at OD650ft. which connects undoubtedly with the adit below. The water for this has been brought to it by a substantial leat from Barrow Gill. The decision to undertake to ventilate the adit in this way indicates that it was a very serious proposal and the intention must have been to drive all the way to undercut the Barrrow Mine and de-water it, so precluding the need for expensive pumping machinery. Every effort has been made to find the company or miners responsible for this working but to no avail.

What we do know is that Barrow Mine was worked over a vertical height of around 700ft. and was opened up by possibly five levels from OD316ft. to OD960ft. Two main veins have been exploited over a period from c1570 to c1889 and at a conservative estimate, a minimum of 1,800yds. of level were driven; of this total, 1,400yds. were in fact driven by c1700. To the mine explorer and historian the site reveals virtually every type of mining technique from hand-chipped levels, hushing, bellpits and shafts, wonderful leats and early roadways - a feast of history.

After the war, the area beside the road at Barrow Mine became an open aggregate quarry and reports suggest that the mountain side was literally scooped away for basic hardcore. Over the years, many hundreds of tons have been removed and the demarcation of the working can be clearly seen. Unfortunately this work has destroyed at least one of the ancient levels, and possibly some of the early dressing floors and ore chutes. Around 1960, a council lorry decided to park directly over the No. 1 Level while the driver ate his lunch - to his surprise his lorry started to sink down as his rear wheels sank into the old level beneath. The earth moved for him all right and as his frantic attempts to make a getaway failed, a rescue truck had to be called to extricate him!

Below the road are the remains of the Tebay dressing floor, still confined by its wall but directly above, the location of the levels is difficult to ascertain although the tell tale zig-zag tracks are a give away. Nearby are the leats hidden in the heather and grass which brought the much needed water from Stonycroft Gill.

Across the road at Uzzicar, the engine shaft was still partially open as late as 1987, the side board timbers visible and a carefully dropped stone indicated the void below, before plopping into the still waters. It was our intention to clear the shaft and descend it, in the hope of gaining access to the 8fm. adit level and any other workings off the shaft. Unfortunately, before this expedition was mounted the shaft was filled and bulldozed. A few years later, the northern Footway Shaft partially opened up and again this was secured in about 1995 and the whole site was liberally landscaped.

During the course of our research into the mysteries of Barrow Mine, we spent a great deal of time surveying with tape-measures and GPS navigators to try to unravel the mystery of the site. The c1690 document of David Davies gives us some bare facts and certainly the levels on the face of Barrow, of which there are four, are easily identifiable; there is a possible fifth removed by later quarrying and a possible sixth now lost near the summit ridge. However, a reference is made to a level driven at the lowest possible horizon, below the OD388ft. adit and being driven off the vein, with three shafts. This is surely the adit due east of Uzzicar Farm.

With regard to the 1690 levels, these would be the workings and the horizons based on David Davies' report and clearly reveal that No. 5 Level was driven after his time, possibly in 1755. When one attempts to apply these horizons they do not correspond exactly with what is visible on the ground, bearing in mind the OD for No. 0 Level and the No. 1 Level are in line with the Ordnance Survey. However, if these horizons are worked from the summit ridge at OD1000ft. a different set of

Extent of Barrow Mine 1690 David Davies

The depths between the levels given by David Davies of 72ft, 36ft, 156ft and 168ft give the following ODs. These horizons start from the Uzzicar crosscut, however, if we follow this pattern No. 3 and No. 4 Levels do not correspond to what is on the ground.

No. 4 Level   OD748ft.
No. 3 Level   OD580ft.
No. 2 Level   OD424ft.
No. 1 Level   OD388ft
No. 0 Level   OD316ft

Extent of Barrow Mine 1878

Based on the above David Davies horizons of 72ft., 36ft., 156ft. and 168ft. starting at the road level, the visible workings are correct on the ground, however this then throws into the equation what of the No. 0 Crosscut Level attributed to David Davies and the shafts which are certainly there.

No. 5 Level   OD820ft.
No. 4 Level   OD652ft.
No. 3 Level   OD496ft.
No. 2 Level   OD460ft.
No. 1 Level   OD388ft.

We hope that you enjoy trying to work it out!!

Barrow Mine looking from Low Level up to the Sand Vein. Ian Hebson Collection.

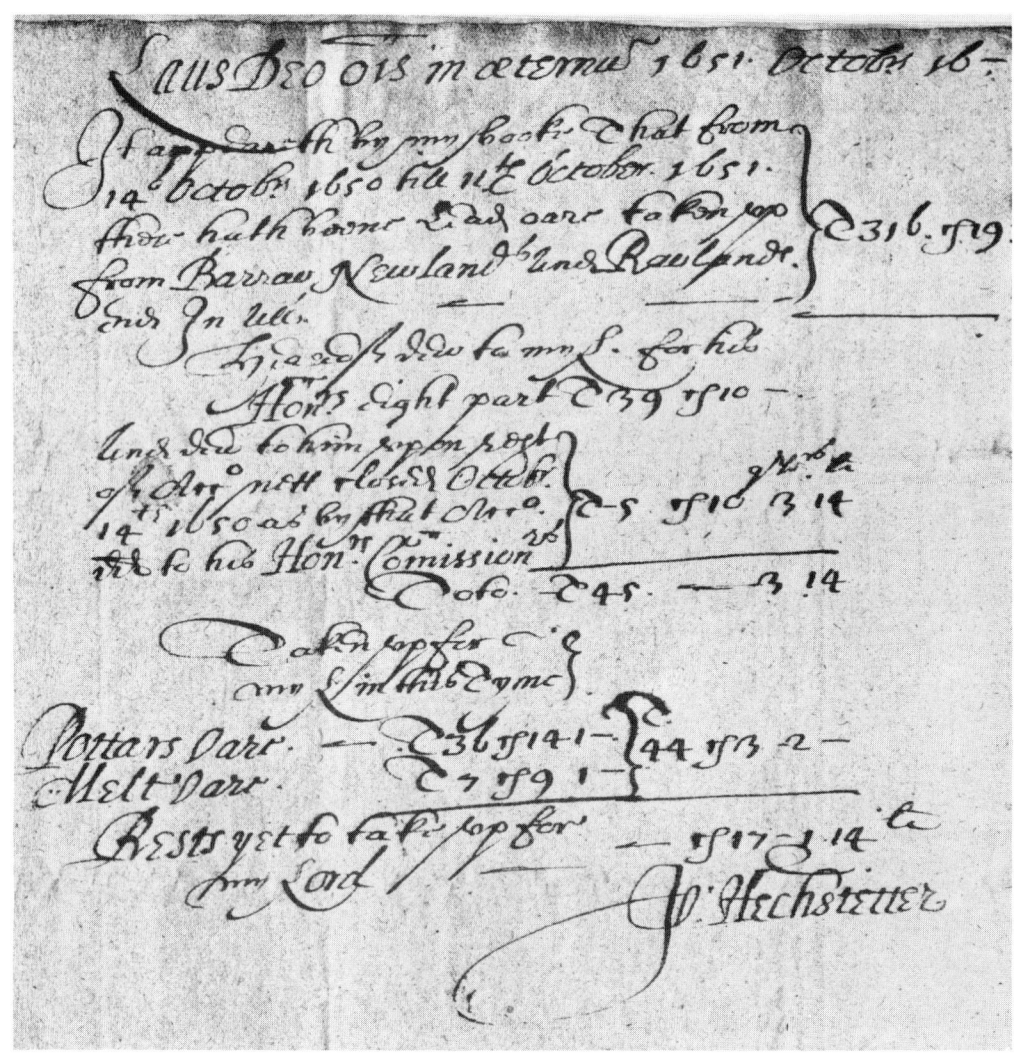

Joseph Hechstetter working agreement for Barrow, Rowling End and Newlands 14th. October 1650 - 11th. October 1651. Also details of tonnage and ore smelted.

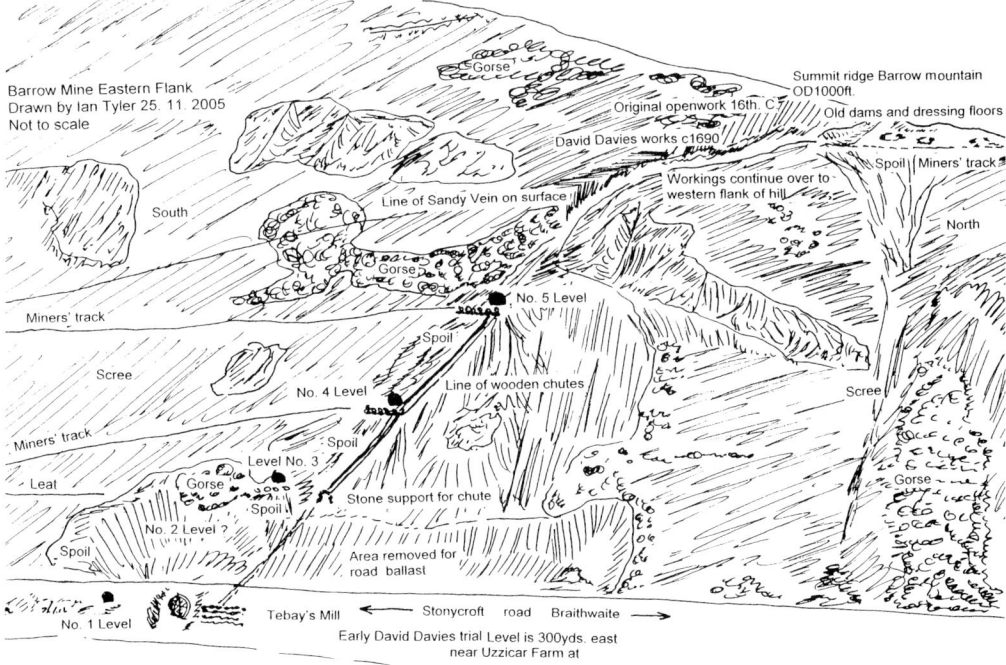

Top: Barrow Mine. Ian Tyler Collection.
Bottom: Plan of Barrow Mine. Drawn by Ian Tyler.

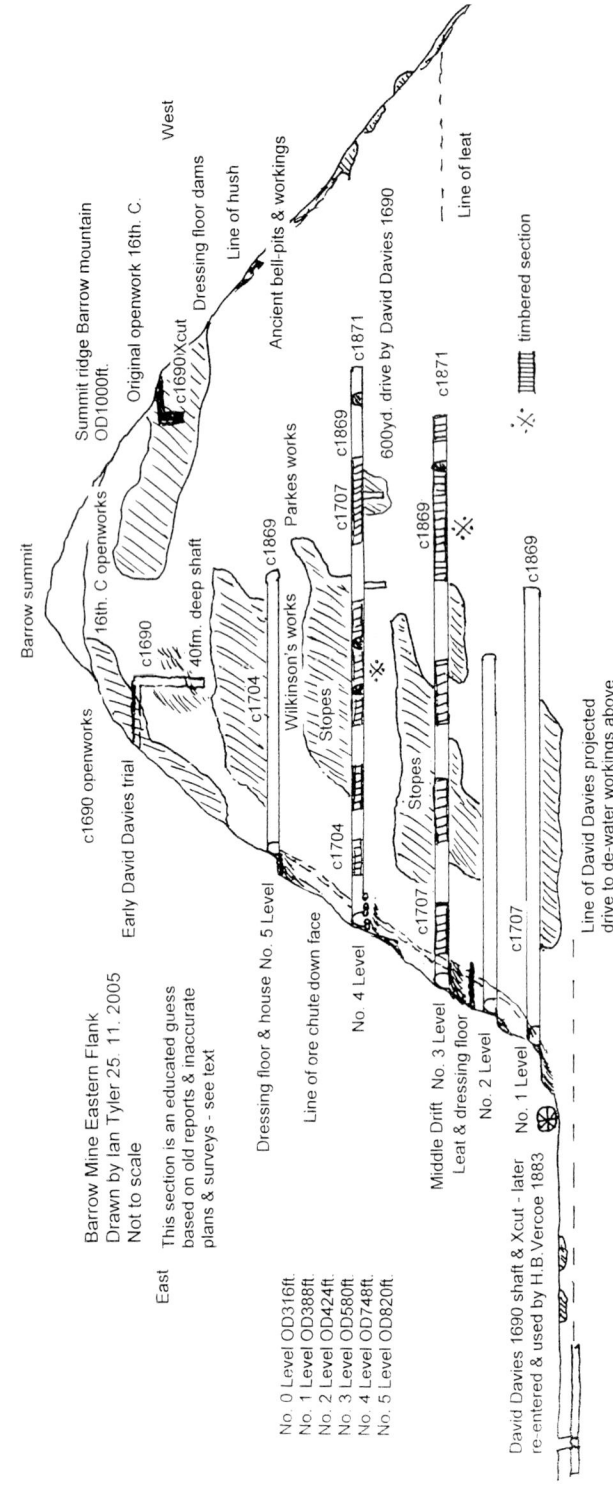

Section of Barrow Mine. Drawn by Ian Tyler.

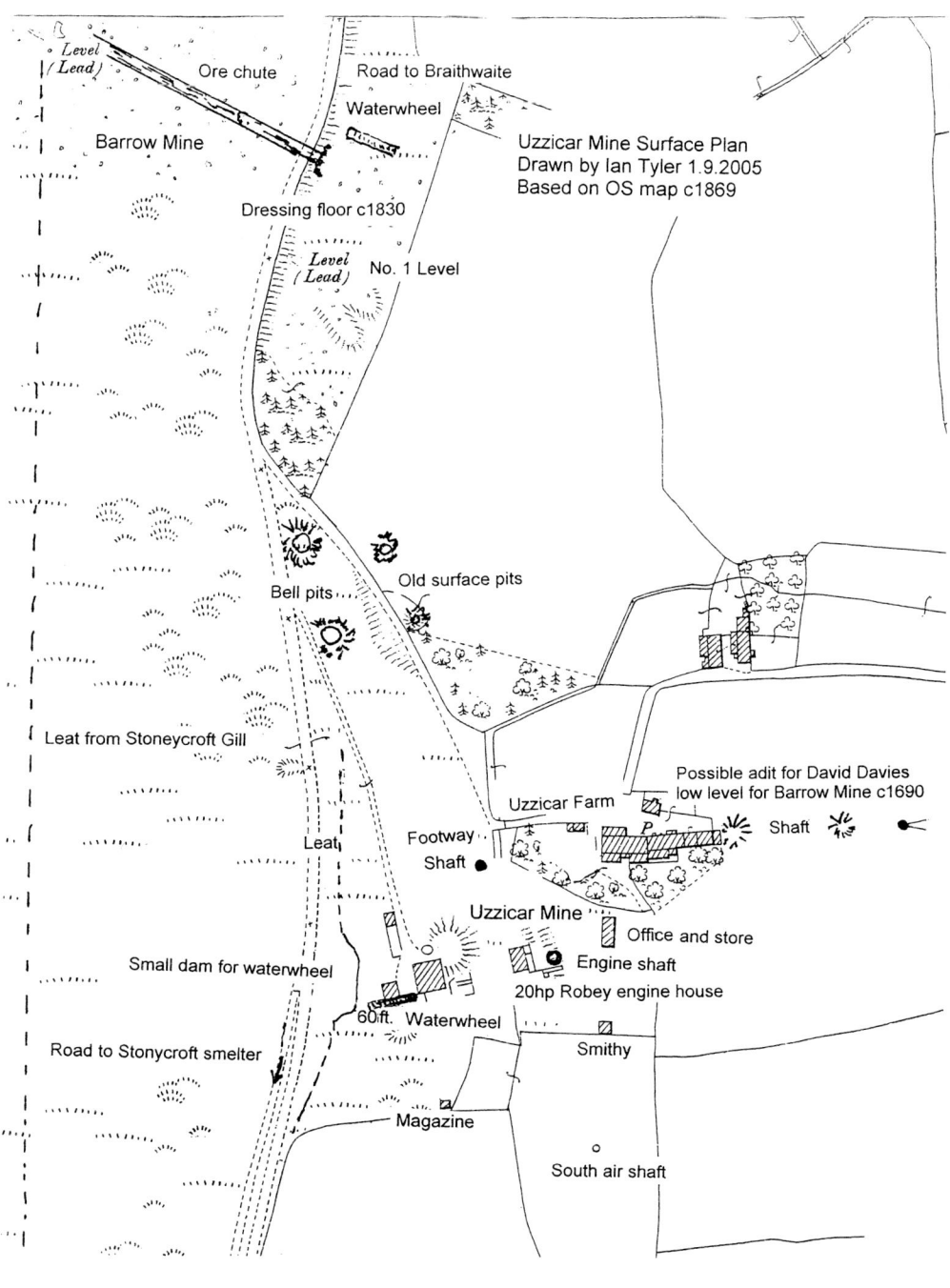

Uzzicar site plan. Ian Tyler Collection.

Top: Uzzicar, Footway Shaft opened up 1984. Ian Tyler Collection.
Bottom: Uzzicar Mine, 42ft. engine shaft and smithy. Ian Tyler Collection.

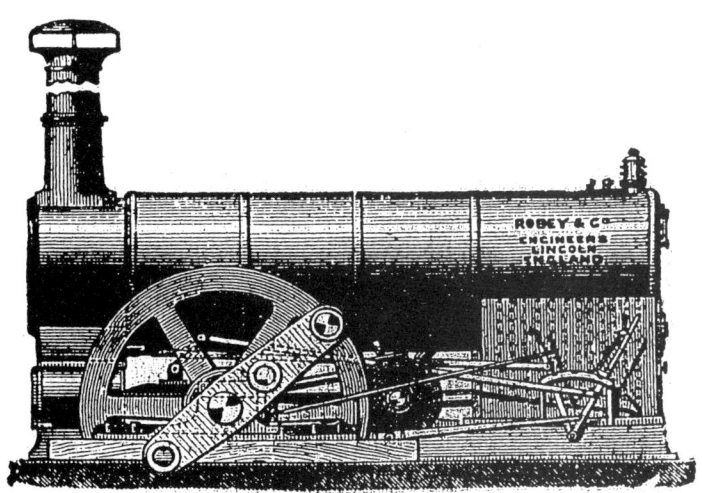

PATENT "ROBEY" WINDING ENGINE.

Top: Looking south from bell pit workings towards engine shaft and smithy - note air shaft in field. Ian Tyler Collection.
Bottom: Robey steam engine of the type installed at Uzzicar.

BARROW LEAD MINES,

Near BRAITHWAITE and KESWICK.

CATALOGUE

OF THE WHOLE OF THE

MINING PLANT,

Etc., now at the above Mines, and comprising—

First-class "Robey" MINING ENGINE and LOCO-TYPE BOILER Combined, with two Cylinders, 6in. by 12in. stroke, and powerful Hauling Drum; One 60ft. and One 20ft. Water Wheels, with large Pitchpine Beam Supports and Wood Water Troughing to same over one mile long; Two Shaft Pumps, with ranges of 10in. and 9in Iron Pipes, fifty yards deep; Massive Pumping Beams, comprising some excellent heavy Pitchpine Beams and Iron Fixings; Pit Head Gear, with 5ft Pulley, &c.; Grinding Mill, with heavy Iron Rolls and Massive Gearing; 16ft. Iron Elevator Wheel, Four Jiggers, Washing Boddle, Blake's Patent Stone-Breaker, 500ft. Iron Tramway Rails and Hauling Drum, Shafting, Piping, Weighing Scales, Barrows, Smithy Tools, Circular Bellows, Grindstone, Scrap Iron, &c.; Stone, Brick, and Timber-built Erections, comprising a quantity of good Building Materials.

-Also all that PLOT OF FREEHOLD LAND, containing about One Acre (more or less), at present forming site of the Barrow Mines aforesaid,

WHICH WILL BE

SOLD BY AUCTION

BY

EDWARD RUSHTON, SON & KENYON

On WEDNESDAY, SEPT. 2nd, 1896,

On the Premises as above.

May be viewed one week prior to sale. Sale to commence at 12 o'clock noon

CATALOGUES and other information may be had from the AUCTIONEERS, 13, Norfolk Street, Manchester; or from Messrs. PILLING & Co., Chartered Accountants, Booth Street, Manchester.

Barrow sale poster.

Top: Ladstock Mine south adit and stope on Combe beck. Ian Hebson Collection.
Bottom: Ladstock smelt mill beside Comb Beck worked until c1820.

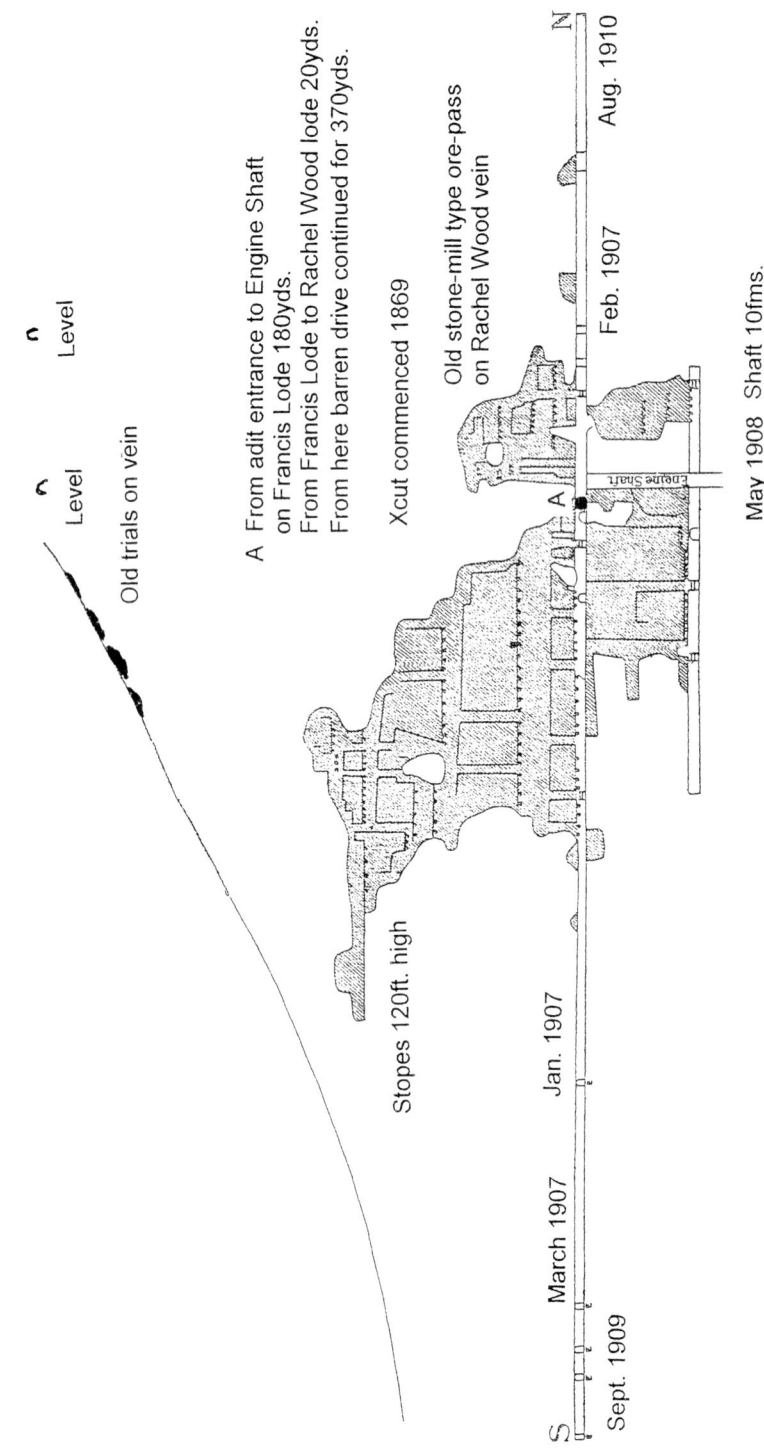

Rachel Wood Mine. Re-drawn by Ian Tyler.

Adit entrance to Rachel Wood Mine. Ian Tyler Collection

Top: Rachel Wood main adit looking 200yds. back to day from engine shaft. Ian Tyler Collection.
Bottom: Looking down into the engine shaft. Ian Tyler Collection.

Rachel Wood Mine, winding/hopper gear Engine shaft. Ian Tyler Collection.

Rachel Wood mine, stopes on vein looking east. Ian Hebson Collection.

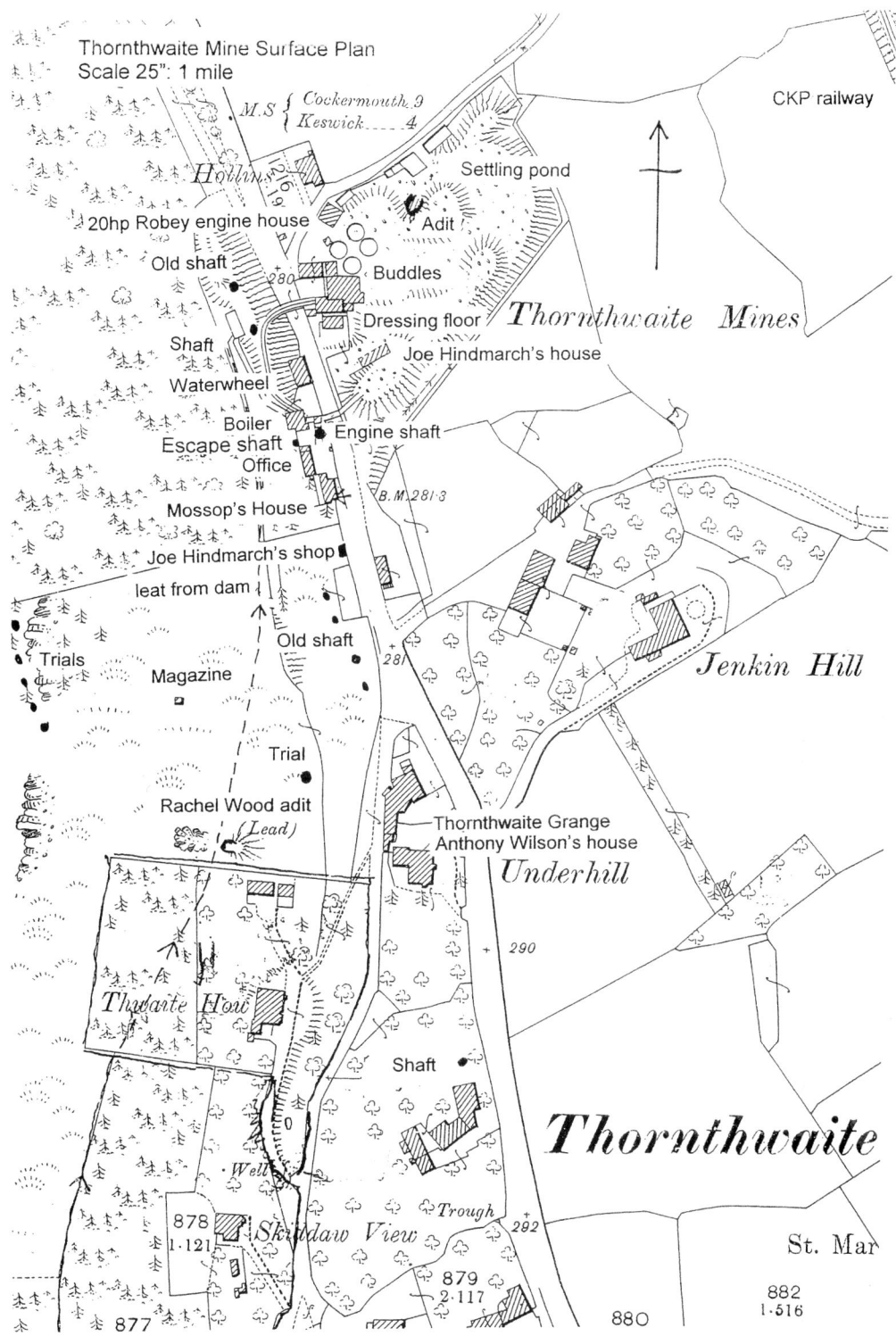

Plan of Thornthwaite Sett. Re-drawn by Ian Tyler..

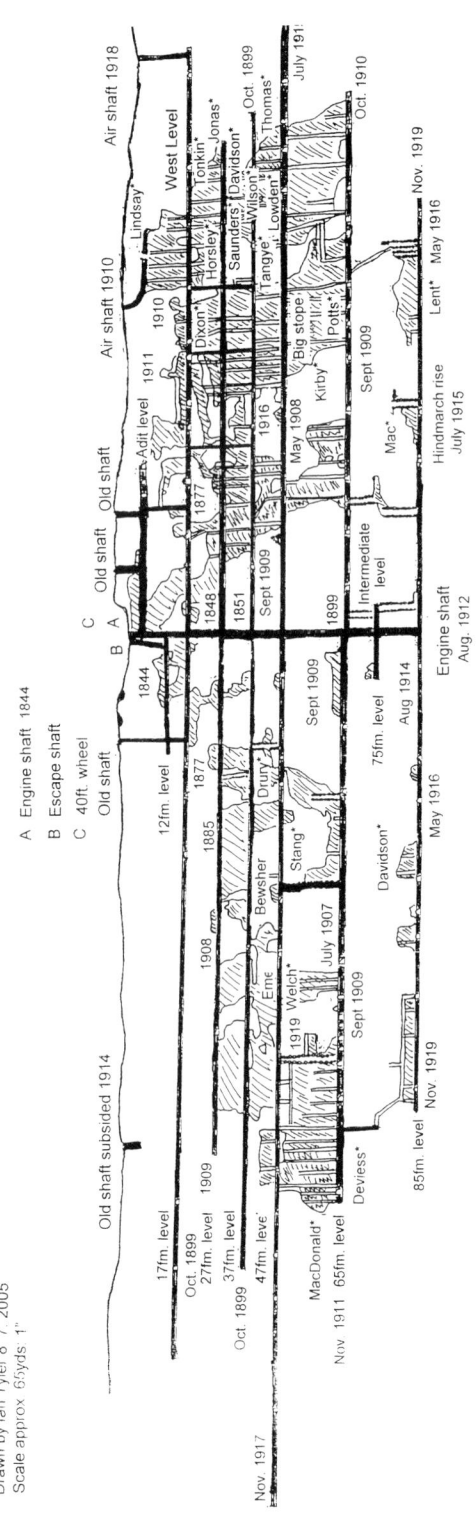

Section of Thornthwaite Mine. Drawn by Ian Tyler.

Top: Thornthwaite Mine - note 26ft. waterwheel. for pumping - note headframe beyond. Courtesy of Beamish Museum.
Bottom: Thornthwaite Mine, headframe and the bridge supplying ore to dressing floor. Courtesy of Beamish Museum.

Top: Thornthwaite Mine, escape shaft/ladderway near Engine Shaft. Ian Tyler Collection.
Bottom: Wooden house built by A. Wilson for Joe Hindmarch. Ian Tyler Collection.

TELEGRAMS:
"THORNTHWAITE MINES, KESWICK."
(DELIVERED FREE.)

GOODS AND PARCELS:
BRAITHWAITE STATION, VIA PENRITH.

ANTHONY WILSON,
Managing Director.

FROM THE **THORNTHWAITE MINES, LIMITED,**
NR. KESWICK.

28 OCT 1915

Dear Mrs Sanders, Could you supply me with a Photograph of Ted, his age, number etc. I am making a large framed Photo Roll of Honour for the Mine, & I should be very thankful if you could let me have a Photo of him

Yours truly
J H Davies

TELEGRAMS:
"THORNTHWAITE MINES, KESWICK."
(DELIVERED FREE.)

GOODS AND PARCELS:
BRAITHWAITE STATION, VIA PENRITH.

ANTHONY WILSON,
Managing Director.

FROM THE **THORNTHWAITE MINES, LIMITED,**
NR. KESWICK.

June 23rd 1916

Dear Mrs Sanders,

The War Fund Committee here hope you will accept the enclosed £3 as some little token of their interest & sympathy on your behalf. They sincerely trust that you may receive definite news of your husband, & wish me to convey their best wishes to you.

Yours faithfully
J Harvey Davies

*Top: Roll of Honour for miners from Thornthwaite Mine who went to war. 1915.
Bottom: Letter from Thornthwaite Mine signed by Harvey Davies in sympathy for the death of Edward Sanders at the Front, 1916.*

Top: Thornthwaite/ Braithwaite/ Force Crag miners drilling competition at local sports day c1920.
Bottom: Memorial plaque for Anthony Wilson at Thornthwaite.

Laal Joe Hindmarch outside his paper shop at Thornthwaite c1920. Courtesy of Eric Hindmarch.

Top: After the bike came the van c1920. Courtesy of Ian Hindmarch.
Bottom: Laal Joe Hindmarch - small in stature but a powerhouse of a man c1920. Courtesy of Eric Hindmarch.

Woodend Trial - note slab sides of level are understoped. This working could have been fire-set. 17th. C. Stuart Clement Collection.

Ancient Bell-pits just below the Gale and Potter Woodend Trial 17th. C. Ian Tyler Collection.

Remains of engine beds and foundations of Silica Brickworks. Ian Tyler Collection.

Silica Mine. Part of silica vein 50yds. wide x 15ft. high. Ian Tyler Collection.

Ladstock Mine and Rachel Wood Mine

Ladstock mine is to be found above the old hamlet of Ladstock where, besides the ample waters of Comb Gill, industry has flourished for hundreds of years. A thriving mill created work in this quiet backwater but mining activity is thought to have commenced here in the 16th. Century and because of this, an ancient smelter had been constructed in Comb Gill. Here the Old men have started their working on two parallel lead veins known as the Beckstones and Ladstock lodes, both coursing NNW/SSE.

The earliest workings are pre-gunpowder on both sides of the gill and the early German miners are recorded as working the area, however there are no specific dates or locations apart from the single name "Thorntat", obviously a very early spelling of this name. Certainly at this location the early prospectors could not have failed to see the vein clearly exposed in the bedrock in the Comb Gill bottom. The workings have been known over a considerable period and although early records are very scant, it would be reasonable to assume that the subsequent workings were started around 1750.

The early open works are to be found on the southern side of the gill where, on the westerly vein exposure, the miners have cut a large open stope some 30ft. deep and 60ft. long. Just below this working is a similar opencut where the parallel vein has been opened out over a similar distance. This was called "Priest's Milkhouse" but why the working was given this name is a mystery; it is these workings that one could link to German prospecting. In the gill nearby are the remains of a bridge, and nearby is a rectangular stone lined pit which may have been a waterwheel pit or an ore washing trough.

Once these easy pickings were over, proper underground work commenced and it was the westerly vein which was driven forward on both sides of the gill. On the northerly bank of Comb Gill, a pre-gunpowder level 3ft. 6ins. wide and 6ft. high has been driven forward a distance of 35yds. and the floor understoped for at least 15yds. and taken down 20ft. in the sole. At the entrance is the remains of a small hut, possibly a smithy or bothy.

This has been a rich mine site and through the nearby hills run at least ten veins and numerous stringers. The old men would attack virtually any exposure for a few hundredweight of lead. It is because of this level of activity that they constructed a smelt mill beside Comb Beck, sited just below the mine. A guide to its age is that it was working in 1798 and it is reported to have smelted lead up until 1849.

On the opposite bank a more serious attempt has been made to open up the vein by traditional mining methods and the new adventurers just followed the Old Men's direction on the vein. A substantial orebody was discovered in the sole near the entrance so work commenced here and a meandering level of similar dimensions to the northern working was driven forward. At 20yds. in the vein improved, work commenced in the sole and the old men went down 20ft. in good ore and pushed forward in the vein at this horizon north and south. Rather than carry the rubbish out of the mine they filled any old drives with the waste rock. Here the Old men were in good ore and continued to go below their existing level by another 20ft.

where again they pushed forward north and south, again backfilling the workings with deads much of which was rich with zinc and lead which would lead us to believe that the miners were indeed in a bonanza lode.

The mine here is trapped between two becks, Comb Gill to the north and a small unnamed stream to the south. Because of this situation, the water make must have created a problem, so the ancients sunk a vertical shaft to aid the de-watering of the working. This was a crude affair and a jack-roll and bucket was the order of the day. No doubt it was probably the water that beat the Old Men and forced them to abandon the mine.

The Keswick United Silver Lead Mine Company took over the sett in 1869 which also included Beckstones, Rachel Wood, Thornthwaite. The old Ladstock. Mine was to be reopened in February under the guidance of Captain Francis and the first job was to de-water the old mine. The Old Men's bell pit was now fallen in and efforts were made to clear the rubbish but this was wasting valuable time, so Captain Francis decided to sink a new shaft, a few yards to the north; to reduce pumping a new adit level was driven to intersect the shaft from the nearby stream.

The miners only had a few feet to sink and within three months the shaft collar had been timbered and secured, the shaft increased in depth and a stronger 60ft. rope was brought up from Thornthwaite so a bigger kibble could be used. The workforce was increased by miners from Thornthwaite and with the extra men, the shaft was soon down into the Old Mens' flooded workings. Within a couple of weeks the men had cleared the water and commented on the small size of the levels, some being only 5ft. high and 2ft. wide. They were pleased to see that in various places lead and blende was still visible in the vein, and to the delight of Captain Francis, much of the pack-walling had a reasonable mineral content - the ancients had not entirely cleaned up! Captain Francis now gave instructions for the adjacent Bell Pit Shaft to be cleared, and over the next few months 40 tons of ore had been recovered.

The new shaft was now down 60ft. and Captain Francis was much encouraged by his venture, indeed, Ladstock was playing its part in the Company's success and was creating more share interest in this undoubtedly profitable venture; its future promise was written up in glowing terms in the Company prospectus.

By the end of 1872 however, the Company had finished with the working, little real mining had been done and certainly there had been no development work other than access to the lode. The mine had literally been robbed of any visible ore and this had gone through the awaiting crushers at the all important nearby Thornthwaite Mine.

Today

The hamlet of Ladstock has changed over the years, even as recently as the last twenty, and the old mill is now a series of private dwellings. The site of the smelt mill has long since vanished although the old road to the mine was for years known as "Smelt Mill Brow". It is thought that the last house near to where the track has been hewn out of the solid rock, is actually on the site of the old smelter. Another interesting adit entrance was visible just above the old mill and we always wondered if this was an old crosscut to the Ladstock Lode, however in the last ten years a house has been built on the site so we shall never know! The workings are still there and as described, however entry is only by the authority of the Forestry Commission.

Old Rachel Wood Mine

The original working of this mine was again by the ancient miners of the late 18th. Century and was carried out directly on the back of the Rachel Wood Vein on Red Crag in a series of three pits on a friable rocky outcrop. The workings, in line on the back of the vein, extend over 30yds. and all three workings were connected underground through the stopes. All the stoped areas are back-filled with the mine waste placed between the hanging and foot walls of the vein on timbers, thus creating square stone shafts. This provided an economic way to use the rubbish and also helped to support the hade of the vein. These shafts allowed access by ladders and hauling with jack rolls, the depth to the first sub-level being around 25ft. At this depth the ancients had put in a false floor to connect to the other shafts, then continued working downwards in a similar manner.

The Old men had certainly proved the vein to a depth of at least 40ft. by this method and over the years, a considerable amount of lead had been extracted but these values as far as we are aware are unrecorded.

Further up the hill are two short trial workings on the vein, the first, at OD800ft., is a considerable opencut which then enters steep ground into which an 8yd. level has been blasted. To the north, in Seat How Gill, is another small trial, 11 yds. long. Both these workings appear to be have been driven as prospecting trials by a later mining operation.

The Rachel Wood Crosscut

The Keswick United Silver Lead Mine was formed in 1869 and took over the sett under Captain William Francis, who was obviously aware of the old workings on the back of the vein. Realizing the potential of the lode and its closeness to the Thornthwaite Mine, the Company directors approved the driving of a crosscut at OD366ft., 86ft. above the Thornthwaite Mine.

The driving was commenced in 1875 in steep ground where the ground cover was thin, and the miners constructed the entrance out of local stone and stout timber. After a 30ft. timbered entrance, the men were in good development ground and as they proceeded to blast the 6ft. 6ins. x 5ft. wide tunnel forward, the waste rock was not just dumped at the entrance but was used to make the foundation of a tramway round to the Thornthwaite Mine dressing plant some 250yds. away. At this point, a strong wooden chute was constructed so the ore could be tipped from the tubs the 50ft. or so down to the Thornthwaite Mine dressing floors. The level was railed out to a gauge of 20ins. and heavy, iron, front tipping mine tubs were used similar to those at Greenside. This was a very serious undertaking and showed a great deal of commitment, as the Company knew the orebody would not be intersected by the crosscut until the miners had driven at least 200yds. This would take at least 2 years of constant work by a good team of miners, however, blind heading drives cost money and the Thornthwaite Mine was not producing as was initially speculated. A couple of short trials were made off the crosscut on the hundred yards of progress, when Captain Francis, under instructions from the Board, was told to stop the development work and concentrate all his efforts on Thornthwaite.

It was to be it was to be many years before the mine was to see further activity when a new company, The Thornthwaite Lead Mines Ltd. was formed by Anthony Wilson and F. W. Crewdson in 1890. It is almost certain that it was this company which decided to reopen the old crosscut, once cleared out and made ready. The miners drove the level forward on a dead straight heading and after a year or so, they intersected an E/W vein containing good lead and zinc ore at 180yds. inbye. This was identified as the Francis Lode and a further 12yds. on, they cut the Rachel Wood Vein which ran parallel; here the lode was of immense proportions. From this point the miners could look due south and see the pinprick of daylight of the portal 200yds. away.

Over the next few years, the Francis Vein was worked a few yards E/W and to the east of the cross cut a shaft was commenced. Here the rock was hard and a minimum of timbering was required. The shaft was cut to a good size around 5ft. wide and 10ft. long and divided into two sections, one for hauling and the other a ladderway for the men. In the cross cut to the north, the miners chose to drive a heading east in the Rachel Wood Lode where they hit a good pocket of ore and commenced stoping upwards using the old method of heavy timbered false floors and "stone mills". Meanwhile, in the sole the men commenced sinking down on the vein and a small pocket of ore was removed; access to these workings was by a small ladderway. To the west their efforts were rewarded with even more success for here the lode was really big and in places was upwards of 8ft. wide.

During 1900, the Company's name was changed to Thornthwaite Mining Co. and a further name change was made to Thornthwaite Mines Ltd. in 1901. This of course did not affect the mining operations and was the result of Board Room politics which by now saw Anthony Wilson as the man well and truly in charge. Over the next few years, the underground preparation moved forward, however, by February 1907, the heading and stopes in the eastern drive in the Rachel Wood Vein which had shown so much promise, had come to a halt. Here the vein had pinched in to barren quartz stringers but westward the drive was good and was now 80yds. in. Some stoping had been done both in the sole and in the roof of the level and a considerable amount of good vein material laid bare. The drive was continued and the level cut to a good size 6ft. high and 4ft. 6ins. wide but again, as in the east, the ore started pinching in. Anthony Wilson instructed his men to continue and within 6 months the men had blasted forward a distance of 90yds., but the vein had pinched in to virtually nothing.

The entrance portal to the mine during this period was completely restructured with the aid of concrete and the old timber legs were taken out and the level concreted inbye to the bedrock. Above the new entrance was mounted a stout concrete lintel which sported the new Company's initials, 1908 TML, and also served as support for the iron pipe bringing water down from the dam up in Comb Beck. The hauling shaft was down a distance of 10fms. and a further manway shaft was sunk on the Rachel Wood Lode to the same depth and connected to the shaft bottom; this work was completed by May 1908. The Francis Lode both east and west had proved poor and so all the attention was now turned to the stoping of the Rachel Wood Lode west. Over the last few years the productivity of the mine certainly contributed to inflating the production figures of Thornthwaite Mine.

Development continued in the Rachel Wood Lode West, the heading was railed out and at the crosscut intersections of the Francis and Rachel Wood lodes, turntables were installed for the easy transfer of tubs and the loading process at the shaft top (see diagram). All the hauling was done by compressed air winch, and the development of all the headings was done by compressed air rock drills using blasting gelignite.

The stope in the Rachel Wood West had now reached a height of 120ft., the old stopes to the east were now worked out, the workings below in the sole had bottomed out at 60ft. and ore was being stoped out. In desperation, in 1909, both the Rachel Wood Lode east and west headings were again driven forward west for a further 90yds. but no lead vein was encountered but near the forehead of this barren drive a considerable leader of water was cut and the work ceased. To the east things fared no better; 70yds. were driven over the next year and three stringers of lead encountered. In frustration the Francis Vein was driven on east beyond the Engine Shaft, however this started to curve north, no workable ground was encountered and it eventually intersected the Rachel Wood Lode.

By August 1910, the decision to continue the adit level forward was taken and by 1912 the drive had advanced 50yds. and no veins had been intersected. It is interesting to note the track was laid to the western side of the level and 6in. light ventilation pipe was attached to the other level wall with double pins. Whilst this work was being done, the stopes both in the sole and roof of the Rachel Wood Lode were being taken down. Over the next seven years the work continued recovering ore from the proven ground and so did the drive..... a further 285yds. of completely barren ground with the exception of the intersection of the east and west Ladstock Veins. Unfortunately these were no more than stringers and did not reveal the quality of the lode seen by the old men years before. Towards the end, leaders of water were cut and some timbering had to be done, and then to cap it all, the heading entered smashed and broken ground and here the drive finally ended in August 1919.

Bad and stale air in a blind heading occurs in just under 100yds., and this drive continued from the Rachel Wood Lode a total distance of 335yds. The conditions here must have been appalling for the miners; there was the dust and the filth from the drilling and blasting, the noise in such a confined area would undoubtedly have contributed to the miners discomfort and the air must have been almost unbreathable; the water from the springs at the end of the drive would have been a real boon. On top of all that, the waste rock would have been trammed all the way out to day, a total distance from the final face of 502yds. by hand! The level from the Rachel Wood Lode is cut at a fairly steep gradient, no doubt to help with the tramming of the dead rock and to allow the free movement of water which would have helped the piped ventilation.

By December 1920, all mining had stopped due to a slump in metal prices and the abandonment plan was drawn up by the surveyor John A Hill..

Today

The mine entrance is gated and strictly under the management of the Forestry Commission, but we entered the working years before these restrictions. Initially one cannot fail to notice the straightness of the drive, no kinks no turns, and the massive stopes on the Rachel Wood Lode from which a heavy duty chain dangles from the roof where the shadow of a higher adit tantalizes the mine explorer. The skill of the miners can be seen in the huge packwall and the stone mills, undamaged by the hundreds of tons of ore which had been thrown down them to the waiting tubs. Perhaps the most impressive thing is being able to peer into the ice blue water of the main shaft and to see the old wooden ladders disappearing into the depths. On the surface, above the forestry road, is the site of the old powder store now hidden in a brambles and shrubs and below the main adit in the woods is a small trial adit. This is completely run in and was probably driven around 1880. The Rachel Wood Mine has its secrets and will not be giving them up easily, I fear.

Thornthwaite Lead Mine

1 Engine Shafts and Deep Mining

The site of the mine lies beside the old A66 Keswick-Cockermouth road, and to the east lay the reaches of Bassenthwaite Lake while to the west the land rises steeply and is dominated by the mountain of Lord's Seat. The few hundred yards to the lake gives but a 60ft. height differential, so consequently any of the mine workings below this could be expected to be wet.

The mine sett is bisected by at least 5 mineralized veins. Of these, two hade NNW/SSE, and from east to west are Brandlehow Vein and Yewthwaite Barrow Lode, (generally referred to as the Thornthwaite Lode) running parallel; 600yds. to the west are the east and west Ladstock Lodes which also run parallel and bisecting all these at NW/SE is the Rachel Wood Lode (see plan).

Thornthwaite Vein is the northern extension of the Barrow-Yewthwaite Vein which we know had been worked successfully from very early times at Woodend, Barf and Beckstones. Indeed so industrious had these early trials been, that a lead smelter had been constructed at Ladstock beside Comb Beck and was recorded as working in the early 18th. Century. The main ore recovered was lead, with a silver content which varied on average from 5 to 12ozs. per ton. Zinc was also mined later in considerable amounts from Thornthwaite and Rachel Wood, but the early miners discarded it as worthless.

Early adventurers discovered the vein in the outcrop rocks between the Hollins and Spout House. Later a small adit was driven at OD278ft. to the vein and was probably worked a few feet north and south. The ground cover being no more than a few feet here, the miners holed out to surface in at least two places. This operation would have required only a small hand dressing floor, and the adventurers soon realized that there was no efficient water supply. To solve the problem, they reached an agreement with the owners of a carding mill at Ladstock to take a leat off the mill race to the mine, however, the output from this trial produced a only meagre single ton of ore in 1829. It is not clear who these adventurers were.

During 1836, the Thornthwaite sett was acquired by Messrs. Isaac Sealby, John Tebay and John Reed, all respected mine adventurers. The lease was for 7 years at a royalty of 1/8th. and the Company also held leases for the mines of Brandlehow, Barrow and Newlands, however there is no indication that any work was done here by them under this agreement.

What certainly would be the case at Thornthwaite was that the working would have to be by engine shaft, which would need capital and expertise... deep mining costs money and the next adventurers obviously concluded this. A new agreement was drawn up on the 22nd. of September 1842 in favour of Messrs. William Clemence Snr., William Clemence Jnr., John Floyd and Mr. Ellice. Their plans were to be more adventurous, realizing that because the vein ran basically N/S there would be little advantage in attempting to work it by a crosscut, there being little or no ground cover and so an engine shaft would be the only way forward. This would require water and lots of it, to turn the waterwheel to operate the pumps and for shaft hauling. On inspection of the sett it was soon noticed that their intended main water supply had been diverted back to the carding mill for use there, during the interim period since the agreement had been reached, a situation which had gone unnoticed while the mine had lain idle. A legal dispute ensued as Mr. Clemence argued for the re-diversion of the supply, and in court he was successful, although it was apparently an arbitrary settlement and some of the water was still to be made available to the mill.

With the water problem now solved the position of the engine shaft was selected at OD280ft. directly into solid ground and just off the vein, and by 1844 the shaft was down to 17fms. A level had been taken off at 12fm. and was being driven north and south and was soon in good ore; things looked instantly promising. A 22ft. waterwheel was erected for the purpose of winding and pumping and a further smaller wheel then used the discharged water to operate the crushing and mill machinery, while the water from the discharge race was used on the washing floor.

During April 1844, William Jones, a mining engineer from Chester, had been invited by Captain Clemence to give an unbiased opinion of the workings, appraise the value of the lode and then, based on these findings, produce a full survey. Arriving at Thornthwaite Mine, Captain Clemence and Mr. Jones descended to shaft bottom at 17fms. There by the light of flickering candles, they walked, stooping, to the forehead where a full 3ft. solid mass of Black Jack (zinc) sparkled in the main heading face. Another level was examined 50yds. south, which ran parallel to the main lode and showed good gossan, an indication that mineral was evident. Returning to the shaft bottom, the men climbed the vertical ladders to the 12fm. Level above, in which understoping was taking place; this area of the mine had already produced over 100 tons of ore. The proposed investment by the company was to be around £3,200 which William Jones considered to be a sound investment, and he recommended they continue to sink the shaft without delay, and commence stoping in the sole of the 17fm. Level. However, he did observe that the 22ft. waterwheel would have its limitations, and would struggle beyond 40fms. Jones pointed out that a larger wheel would have to be installed should the engine shaft be sunk below this, and he thought a 40ft. wheel would provide enough power for all their future requirements.

By 1847 the operation had invested a total of £5,000 in opening up the mine, but despite sales of ore, the venture required still more capital. Every effort was made to bring in new investors, but the market was barren and reluctantly they decided to sell the mine as a going concern. Within less than a year the lease was reassigned and a new company, the Keswick Mining Company, was formed and registered on the 28th. of August 1847. The new directors were Messrs. Richardson, J. J. Maw, T. T. Richardson, J. G. Marshall, H. C. Marshall, P. Langton and C. Merryweather and the lease was for 21 years at a royalty of 1/10th. to 1/15th. These men, on the advice previously given by Mr. Jones, decided to install the larger waterwheel straight away, which would also be geared up to work two setts of crushing rollers. To supplement their income whilst mining was in suspension, they reworked the old Beckstone Mine dumps. Once the new 40ft. pumping wheel was erected, the shaft was cleared of water and sinking recommenced with all possible speed, (fortunately hard rock mines rarely deteriorate when flooded due to water make, however this is not the case in coal).

By 1849, the engine shaft was down to the 27fm. horizon and levels were being pushed out north and south. The 17fm. Level was being worked south and 4 miners were engaged sinking a sump, while in the forehead another team of miners were in rich ore. In the northern heading, 2 men were pushing on where the orebody was improving, Just when things seemed to be looking more favourable, the miners working the sump in the 17fm. cut a vast leader of water and this was causing major problems. The men rigged up a hand pump but the make was too great; nothing could be done, the working was drowned and the water ran the length of the level and cascaded to the shaft bottom. This made conditions untenable for the men working in the 27fm. Level, and the only solution to regain this ground was for the men to commence a rise in the 27fm. Level so they could come along underneath and de-water it; the water would then drain out freely into the engine sump. The eventual connection was made in August 1850 ...probably with spectacular results. This was good news and the orebody over the height of 10fms. was now prepared and ready for extraction.

By November 1850, miners were working the 10fm. south while below in the 17fm. two men clearing debris discovered two stringers each bearing 4ins. of ore; at the same time, six men were continuously engaged in sinking the engine shaft. Here the conditions were truly appalling and the miners complained bitterly about the conditions to the mine captain, Mr. Merryweather. It was constantly wet underfoot due to the water still pouring down from the old sump, the rock in the sole of the shaft was desperately hard, the jumpers were easily blunted and consequently the rate of descent was slow. Merryweather understood the men's predicament and assured them that things would get better, and the water would eventually abate at some point. An advert was placed in the local papers for a 20/30hp. steam engine which would generate enough power to operate both the winding and some of the crushing plant; although this would not help the men stay dry, it would provide faster hauling and the possibility of drying wet clothes in the boiler room, however this could be some time in materializing..

The area of land leased by the Keswick Mining Company was encompassed by various other tenants and landowners, who no doubt saw the introduction of mining adjacent to their fields and woodland as a nuisance, and were quick to advise their legal representatives of any wrong doing. In January 1851, Joseph Thompson and Ann Fisher sued the company, and received the sum of £15 12s. 6d., for the damage done to their land at Sourmire. What the company had done is not clear, possibly the constant heavy cartage had ruined the road or there had been the accidental demolition of a wall, but whatever it was, it had upset the natives. The company however had more important dealings in the offing by acquiring more leases, and by May 1851, the Keswick Mining Co. had a sett which extended in area 6 miles long and 4 miles wide and they now owned the prestigious mines of Brandley, Barrow and Stonycroft plus three smaller workings, making it one of the largest mining companies in the area.

The sinkers in the shaft had arrived at 37fms., but at the moment of triumph of arriving, the miners driving in the 17fm. Level cut another massive leader of water. This had the effect of taking the water from the forehead of the 17fm. through the 27fm. workings and down into the 37fm. engine sump. By October, six sinkers were still grafting but the shaft over the last 20fms. had been taken down in bare rock, not cut to full size, and had not been fully timbered. This may well have been done to see if the vein was actually rich enough to develop, and also to save money. It was now decided that the engine shaft should be fully completed before further development was done, including sinking the shaft further. Miners set to work on the widening of the shaft and carpenters were employed for the process; dividing it into the separate compartments of winding, pumping and a ladderway became a priority. This work took nearly 18 months to complete, and by 1852 the shaft was completely finished and the 37fm. Level driven on. But the great expectations of this deep level were unfounded, in fact the recovery was very poor, so much so that in January 1853, a share call of £1 was made by the company, and it was recommended that the mine be examined by another independent engineer, Captain Mitchell of the Merllyn Mine. His report was perhaps more truthful and to the point, and stated what they did not want to hear. He asserted that the mine was a poor prospect and although good ore reserves were visible in some faces, this was insufficient to secure the future of the mine. The only answer was to sink the engine shaft to at least 50fms. to prove a satisfactory orebody.

The directors thought this prudent, and the accounts presented by the chairman Alexander Graham revealed the previous month's balance of £46 8s. 5d. and a current balance of £249 8s. 5d., which offered a glimmer of hope. But things underground could not have been worse: the new 37fm. levels at shaft bottom in both the north and south headings had not improved in driving, and showed virtually barren rock in the face. In this area of the mine they had hoped for a bonanza strike.... all they had was water.

2 Gold Fever

At the end of 1853 the cry went out that gold had been found by a Mr. Calvert in a stream near one of the company's recent acquisitions, and speculation was rife. At the company meeting in December, Mr. Calvert was invited to make a presentation and when he described the location and value of his find, shivers of excitement ran through the assembly. For obvious reasons, the exact location of the strike was not revealed but based on this information, 5cwt. of ore was dispatched to a company holding a Berdam's machine (for gold separation) in the hope that the sample would turn the company's fortunes round overnight. The next item on the agenda however, were the company accounts which showed a balance of £111 1s. 3d. and it was recommended that a further call of 4/- should be made on the 6,005 shares. In order to further streamline the company, a proposal was made to sell off one of the recently acquired mines, but this was overruled. The meeting eventually closed and as the gentlemen retired for refreshments, there was much talk in the room of gold and the wealth it could generate for the company. They only had to wait a few months, and in April 1854 came the results from Messrs. Berdam & Parkes on the ore sent for sampling; the company chairman was presented with a bill for £24 13s. 6d.... but there was no gold.

This was a cruel blow, but in the hearts of the mining engineers there must have been more than a bit of apprehension and caution, and it was now back to stark reality. Underground, the 37fm. was the only heading being worked and was costing 37/- a fathom to drive. By June the miners were complaining that the rock was tremendously hard, the ore poor and water was still seeping through the vein; the only glimmer of hope was that small amounts of Black Jack were visible. The months went by with little improvement, all the stopes in the 17fm. had been cleared and almost all the known reserves had been worked out. The situation was becoming serious and the harsh words of Captain Mitchell's report were now coming true. By November 1854, due to such meagre results, the attitude of the directors had become very negative and some of them were suggesting selling up. The miners were suffering terrible hardship in the underground workings where the bottom of the mine was swimming with water, and the lack of a good orebody was also affecting the miners in their pockets. They were just driving barren headings north and south in the 27fm. and 37fm. levels and the orebody in the 17fm. had been stoped out and robbed. Reluctantly the directors decided they had no alternative but to wind up the Thornthwaite Mine and put the plant up for sale.

Machinery for Sale 17th April 1855

40ft. waterwheel 3ft. 6in.	Crushing mill with double rollers
3 lifts of 9in. pumps	4 head stamps
Horse whim	Tubs and buddles
Capstan	Complete smith's shop
20ft. waterwheel 3ft. 6in.	Store house

By 1860 the company was in serious trouble and of its several mines, only Brandlehow was working. There had been little interest in any of the workings advertised for sale and so the whole of the company's assets were put on the open market; interested parties were directed to apply to Mr. R B Shepherd of Portinscale who was representing the company, while details of the lease could be obtained from Mr. John Watson at George Yard, Lombard St., London.

Years passed and it was not until the 20th. of December 1869, that Captain William Francis negotiated a 3 year Take-note with the landowner Mr. R. D. Marshall at a dead rent of £20 and a covenant of 4 men to be engaged throughout the period; this could be subsequently ratified into a 21 year lease. The new company was called the Keswick United Silver Lead Mines Company and during the initial three years the company employed two reliable mine captains, Henwood and Muse to inspect the mines for completely impartial reports. These were more than favourable and both men were convinced that good ore lay deeper, north, south and to the west. The speculators went out to secure the Board of Directors and on the 27th. of January 1872, The Keswick United Silver Lead Mines Company Ltd. was formed with a capital share of £30,000 made up of 6,000 £5 shares. The sett contained Rachel Wood, Ladstock, Beckstones and the jewel in the crown, Thornthwaite. The Board was made up of Joseph Allen of West Hackney, John Bell, M.A. of Blackheath, William Burnett of 24 Gresham St., London, Henry Dawes a railway and rock boring contractor of 44 Sloane St, London,, Henry Molyneaux of 7 Leighton Rd., Kentish Town, London, James Farie of 5 Willow Cottages, Canonbury and Frederick Snelling of Stratford. The royalty was 1/14th. of ore raised and the mine was to be under the supervision of Captain William Francis. Unfortunately, chairman John Bell had to resign his position, due to ill health, shortly after his appointment.

To further impress the speculators in the Company, none other than Mr. Bryce McMurdo Wright Jnr. of Great Russell Street, London, an eminent and well respected mineral expert, was invited to the mine to give his observations; he freely declared that he was most impressed and lead was assayed at 82% with a silver content of 4.5ozs. per ton.

During 1872, an adit level was driven to the engine shaft from the east beyond the dressing floors at OD220ft., and came under the turnpike road. On connecting with the lode, the ventilation would improve dramatically and save a considerable lift on the existing pumps, also allowing deeper sinking. Further development work commenced in October, and a trial shaft 120yds. south of the engine shaft was put down on the back of the vein. This was timbered across the vein and the bedrock of the hanging wall and footwall were considered sound. The location of the new shaft was very near to where the original workings had been and some of the work here was carried out by Captain Francis himself. Prospecting a further 40yds. south near an old farm, they found good evidence of the lode and by 1873, William Francis declared to the Board that all his initial exploration had now been completed. His intention now was of sinking the engine shaft and he reminded the Board that a previous company had considered the purchase of a 30hp steam engine. This idea was put on hold however, and instead of continuing in the shaft it was decided to try the old Rachel Wood Lode.

During 1875, the Rachel Wood crosscut was started at OD366ft., possibly as an alternative to prevent the enormous costs of pumping, but also to exploit a lode which had already been proved by the Old men on the hillside above. In theory this made good sense and would give the Company another source of ore which could be trammed the 250yds. from the portal and sent down wooden chutes directly to the crushing mill just 25ft. below. After driving a considerable distance however, the Board decided the venture was costing too much money for no return and instructed Captain Francis to channel his efforts into Thornthwaite.

By January 1877, new development work in the 17fm. Level had gone well and the main lode had been intersected 60yds. south of the shaft. A further 50yds. on, the men claimed that the air was poor and so a ventilation rise was commenced up to the 12fm. Level above. This was not achieved without a great deal of hardship as the rock was extremely hard, the men were stifling in the blind heading with no fresh air and soon became tired in the appalling conditions. The 30ft. rise consequently took much longer than anticipated and on completion, the miners were transferred down to work in the 27fm. whilst the 17fm. stood idle. This was an ill fated decision as the miners working the 27fm. heading were suddenly engulfed in a vast inrush of water, sweeping them off their feet as the icy water spewed from the ruptured face. The miners, sodden through, picked themselves up as the water cascaded down the engine shaft and luckily, none of the men were carried that far. Once the water had abated, the severity of the inundation could be seen; much of the level was unstable and had to be timbered to secure it for a distance of 30ft. Fortunately the company had recently installed new 10in. pumps with a 60ft. lift, and these prevented a major flooding in the engine shaft. The new pumps were put under further test over the next few weeks as it rained incessantly, but they proved more than adequate. The dressing floor modifications were going well, the waterwheel had been erected and new tubs, jigs, grates and a crushing plant had been installed and were all undercover, so work on the dressing floor could continue in all weather.

Even so, not all the shareholders were happy and one such city gent wrote to air his views via the Mining Journal of March 1878, as he obviously had been lost from the Company mailing list. He demanded to know:
1. The original amount of purchase either in cash or shares.
2. The amount expended on directors' fees, rent, salary, incidentals to date.
3. The amount expended on the mine to date, inclusive of bills, labour, agent's salary and total monthly expenditure.
4. The amount of ore raised and sold from commencement of company.

A reply was sent through the Mining Journal stating that the Company had never failed to send out annual reports or balance sheets to shareholders. The complaining shareholder had evidently moved and had not sent the Company his new address; he would be more than welcome to the balance sheet for 1877 providing he would supply his new address!

In 1878, at their fifth AGM, the Board of The Keswick United Silver Lead Mines made their report to the shareholders. It did not make for stimulating reading: sales of lead ore had been nil and only a small amount of blende had been sold which had brought in a meagre £319 17s. 7d. Funds were desperately needed to keep the mine operational, but shareholders were reluctant to accept a further call despite the fact that the Board had been financing the operation personally to ensure their ultimate success, and to the detriment of their other businesses. During June, the Directors decided to have one last effort to save the mine and with the help of one shareholder, they managed to raise £300 to release the ore from the middle ground of the 27fm. The lower part of the mine was flooded, as a lower part of the pump had failed and efforts were made to purchase a further 20fm. section second-hand. The only ones available were in Cornwall and it was therefore decided to buy new from Pratchitt Bros. in Carlisle. Only 10fms. were ordered and delivered and were eventually installed, but there was much delay due to rain.

The next report, of March 1879, confirmed that at last the new ground in the 17fm. was being stoped out and the new winze south was nearly down to the 27fm. Level, a block and tackle being used for hauling. In the north the 27fm. was now advanced but the miners were using wheelbarrows which were useless and inefficient; a tram road must be laid for such an important level. By May, despite the personal efforts of the Board, the shareholders appeared to be holding back at a crucial development of the mine, the situation being further aggravated by the fact that lead ore prices had slumped and the returns were a lamentable £225 14s. 4d. The Directors were becoming increasingly frustrated and told the shareholders in no uncertain terms that the mine had been kept afloat by one or two loyal shareholders and the Directors themselves. This year, a further £660 had been invested bringing the total to £4,570 11s. 9d. and not a farthing of interest had been asked though no doubt they would all want to share in the success! The situation however, was grave with £160 owing to the men in wages and other costs outstanding of £180. As a consequence, the Directors suspended work and informed the investors that to save the mine, a minimum of £1,000 was required to re-float the Company. It appears that the shareholders kept their hands firmly in their pockets, as by the 14th of October the Company was sliding into serious financial difficulties and was £600 in debt. It appears the lease was transferred on the 1st. of November 1879 to Messrs. Francis Macdonald Robertson, Thomas James and J. Clemments, but this venture seems to have not really moved forward and the mine closed.

3 Gleaming Galena

A new lease of life occurred in December 1882 when the lease was reassigned to Messrs. Henry Buchanan Lobb and Michael Reed who formed the Cumberland Lead Mines Ltd. and who, confident of their success, wrote to their new landlord Mr. Marshall, telling him of their ability to raise £15,000 capital of which they already had £10,000. They intended to upgrade the dressing floor and had already ordered a new set of Green's and Thomas separation machinery, circular buddles, a Marsden stonebreaker, a new 36ft. x 30ft. waterwheel, a 40hp. steam engine and a 30hp. Robey engine, all at a cost of £3,000 and which they expected to be on site the following month.

Under the direction of Captain Lobb, the son of H. B. Lobb, the mine was to be developed further and the shaft was to be sunk to the 50fm. horizon to open up new ground. The existing 17fm., 27fm. and 37fm. Levels were to be developed north and south and to facilitate this work in the quickest time, the Company had invested in four of the latest, state of the art, air rock drills; this advancement would give the new company every chance of success.

They did not have long to wait for their hard work and investment to pay off and during 1883, the "Bonanza Lode" was cut in the Thornthwaite Lode in the 27fm. Level, where the gleaming galena stood 12ft. thick in the face! The owners celebrated the finding of this in July, by treating all their employees to a slap up dinner at a posh local hotel. The Company was now assured of unbelievable success and the papers and chronicles described the new discovery as phenomenal and the value to be of the highest importance for the entire district.

In 1885, the opening up of the mine was still continuing and the 17fm. Level was being driven on what was known as the Dropper Vein, where the miners were crosscutting and the lode was 25ft. to 30ft. wide with an estimated potential of around 4 to 5 tons of lead per fathom and ¾ of a ton of zinc. It was realized that should the orebody continue at this magnitude the mine would be employing upwards of 90 miners. By the following year, the mine had been developed from the shaft 258yds. in the 17fm. Level, 176yds. in the 27fm. Level and 202yds. in the 37fm. Level and in all, over a mile of tunnels had been driven to open up new ground over a vertical height of 230ft. Many of the main levels were now also railed out including the full extent of the 37fm. Much of the new plant was now installed and the new 36ft. waterwheel was working well, along with the 30hp. Robey steam engine which was sited at the shaft top and was being used for hauling; the installation of the waterwheel reduced pumping costs by £50 a month.

A cash flow problem arose in August 1887, when three of the miners actually sued the Company for shortage of wages. Joseph Ray and Edward Edwards were underpaid £2 9s. 6d., and Thomas Lancaster by £1 5s. 0d. The case was resolved in the local court and our three miners did receive their dues!

During March 1887, Mr. Hindmoor, an experienced miner, was preparing to fire charges but on picking up a detonator to place in the charge, the device exploded prematurely. Mr. Hindmoor's hand was badly damaged and some of the blast was directed towards his face, severely injuring his eye. This type of injury was all too common in these early days of explosives, the hand and arm raised to protect the face in that last split second of instinct often left the miner with dreadful injuries.

Sales of lead and zinc ore during November to December 1888 appeared to be fairly regular, the lead ore fetching around £9 10s. 0d. and zinc, although varying, balanced out at £4 a ton. Cartage to Braithwaite station was 2/- ton and the royalty paid to Mr. Marshall at 1/14th. was £61 19. 3d. The mine was working steadily and in the last 2 months of 1888 had sold 170 tons of lead and blende for which they had been paid £884 10s. 0d.

On the 8th. of January 1889, the men had entered the mine to make their way to their various workplaces and Edward Brown and his mate were walking along the level to commence repairing some roof timbers. The pair started to remove one length of timber and replace it with a newly cut length, when suddenly, tons of loose rock detached from the roof. Edward was directly underneath and never stood a chance, but his mate was more fortunate and managed to side step the rush. Dazed and shocked he called for help and men came running from different places where they had been working. The men tore at the rock feverishly with their bare hands to free their trapped mate but he was dead, crushed to death by the weight of the rocks. His broken body was carried to the surface and laid to rest in a nearby cottage. An inquest was held the following day and Accidental Death was the verdict. The underground foreman, Robert Williams, visibly upset, confirmed that the day before he had inspected the level where the men were working, and reported to Mr. Lobb that the area appeared to be safe, as indeed it had seemed.

During July 1889, Mr. Lobb received a short, sharp letter from Messrs. Saul, Solicitors, demanding to know by whose authority the Company workmen had disturbed a considerable amount of ground on Jenkin Hill. The property, which was not part of the Company's tenure belonged to a Dr. Thompson, who had leased it to one Jonathon Birkett. The letter insisted the land be reinstated to its original condition forthwith, otherwise proceedings would be brought against the Thornthwaite Lead Mining Co. The letter concluded with a bill for £10 7s. 6d. which was to be settled without further communication!

Shortly after this incident, Lobb Jnr. decided to leave his position to go and take over the Hilton Mines near Appleby and a memorable leaving do was held at the Swan Hotel for himself and his wife where they were presented with a marble clock and side ornaments and a silver biscuit box. During the evening, the new incoming managers Captain John Nichol and Captain Garnish who would take over in February 1890, were presented to the assembly and Mr. and Mrs. Lobb said their good byes and prepared to leave for pastures new.

Thornthwaite and its environs are heavily wooded and an ideal spot for a little poaching and local miners Nicholas Hand and his mate William Thomas, when not toiling in the bowels of the earth, found respite at weekends supplementing the food pot with a spot of poaching. Indeed, as locals, they more or less saw it as an ancient right but unfortunately, Mr. Clemmentson the land owner had a different slant on things. He was tightening his grip on lawbreakers, and by a stroke of bad luck the pair were caught in a pincer movement by his gamekeepers Walker and Gate in March 1890 and were subjected to the full force of the law!

A spectacular accident happened during July when, six miles away at Threlkeld Station a goods train of seven wagons, three of which were loaded with quarry stone was caught and bumped by a passing train which had the effect of releasing the brakes. Station staff looked on aghast as the wagons commenced to roll forward on the gradient... this was virtually continuous all the way to Keswick. Within minutes the goods train was on its way and gathering momentum and before anything could be done to alert Keswick, 4 miles away, the runaway was already whizzing through the station to the consternation of the passengers waiting for the 5.45! A quick thinking railwayman contacted the Braithwaite Station staff and they rapidly prepared a siding; eventually the runaways came cruising round the bend and into the prepared siding with spectacular results! It was an embarrassment to the officials of the Cockermouth-Penrith-Keswick Railway but thankfully a disaster was averted.

During October 1890 a further problem occurred over remuneration when William Barker, who had been employed By Captain Lobb as an engine fitter at £2 a week, felt that he was being singled out for unfair treatment under the new managers John Nichol and Captain Cornish and was suing the Company for £8.

4 *Laal Joe*

March 1892 saw a veritable influx of mail land on the desk of the mineral agent in his office at Cockermouth Castle and also at the Company offices. It appeared that more than one local resident had noticed the light grey plume of effluent washing its way into Bassenthwaite Lake, and over the next few weeks the letters became more heated and the local anglers became involved. By April the Company was accused, by their negligence, of causing the deaths of many fish as a result of slimes being released into the lake and it was a fact that no pike were being caught. One fisherman, who had held fishing rights and a boat on the lake for years, was so incensed he was refusing to renew his lease! By June, Messrs. Saul, Solicitors of Carlisle were involved and the Company was quick to respond requesting Dr. Hellon, a leading environmentalist, to analyze the water. In the end the long awaited report arrived and its conclusion was that there was nothing in the water that was really detrimental to aquatic life. The Company, in an effort to prevent any further problems, constructed a further two settling ponds, however the stone to do this was removed without permission from Barf Beck causing further aggravation. The miners engaged in this work were told, in no uncertain terms, to find another source of stone.

In 1893, the driving force of the company, Henry Buchanan Lobb, died and with the captain gone from the helm, nobody seemed to want to take the project on; on the 4th. of August 1893, the plant was put up for sale. Two local businessmen could see the potential and in 1894 the mine was taken over by Thornthwaite Mining Ltd., the directors being F. W. Crewdson and Anthony Wilson of Thornthwaite. Anthony was a very experienced mining entrepreneur and, living in the area, had his finger directly on the pulse. His involvement coincided with the closure of the nearby Uzzicar Mine and he wasted no time in putting in an offer for the remaining plant. This consisted of crushing rollers, waterwheels, various pipes etc., however Anthony made it clear that the cost of dismantling it would not only be costly but dangerous and offered £25 to clear the site and demolish the building, but his offer was apparently rejected.

Meanwhile, at Thornthwaite, the mine foreman was instructed to commence sinking the Engine Shaft and over the next few years progress was rapid, mainly due to the fact that the air rock drills could make ground much faster than hand drilling, and the Robey winder was very efficient in removing the development muck. Off the shaft, the 17fm. Level was now advanced 360yds., the 37fm. Level was at 325yds. and the new 47fm. Level was well established and driven 295yds. The Engine Shaft had arrived at its new horizon of 65fms. and levels driven off a total distance of 473yds.

A great deal of new ground was being developed and blasting was taking place every day. Once the holes had been drilled then they had to be charged, a dangerous task which had to be carried out by experienced men. One such was "Laal" Joe Hindmarch, a local man and a miner for many years along with many of his family who had also worked at Force Crag Mine. Joe had laid the dynamite charges and retired to a safe distance where, in the safety of an inbye, he counted the number of blasts. Whether he had miscounted or caught an echo is unknown but as he walked back to the face, a rogue charge exploded with terrific force, blasting straight into his face and throwing him to the ground. The delayed discharge was heard by his mates who rushed to the scene to find him alive, but only just. His face was badly disfigured and the men carried him carefully up to the surface. The doctor came immediately and dressed his wounds but the blasted splinters of rock were just like shrapnel, and were to cost Joe his left arm, the sight in one eye and an injured leg. He did survive, a fact which was put down by many of his mates, to his small stature; a larger man would have taken the full force and been killed instantly.

Anthony Wilson had known Joe and his family for many years and realized Joe's days of mining were over, so he set him up in business in a small shop not far from the mine opposite Todhunter's farm, selling papers and general goods. Anthony also had a small wooden house constructed on the mine property for Joe and his family. The years went by and the small business developed, but the paper round, and the tedious job of collecting them every morning at 7.30am from the railway station a mile down the road, on his carrier bicycle, in all weathers was becoming a chore. One day, very near Christmas, when the weather was wild and wicked, Joe was making his early morning sojourn to the station to collect the papers. On the return journey, the front carrier of the bike well laden, a neighbour, spotting him shouted, "It's time you gave that bloody job up at your age, Joe ". Without further ado, Joe grabbed the papers and threw the lot up in the air and into the howling wind ... "Yer bloody right"! he yelled over the noise of the wind, "... you can do it"! Laal Joe liked a drink or two at the local, The Black Swan, (now alas, gone), and one memorable occasion, after a few pints with a mate, they looked set to be a while getting home! Joe's mate, feeling paternal, insisted on seeing Joe safely back to his house and they wobbled merrily down the road together. On arrival, Joe then felt his mate needed a bit of assistance getting back to *his* house. They spent some considerable time, weaving hilariously around Thornthwaite seeing each other home! Though Joe was a small man, his wife was quite large, 6ft. 1in. actually, and was affectionately referred to by her diminutive husband as "Laal Skidda"! Happily, the Hindmarch emporium still trades in Braithwaite nearly 100 years on, mind you, they did arrive with the German miners over 400 years ago!

The new year of 1900 did not start well at the mine, the mill flow process had recently been modified to upgrade production, however in reality the mill was not flowing well! The new crushing arrangements were inefficient and could not manage the run of ore now coming from the mine where the men were at this time in some very rich areas of ground resulting in this unusual state of affairs. The result was that Anthony Wilson had to make a drastic and unpleasant decision - he would have to lay off twenty miners of the sixty five employed. Anthony explained the position to the men, who were given a fortnight's notice, and he promised that the Company was arranging to acquire new plant to rectify the problem and all the men would be re-employed.

Captain William Francis had, for many years, been involved at the forefront and development of many Lake District mines, and he had certainly enjoyed success here at Thornthwaite. Now, with age creeping on, this active mine captain decided to retire and make way for a new man, although, because of his vast wealth of experience he would be retained in a consultancy capacity. The new mine manager would be Jonah Hodgson who had recently been employed as the manager of the Wyndham Iron Mines in West Cumberland.

In September 1901, 28 year old Harry Bennett, a miner at Thornthwaite and evidently very hard up, decided he would misappropriate the petty cash from the mine office. His attempt took place during the evening of Monday, the 10th. and the total haul was 32/6d. When Harvey Davies, the office clerk, arrived for work as normal on the Tuesday morning, he found that the inner office door had been opened and two of the planks in the door were damaged. He then noticed the cash drawer had been broken into and on checking his petty cash he established that 32/6d. was missing and that amongst the stolen money was a 2/- coin stamped Woodend. He then went and told Captain Francis and Anthony Wilson, the police were informed and PC Reid arrived. He made his inspection, ascertaining from Mr. Davies that the office and cash were secured at around 4.00pm. the previous day and he then crossed the road to the engine room where he found a large screwdriver made from an old file lying on the work bench, paint from the office door still adhering to it. PC Lindsay checked around various shops in Keswick and by chance he called in at Moses Dalzell's, the clogger in Museum Square who remembered selling a pair of clogs to Harry Bennett for 2/11d. It wasn't until the following day, when checking his cash that he noticed the Woodend coin and took it to the police. Moses Dalzell could not positively identify Harry Bennett but his apprentice John Parker did verify the man as the customer. Based on this information, P.C. Reid arrested Harry Bennett for the theft on Sunday night at his lodgings, and when asked about his clogs, he admitted that he had purchased them at Dalzell's. The case was brought before the Magistrates' court, with Mr. Spedding JP of Mirehouse in the Chair. Harry Bennett protested his innocence, saying he was with his two mates, Sam Hudson and Joseph Tickell that evening, and that he had not stolen the money from his employers. All the evidence pointed towards him but perhaps he took his two mates to the pub with his ill-gotten gains because Mr. Spedding dismissed the case on insufficient evidence. He did however, recall Moses Dalzell to advise him: "you came here and gave evidence in a most unsatisfactory manner, you are an unwilling witness and uncertain, consequently you will not be allowed expenses. Let Harry Bennett be discharged forthwith"!

A year later the Company name was changed to Thornthwaite Mines Ltd., and the Company pursued the underground programme with vigour so that, by 1903, production was increasing dramatically. The healthy market in zinc ore was certainly a help and 639 tons were brought out along with 128 tons of lead. The workforce was now 59 men underground and 19 in the mill making a total of 78. It can be assumed that the men who had been laid off had been reinstated ... Anthony Wilson was a man of his word.

Without much warning, in 1904, the young Mine Captain Jonah Hodgson, after a short illness, passed away. In the few years he had been at the mine he had won the respect of the men and that of his senior colleagues and his death came as a sad shock. Jonah was a West Cumbrian and the day of the funeral commenced with his body being taken from the house at 9.00am. carried to the station and then borne by train from Braithwaite to Whitehaven. Out of respect and loyalty, the miners had given up their day's wages to see their young boss have a good send off and nearly two hundred people lined the streets to see the cortege pass. Local Engineer J. L. Sealby sent a carriage full of wreaths and the tiny station at Braithwaite was packed with mourners, Mrs. Hodgson being supported by friends and by Anthony Wilson and the Directors of the Company. The miners were represented by Messrs. Waite, Reed, Cunningham, Askew, Hodgson and Davies. As the locomotive pulled away, all the assembled bowed their heads in respect until the train was out of sight.

By 1907 the mine was progressing really well with production at over 1,400 tons of ore and looked like increasing, but Anthony was a prudent man and during November of this year, to have an independent assessment of the Company's mines. To this end he employed the services of the local geologist William Hemmingway of Mungrisdale, who duly produced his interim report, suggesting that to advance prospects, the shaft must be sunk deeper and the works progress southwards beyond Comb Beck; development work must continue in the Rachel Wood mine north heading, and the vein should be prospected in the sole. Prior to this work being done a new concrete portal was erected to secure the mine entrance.

5 Battered & Bleeding

On July 8th 1908, miner William Clark walked as usual the mile or so to work and entered the mine but, as he descended the ladderway, he slipped and fell 20ft. to the next station. He landed extremely badly breaking a thigh, and his cries for help brought fellow miner Thomas William Sanders running to his aid; Thomas summoned the under manager who supervised the rescue. William was strapped to a board and hauled up the manway to the surface where he was taken to the ambulance room. Extra blankets and hot water bottles were supplied by Mr. Mossop and Mr. Fidler who administered First Aid but it was decided that William would be better off at Keswick Hospital. He was placed on the mining stretcher, and then carried by his mates post haste towards Keswick. Mercifully they were met at Braithwaite Bridges by the Ambulance Litter, being brought by Messrs. Todd, Stuart and Temple who then took the patient to Keswick Hospital. William remained there until August 24th, when he was transferred to the Carlisle Cumberland Infirmary and four days later an operation was carried out on his thigh bones to knit them together with wire. Unhappily, this was unsuccessful and a subsequent operation was carried out on the 30th of September but the bones would not still knit together and the patient developed blood poisoning from which he died aged only 43. Mr. Leck from the Mines Inspectorate subsequently held an inquest at Carlisle and Anthony Wilson attended to give evidence on behalf of the Company; the verdict was Accidental Death.

Only a year later, in September 1909, at around 1.30pm., three miners, Edward Grisdale, John Lowden and Arthur Lewthwaite had just finished their bait. Making sure all had their candles lit they started off down the ladderway to the 37fm. Level, Edward going first followed by John who was carrying his pick. Some way down, the ladders ran alongside a mill, a section which was exposed for about 5ft. Edward arrived first at the bottom and proceeded along the level, when he stopped to take a stone out of his clog. Arthur came along and asked where John had got to, to which Edward replied, "he was following me but I have not seen him". Assuming he must have gone to collect something, the two men walked down the level to the hoppers which were to be drawn, releasing the draw bar to fill the tub with ore. To their horror a battered and bleeding John fell out down the chute moaning, "get me out Arthur". The men raised the alarm and a telegram was sent to the Keswick Ambulance Service. Dr. Graham arrived and administered First Aid, and after being made as comfortable as possible, John was taken to his home at Park View, Keswick where he lived with his mate of 9 years Robert Saunders. Unhappily, John later died of his injuries. As a result of his death, an inquest was held by the Coroner Mr. Atter and also in attendance were Mr. Leck from the Mines Inspectorate and Anthony Wilson. The inquest revealed that John had been suffering dizzy spells over the past year and he had told his friends that these had sometimes occurred whilst riding his bicycle in the town, and that it was a worry to him. His sciatica was also giving him some problems but on the day of his accident all his mates verified that he was in good spirits. So how did the accident occur?

Had he had a dizzy spell and fallen through the exposed section into the mill and then down the 40ft. onto the ore in the bottom of the hopper, thus sustaining a fractured skull and the terrible injuries which would later cause his death? This would seem to have been the sensible conclusion. The company was questioned as to why they had not secured a safety fence over the exposed section of mill and Anthony Wilson stated that timber and equipment for doing this type of job was at hand should the men have felt the need to protect the section. In fact some miners concurred that, as they knew it was there, it presented no real problem, however in hindsight perhaps they should have put a piece of timber in place. Mr. Leck echoed the miners' feelings; he had inspected the area of the accident and thought it was alright, the ladder was of good quality and more than ample for the job. Consequently the findings of the court brought in a verdict of Accidental Death.

One of the most successful years was 1910, when 1,609 tons of lead and zinc ore valued at £30,000 was produced by the 50 miners underground and the 25 men in the mill. The engine shaft was now down to the 65fms. and the recent ore strike was referred to as the Big Stope. This main working area was between the 47fm. Level and 65fm. North. Other good deposits were in Lindsay stope on the 17fm. North, whilst the Emmerson stope on the 47fm. South was enjoying a run of success but generally, the area north of the Engine Shaft was now the main area of production, and things looked like they could even improve even more! The 65fm. Level South struck a huge bunch of ore which was solid to the 47fm. Level above, and became known as the Alfred Deviess stope; it was fairly common practice in big mines to name the working areas after the miners, foremen or directors. Ironically in the north face, the stopes were just as rich and this culminated in the largest production in any year since the mine opened of 1794 tons which produced 8,722ozs. of silver, which was a very nice bye product.

In 1912, the engine shaft continued downwards and by August arrived at the 85fm. horizon and levels are being driven north and south in the vein. As we know the engine shaft is sited on the west side of the road and the mill on the east but over the previous few years there had been various advancements and the two areas were now connected by two iron trestle bridges spanning the main road. The ore was brought to surface in mine cars of 14cwt. capacity and hand trammed from the shaft top over the road bridge, where the tubs were tipped into the waiting grizzly. The oversize was lifted into a Blake Crusher, the ore washed and sent to a second crusher, then into a 2ft. x 12ft. trommel, then to the jiggs. Next it was lifted by a cup elevator to a set of 2ft. Cornish Rollers and from here, the finely crushed ore was dispatched to the Luhrig separator or classifier and the slimes to Wilfley and Buss Tables from where the slime residue was then passed to catchpits which were 12ft. to 20f.t deep (Thornthwaite was, in fact, the first mine in England to have Wilfley Tables). In an effort to ensure there was no leakage of the slimes into Bassenthwaite Lake, they were dispatched from one process to another by wooden launders lined with glass to improve the flow however, the quartz particles literally wore the glass away and of course any severe vibration or sharp knock broke the glass. This was an unsatisfactory solution and the longest one could expect them to last was six months so the system was replaced with glazed 6in. pipes.

By 1913, further modifications had to be made because the shaft was now down to 105fms, 450ft. below the level of Bassenthwaite, and consequently a new hydraulic Bull engine operated the pumps which were now installed and capable of raising water at a rate of 350 gallons a minute from shaft bottom. This was done in series by a 13in. ram pump from the 85fm. Level and by a 15in. pump from the 65fm. Level, to the surface. The water power for the pumps was supplied from a recently constructed 30ft. high concrete dam, the reservoir site being 500ft. higher up Comb Beck with a capacity of 1,000,000 gallons. A further power source was a 45hp. Pelton wheel, and a gas suction engine supplied power for various items of machinery; the air compressor provided air for up to seven air rock drills being used underground and had been the reason for such rapid development over the past years. The slime plant was worked off an 8hp. Pelton wheel.

It is more than probable that it was during this period that the adit level, which passed under the Keswick-Cockermouth road, was reinforced with concrete and steel girders. This road was now seeing much heavier traffic, traction engines weighing upwards of 10 tons with their heavy loads of ore to be dispatched to the nearby station would be a weekly occurrence ... on a road designed for horse and cart!

The mill of course, was being constantly upgraded and now had two Marsden stonebreakers, from here the ore passed through sizing trommels, then two sets of Luhrig high speed crushing rollers which reduced the ore to 3/16ths., then into Green and Davidson's jiggs; the slimes were treated on four Wilfley tables, a Buss table, two Luhrig slimers and one Luhrig vanner. The effluent from the mill was directed to slime pits which now covered 2 acres, and were specially designed by Anthony Wilson to ensure no problems occurred. They consisted of double walls made of turf and tailings, so that the coarser material was deposited in a channel between the two walls and the finer slimes were released through pipes into the next pond for collection.

It was not unusual in Lake District mines to have father and son working at same mine and, as in other areas of the country, it was tradition and common practice for a son to follow in his father's trade. Here at Thornthwaite, miner Robert Sanders, originally of Skelton, worked with his son Edward Leck Sander who had been born in Dalton in Furness and had worked for a short time in the Furness iron mines. The family had now moved to Keswick and Robert's brother Thomas William Sander was also working at Thornthwaite. The other side of the family were Lecks who hailed from the Patterdale area, and were descended from the German miners. In fact 17 year old Joseph Leck and his father John Leck aged 52 worked together at the Caudale Slate quarry. On the 17th. of April 1818, in a freak accident, a massive slab of slate detached from the quarry face bringing with it tons of debris and killing both men instantly. The other quarrymen ran to the scene but there was nothing they could do and eventually the mutilated bodies were dug out and removed some days later. Here at Thornthwaite, the 3 members of the Sander family walked to work together from Keswick and most evenings, the family would walk from High Hill and meet them coming home. But the family was soon to be separated. Thomas Sanders was becoming restless and looked across the

Atlantic for his fortune emigrating to Vancouver, Canada where he found work at the Reserve Coal Mine, Nanaimo. With the outbreak of war in 1914, local production virtually halved and many of the men answered the call to arms, including Edward Leck Sander. In the local pub, Edward and his mates decided to do the right thing and agreed to join up together, and the following day the lads went off and joined the Border Regiment.

Some of the older men stayed on at the mine, whilst Anthony Wilson desperately tried to encourage the younger men to stay also. Lead and zinc ore were vital metals for the war effort but his experienced workforce was becoming more depleted. It was a question of pride, loyalty to King and Country, and "their pals" had already gone. All Anthony's efforts were to no avail and his men continued to sign up, but he set up a War Fund Committee and he had memorial books made which included details of all of his employees who paid the ultimate price. Amongst those names was to be Edward Leck Sander. Like so many others, young Edward embarked for Gallipolli and the Dardanelles and also like so many in that hell, he was never to return, reported missing, presumed killed in action on the 21st. of August 1915. His grieving father Robert, too old at 68 years to enlist had only the memories of his son to sustain him, and the thought that at least his brother was safe in Canada. Then the dreadful news arrived that Thomas had been killed in a mining accident on the 26th. of December 1919.

During the war years, Anthony did all he could do to generate the production of ore for the war effort. The 85fm. Level was pushed forward north and south and intermediate ground prepared for a 75fm. Level, but this was never completed. The 85fm. Level was driven on and small stopes were commenced, Davidson's in the south, Mac Stope and Hindmarch's Rise in the north. The 65fm. Level was standing, the 47fm. Level had been pushed forward a few yards but no stoping was done and the 37fm. and 27fm. Levels were standing, but the mine was running down. By 1919, the final stopes were being worked in the 85fm. South and the Lent Stope in the north and a small pocket of ore was removed in the old 17fm. Level; these were the last places to produce ore, this was the final production, and the total for the war years was 1,220 tons of lead and 2,560 tons of zinc.

The war, with its fixed ore prices, created a false economy, and now with hostilities at an end, these prices were removed. As a consequence, ore values slumped which affected the nearby mines of Threlkeld, Greenside and Carrock Mine in much the same way; the development work had been done and further reserves proven, but now there was virtually no market and indeed the government stockpiles were in excess of what the country could use. The situation was further aggravated by an agreement to purchase a minimum tonnage from a number of foreign sources. These deals, made by the Ministry, could not be revoked and consequently our home market literally crashed; it would be many years before we were back to normal. It is for these reasons and not the lack of ore, that the company was forced to shut down.

By 1921, the Thornthwaite Lode had been working for 38 years almost continuously, but now the mine closed, throwing the 120 strong workforce out of employment. The final survey of the mine was done by Mr. John A Hill, surveyor to the Weardale Lead Co., Co. Durham and his work was completed on the 24th of June 1924.

Today

The site of Thornthwaite Mine is now virtually lost in the forest of the same name. The remaining buildings were occupied for many years by a garage, and then by Egerton's as a road recovery vehicle station (recently re-opened 2004). Local mining engineer Willie Shaw always believed that a wealth of ore still lay hundreds of feet down waiting for new adventurers. Anthony Wilson, who operated the mine for many years, lived literally on top of the vein, just 200yds. from the mine. His pink painted house, Thornthwaite Grange, is now a guest house. Anthony Bagster Wilson, JP and Squire of Thornthwaite who, like Willie, carried the pioneering spirit of mining into the 20th Century, sadly died aged 82 years on the 17th. of July 1954 and a small slate plaque in his memory is to be seen in the local bus shelter at Thornthwaite.

Windy Hill, Woodend & Barf Mines

Hidden in the dark depths of Beckstone Plantation, which is now part of the Thornthwaite Forest, and just beyond the village of Thornthwaite, is one of the older mining sites of the county.

Here, when the steep-sided gullies had been denuded of vegetation, and the early adventurers working the old Yewthwaite, Barrow and Brandley mines knew the courses of the veins, they realized further riches must be available on the shoulders of Barf, Thornthwaite and Derwent Fells standing high above Bassenthwaite Lake, and they were to be proved right.

The trials are, in many cases, small pits and openworks directly on the back of the vein and there is evidence, among the vegetation, of tracks and the remains of buildings. Beckstones Mine was a proper mine but has now been lost under the tons of scree on the front of Barf. Indeed the loose ground beneath the Bishop gave way to an easy source of building stone, hardcore etc. and local farmers and builders have obviously worked this area for hundreds of years. The sett was, in the early days, referred to as Woodend, Windy Hill and Barf, and Lord Egremont granted a lease in December 1532 to four men, William Scattergood, Jack Pyzer, William Smaithwaite and Nicholas Hyde, three of whom came from Derbyshire, to search for lead. Their efforts seem to have been rewarded as they were paid the sum of £15 13s. 4d.

A level, driven west into the middle of the crag behind Woodend, is of some antiquity and appears to have been fire-set and hand-worked. The level is extremely narrow, and all the 18ins. of vein material has been taken out between the foot wall and hanging wall. The working has been stoped to a height of around 15ft. including the rubble on the floor, and at the far end of the 35yd. Level, an angled rise has been taken up to surface (perhaps this was a smoke vent-hole?). The level appears to have been subsequently reworked a few years later and has been driven forward with the aid of powder.

It was well over a hundred years before another mining venture took place, and this was 50ft. below the previously mentioned working. During 1704, Mr. Anthony Tissington and his men dug three pits near Woodend and had reasonable success, obtaining some lead ore. A further series of trials was made in the area in 1754, by Robert Piele, Elizabeth Piele, William Gale, Anthony Tissington and Mrs. Isabella Potter at a royalty of 1/14th. Isabella was no ordinary female and she appears to have been an exceptionally hard woman and a strong worker, having been involved in other mining ventures in the area. This venture continued until 1759 and the total lead ore sold was around 35 tons. It is highly probable that these workings were at Windy Hill, which is to be found 300yds. north of Beckstones Gill and on the eastern flank of Barf, where there is a series of very old surface works and open works on the vein. One of these workings has been totally obliterated by a more recent quarry working, but if one examines the face, the lead vein can still be seen. This little company of adventurers also continued their venture on the south side of Beckstones Gill, where the tell tale quartz vein can be found and at around OD650ft. is a series of bell pits and small surface shafts on the back of the vein.

This particular venture seems to have finished around 1764, and the production not as successful as their original venture.. The tonnage recorded at the Estates Office of Cockermouth Castle was 7 tons of lead ore sold.

What is recorded is the fact that the adventurers were back in 1770 and continued until 1787, the partnership of Piele, Potter and Gayle having been together for over 30 years. Anthony Tissington would probably have passed away by this time or if not, he would have been a very old man and certainly his name is not referred to or recorded in these recent operations. Indeed they all were growing too old for their trade and by 1796 the Piele family had been mining in the area for over 40 years. Elizabeth Piele had reached the end of her tether and wrote a pleading letter to Lord Egremont explaining that the family had fallen on hard times and a considerable amount of money had been lost in their recent mining adventures. On top of this their father had died and all that were left were the three daughters, all of whom were now widowed and who were now over 60 years of age, in fact one was 74. What they wanted was a new Take Note and time to recover some ore for sale before any monies were due. What the outcome was is not recorded but I hope it was a favourable reply - I'm sure it was.

Beckstones Mine

The mine here takes its name directly from the gill of that name which bisects the mountain of Barf and Seat How, and which passes under the road just to the south of the Swan, an old coaching inn (now unhappily, developed into housing). As we know, the lead veins here had already been worked by the early adventurers including Beckstones, and the whole of this area is dotted around with small trials and surface workings, but this promised to be a proper mining venture.

With the turn of the century, mining technology was improving, gunpowder was available and underground workings were taking over from shallow pits and trenches. The first attempts were in April 1808, when a company called the Skiddaw Mining Company operated by John Bree and Joseph Bancroft took up a 1 year Take-note at a royalty of 1/6th. to work the vein . Whether or not the intention was to go through the oceans of scree beneath the "Bishop of Barf" and commence underground mining, we do not know. It may be that the two men were hoping to find some easy pickings in the old trials, however the venture did not continue for longer than a year.

A more likely candidate for the job was John Tebay, who took a lease including Barf and other mines in the area, in March 1819. He was a skilled operator and would have had the means to develop such a difficult venture. It is recorded that the vein was encountered but the host rock was Skiddaw Slate and was very friable and unstable, and consequently much timber was required to keep the mine and the entrance secure. Over the next 11 years, a quantity of lead ore was definitely brought out to day, proving that the vein had been encountered. The ore was sold for £2,872. 8s. 11d. and the development costs came to £871 8s. 11d. By 1830 the venture had collapsed and no further work was done, and it was to be nearly 10 years before a new adventurer would work the mine.

The next lease was taken up by a gentleman named J. Walker in 1830 but this seems to have been an under-funded effort and over the next nine years the total recorded output was only 17 tons 19cwts. 2qts of lead. No further activity took place and the mine closed up.

The mine then lay dormant until 1848, when the mine tips were being reworked by the Keswick Mining Company but it is not clear whether this company reopened the mine. The only ore sold was a mere 3 tons 10cwts. in 1849, and the company retained the lease only until the end of that year.

During March 1850, a group of five new adventurers, J. Richardson Jnr., G. Cape, W. J. Laidlow, J. Holmes and J. Martin took out a 2 year Take-note at a 1/15th. royalty but nothing is recorded of their success or failure. Another 4 years passed by before further interest was shown when a 2 year Take-note with a 1/15th. royalty was issued to Messrs. T. Fuller of London on the 15th. of December 1856, but by December 1857, only 1 ton 2 cwts. of lead were recorded as being produced and it was reported to the Estate Office that the mine was now standing idle

Then, in September 1859, a Mr. Richard Eales was offered a Take-note at a royalty of 1/15th. but this time with a covenant that 4 miners must be employed for the duration. During his 2 year tenure, a total of 10 tons of ore was raised however this could have been from any of the old trials on the sett.

It appears that for the next 22 years the sett was unlet, then in March 1883, a Take-note for 2 years at a royalty of 1/15th. and an annual rent of £20, was issued to Captain William Francis of Ladstock House, a well known local mining entrepreneur. This had the makings of a proper company venture and his associates were E. J. Hale of Mersey Docks, W. A. Currie, a Chief Rating Officer of Liverpool, W. Bradley, J. R. Currie of the Silverstone Rubber Company and Bown and Adams, Solicitors. The Company apparently could not raise the capital required and the options were not taken up however, Captain Francis was not to be deterred and during 1887 appears again with new credentials but again, things didn't materialize, even though he was planning a £10,000 investment.

Waiting in the wings was a Mr. Anthony Ede who was anxious to have a lease but for some reason this was refused without question, and no sooner had this application been revoked then, once again, on the 24th. of June 1888, Captain William Francis negotiated a 2 year Take-note with Lord Leconfield, the royalty to vary between 1/13th. and 1/15th.; the rate of the Take-note was £25 for the first 2 years and £30 for subsequent years with an option then for a 21 year lease. The company was made up of John Hudson, Chairman, W. James, William Farr, a cabinet maker, J. Beatrice, Jane B. Smithson, an oil and colour merchant from Sale, William Lingley, a merchant, Thomas Spink, a contractor of Sale and John Smithson, a plumber and glazier from Saddleworth. The company solicitors were John Guest of Bacup, and Captain Francis would be the agent. The company would be known as The Barf Woodend Silver Lead and Blende Company and was prepared to expend a total of £2,000 on the venture initially.

Francis tried to negotiate a better deal on the lease declaring there was little water power, and that he would have to install a steam engine and rent further land to do this. Further to this, he suggested a royalty of 1/17th. and the rent to be reduced to

£20. However, Walkin Thomas, agent to Lord Leconfield, was a hard man and not prepared to reduce the terms which had already been agreed in principal.

Despite all the wrangling, work commenced on July 1888, the main Beckstones Level was the prize and workmen started to remove the tons of loose scree and debris and commence fore-poling through. This was slow work and it took many weeks by the miners and carpenters to break through into the firmer ground, and even then their troubles were not over. The rock here is Skiddaw Slate and it fractured and gave way, so that much of the first part of the level had to be timbered before more solid ground was encountered. It took a year before the miners got through to the old working area, and some 400yds. of level had been cleared and secured. Here a few tons of lead ore were recovered and assayed but only yielded 8/9ozs. per ton; this was not really very rich and Captain Francis was very disappointed at what they had returned in the two years. He realized that there was little future in pursuing the venture, and by 1891 the company had foundered.

Today

The Beckstone Mine is virtually obscured by oceans of silver scree, the huge tips of the development work are now covered in gorse and small trees and the last time the level was visible was 1925. The area is now overseen by the "Bishop" who in his annual coat of white paint has seen all over the years.... what a story he could tell. Nearby in the front garden of "Beckstones" is a stone arched tunnel referred to on some maps as a disused level but so far as I am aware, no records exist of it as a working mine. Perhaps it could be a drainage culvert from the fell above.

Wythop Silica Mine

1 The Secret Valley

This venture took place in the most northerly site of the area covered by this book and its mysterious history lies in the hidden valley between Sale Fell to the north and Broom Fell and Lord's Seat to the south, an area known as Lowthwaite. Here, tucked away in the extreme head of the valley, beyond the ancient dwelling of Wythop Hall on the western edge of Wythop Forest, are to be found the workings of the silica mining venture.

The research into this mine has proved somewhat difficult and to actually locate the exact position of the workings required some persistence, as it is not marked on the ordnance survey map. Further to this, detailed information appears to be shrouded in mystery and rumour. During the time of its working it was evidently supposed that it was a project to provide work during the depression. Another conjecture was that it was a government sponsored, top secret project. One of the companies involved was to be called the Lakeland Syndicate and was possibly confused by locals with a company called the Thermal Syndicate, which was involved in the manufacture of vitreous silica glass for strategic purposes; operating out of Workington, they were apparently involved in some classified work. Based on its remote setting one could easily believe how these rumours started but, as we shall see, these suggestions are completely false.

The first interest in the site was in September 1920 by Mr. Lyon, the manager of the nearby Ruthwaite Baryte Mine who was given permission by the landowner, Lord Inglewood, to drill 2 shot holes in the vein to see if the mineralization was sufficient to commence a mining operation and a further viable business. News of this activity soon came to the ears of a Mr. Wright employed at the nearby Force Crag Mines.

It must be appreciated that all this area of land was thick scrub and undergrowth, and very steep, undulating and rugged terrain which had, for many years, been primarily used for shooting. Lord Barnard who was the Estate Trustee, urged some caution but considered that if they allowed some small exploration for mineralized veins it could do no harm. Certainly the vein structure worked at Thornthwaite Mine must pass through the area somewhere, and there was the possibility that the discovery of a large mineralized quartz vein could create further interest and a more lucrative source of income.

To this end Mr. Wright was allowed the same privilege as Mr. Lyon and was also given permission to inspect the vein. It was shortly after this, in June 1927, that Mr. Scoular a mining engineer engaged with the Braithwaite Mines Ltd., was offered a 5 year lease at a dead rent of £150 and a royalty of 6d. a ton on silica produced, however, nothing appears to have come of this.

During the same month, Anthony Wilson of Thornthwaite, a director of the Thornthwaite mines and agent for a newly founded company looking to open a silica brick making plant, arranged a private meeting at the George Hotel in Penrith with Mr. Frazer, representing the Inglewood Estates. It was proposed by Mr. Wilson that the silica would be mined and transferred from there by wooden chutes or aerial rope-way to the main road, where it would be taken by cart to Thornthwaite mine to be crushed and sold on. Should this prove to be a worthwhile business proposition and the vein be proved at depth, a tram road could be constructed and a plant set up to handle the product on site.

The terms he was offered on that day were a 45 year lease, an annual rent of £25 with a royalty of 3d. on either silica produced or the weight of bricks sold. The production of silica is not straightforward however and there are many restrictions; the air rock drills have to be of the type with water to suppress the dust - the cause of silicosis in miners. Another major problem is that working the quartz is very expensive due to the rock being extremely hard, thus blunting the drill bits, likewise more powerful explosive would be required thereby increasing the price of production per ton. Anthony requested that certain other things be confirmed in writing from the estate office, such as rights of way on and off the property, the right to build a plant and erect a rope-way etc. before becoming involved in expensive legal papers.

These dealings appear to have been a very secretive, as Anthony Wilson would not divulge his clients' names or company address, or it may have been that he was doing the research for himself. He had over the last 40 years been heavily committed to numerous mining ventures in the Lake District and the north of England and may have been looking for a new venture. Indeed it must be pointed out that the manufacture of silica bricks was a specialized and lucrative market, and at that time around 50,000,000 of them were required annually in Great Britain, selling for around £46 per 1,000 thus creating a business of some £2,300,000 - a prize not to be ignored.

During September 1928, Harvey Davies, the manager of the Cumberland Granite Quarry at Embleton was in confidential liaison with Mr. Simon Fraser of the Vane Estates Office at Hutton in the Forest who also knew Anthony Wilson personally and knew him to be a man of integrity. James Gill of Portinscale, however, seems to have been something of a mystery man but he was representing Messrs. Johnson of Leeds Fireclay, A. N. Braithwaite MP, Mr. Seacombe Wills and J. S. Kilner a brick machine manufacturer, and they were at this time known to be forming a company to extract silica. The company was to manufacture silica refractory bricks and fire cement predominantly for iron and steel works, coke ovens etc. Eventually Harvey Davies was able to confirm to the Estate Office by letter the bona fides of all the men involved.

2 A Serious Project

Early in 1929 Mr. R. B. Wright of Messrs. Wright Productions, Rose Gill Mill, Crosby, Maryport applied for a lease to work the silica vein at Beck Wythop, however nothing appears to have happened until the October when a Take-note was drawn up in favour of the directors Messrs. Wright, D. Newcombe Wright, W. H. Butler and H. Gregory. The annual rent would be £25 and the royalty payment 3d. a ton. Before committing themselves however, Mr. Wright decided he wanted further time to re-examine the area on the ground, and to completely establish the exact whereabouts and extent of the silica veins. He had heard that more could be seen of the exposed vein at the Hagg, Ling Fell, Birch Crag, Barf and Beckstones Gill to the south, although some of this land was owned by other people. Wright was anticipating that a deal could be done to extend the size of the sett should the need arise in the future. Eventually Messrs. Wright Co. were indeed ready to sign, but alas, they had missed the boat. They were informed by Waugh & Musgraves solicitors that the sett had been leased to The Lakeland Syndicate Ltd. This had taken place on the 25th. of March 1929, and was for a 50 year term at an annual rent of £75 merging into the royalty of 6d. a ton once production of 10,000 tons a year was achieved, and in excess of this the royalty would reduce to 3d. a ton. A £2 an acre land damage fine would be also be imposed. An approach was made to the Cockermouth-Keswick-Penrith Railway for land to construct a rail siding and another to the Forestry Commission requesting wayleave for an aerial rope-way; these requests were approved, in principle, during April.

In spite of his annoyance at being "pipped at the post" so to speak, Mr. Wright, on reassessing the situation felt sure that he would be able to obtain all he needed from the new company for his own production, without the risks involved in operating the venture himself.

Nearly 3 years on however, the Lakeland Syndicate had not done anything really constructive, apart from spending £500 of the company's capital on legal fees alone. By 1932, the rent was in arrears, apparently due to the fact that the capital anticipated from shareholders' investment had not materialized.

During September 1932, Anthony Wilson was still showing an interest in the project; being a well known businessman, local J. P. and respected man in the community, it was suggested that if Mr. Gill could reassign the lease to him, this would be acceptable to the Vane office. By the end of October 1932, James Gill was still playing for time, insisting that further capital to clear the company debts and arrears would be forthcoming Apparently when equity from Lord Inverforth's Trustees was released to one of the shareholders, this would be enough to clear all the arrears and start developing the works and plant. Indeed James Gill clearly stated that they had already spent a total of £5,000 on tests to establish the quality of the silica etc. Proof of the correspondence was sent to Fletcher Vane's office to substantiate the position.

In September 1933, the Lakeland Bricks (Refractories) Ltd. prospectus was issued and the share offer was £150,000 made up of 80,000 shares at £1 and

280,000 at 5/- making up the full offer. The Directors of the Board were Marcus De La Poer Beresford of Pinner, Maidenhead Brick and Tile Co., George Rupert Dugdale, the London mining engineer and Harry Carlyle Waddington, an Edinburgh accountant. The General Manager would again be James Gill, BSc. of Portinscale, on a salary of £1,500 per year. It was estimated the cost of the plant and railway sidings etc. would come to around £34,450 and a plant of the size proposed would have the capacity to produce 5,000,000 bricks at £7 10s. 0d. a 1,000 giving a return of £37,500, and 5,000 tons of plastic cement lining at £5 a ton, making a further £25,000, a total annual turnover of £62, 500. The company directors had invited their landlord Mr. W. M. Fletcher Vane to join them on the Board but he had declined the offer.

By November, only a small amount of the shares had been taken up and this simple fact resulted in the collapse of the venture, however the project was not completely dead and James Gill pursued the matter with great vigour and managed to arouse the interests of another group of gentlemen. Options were taken up in July 1934 by a new company entitled the Cumberland Silica Bricks Ltd., and on the 16th. of August 1934 their prospectus was floated. The directors were George Rupert Dugdale a mining engineer of London, Ronald King George, a petroleum engineer also of London, and Alec Francis Harvey, an insurance underwriter of Hove. The on-site manager was of course James Gill. The share capital offered was £80,000 comprising 100,000 shares at 10/- and 600,000 at 1/. The reserves of silica contained within the 2, 674 acres of Wythop Park were stated as being 3,000,000 tons and within the established 10 acres, gave proven reserves of 220,000 tons of high grade silica - enough to produce 62 million bricks which would give eventual production of up to 130 years.

Already chemists Messrs. David Kirkaldy & Son of London had tested the product up to a temperature of 1,850 degrees and the following results were published:

<u>*Silica Bricks - Fusion Test*</u>

one or two particles fused at 1800 degrees centigrade
several particles fused at 1825 degrees centigrade
a large number fused at 1850 degrees centigrade

<u>*Crush test*</u>

The average crushing load of six bricks was 4,920 ppsi

<u>*Fire Cement - Fusion Test*</u>

Several particles fused together at 1825 degrees centigrade
A large number fused together at 1850 degrees centigrade.

These results show that bricks made from the product would withstand a temperature of 1,800 degrees centigrade before fusing whereas other bricks being made in the country fused at 1,650 degrees centigrade.

The company had been pursuing Anthony Wilson to come onto the Board but, being a very astute man he decided to investigate the company's claims before making a final decision. He had friends on the Board of Directors of the Consett Iron Works and dispatched to them a parcel of 7lbs. of quartz from Wythop on the 8th of August. Mr. S. Tweedy of Consett, an analytical chemist, subjected the sample to various tests and by the middle of September, he was able to report that the Wythop silica was greatly inferior even to the lowest grade rock which was being obtained from Weardale. This apparently was far superior and their high grade Ganister rock was nearly pure silica. The company continued to pester Anthony to join the Board but based on this information he firmly declined the offer.

Further claims in the new prospectus were deemed inaccurate, and consequently one of the directors of the Consett Iron Company Ltd., on seeing these claims wrote directly, on the 16th of August 1934, to the landowner W. Vane, not to his office but directly to his Regimental address C/O the 6th. Durham Light Infantry at Staindrop. He was evidently pretty incensed at the claims made by the new company, and he insisted on looking at the property and the process to see how they achieved these excessive claims. Further to this, he was prepared to organize and foot the bill for a visit by the directors to view a proper working operation. The company, however, oblivious to all the criticisms levelled at them, pursued their plans. They intended to build a plant of their own design, develop a railway siding on the western side of the Cockermouth-Keswick-Penrith Railway, erect an aerial rope-way and construct a loading wharf which would supply processed products from the plant; the location of this was near to bridge No. 27 at Beck Wythop.

3 Friends Step In

On the 6th of December 1934 it appears the company actually started work on the site, and is also listed in the Stock Exchange year book for 1934. The company soon began to realize what a major undertaking the construction of the plant was. The access for the big lorries bringing materials and heavy machinery up the single track road, very steep and winding in places, from the main Cockermouth-Keswick road was more than a challenge for the drivers. Once the transport had arrived at the actual boundary of Wythop Hall, a new road had to be graded and constructed to the site of the plant another half mile on.

The actual plant covered an area of around 200yds. in length by 20yds. in width and huge concrete engine beds were created at the top of the site for the crushing plant. Directly below this were more concrete abutments to carry heavy machinery for operating further crushing and sizing plant. The area adjacent to and below this was the washing and grading area which appears to have been laid out very much like a mine dressing floor. Below this is a very large flat area, presumably the brick kilns and firing area, near to this was the boiler house which had a considerable chimney.

Around half a mile east from the top of the plant is the quartz vein which is about 50yds. wide and around 10ft. thick and can be followed up the steep hillside for around 50yds. An area here has been blasted out to create a turning and reception area for the railway where the rock would be loaded, either from an underground working or where wooden hoppers could have been erected to shoot the blasted rock into the waiting rail trucks. These would be hauled to the plant up a steady gradient on a 2ft. gauge light railway, laid from the point of extraction to the processing plant half a mile away . This work would be done by a Jung 4 wheel diesel loco Type EL 105, No. 4050 10/14 bhp 2-stroke, which had been recently purchased from the Standard Steel Co. who had apparently imported it from Germany. Just prior to the locomotive arriving at the plant a small siding was made, and then a substantial concrete and steel bridge was constructed to span the ravine down which flows Beck Wythop. Once across, the loco with its train of 4 loaded side-tipping tubs would discharge the rock into the waiting hoppers ready for the crushers to commence their work. Just south of the bridge the beck has been dammed by a well made concrete dam, essential to ensure a good water supply for the plant, particularly in summer.

Certainly the size of plant and process would have created a work force of at least 30 men, although if they had lived at Wythop Mill or Embleton it would have meant a stiff 500ft. climb and 2 mile walk in every day, and there are no short cuts here. An accident occurred in February 1935 to one of the newly taken-on work force. His name was Turner and he was injured whilst engaged in work at the plant; he was taken to Carlisle Infirmary where he was detained for treatment of an eye injury.

There was a considerable stir at the small hamlet of Beck Wythop when, very late one evening, young Robert Hudson was woken by the heavy rain splattering on his bedroom window. As he blinked in the darkness of his room he became aware of a commotion outside. Looking through the curtains he could see a large lorry on its way up to the brick works, laden with heavy machinery and completely jammed across the road at Brook House Beck bridge! It had come up the wrong road and got stuck! After demolishing a hedge the driver managed to extricate his wagon with the help of Robert's father who finally came back in completely soaked to the skin while Robert, now tired of the antics, curled up and went back to sleep.

Indeed the works created quite a stir in the local community, new jobs would be available, and the local school at Embleton went for a day trip to the premises to see what industry had invaded this quiet area of the Lake District. Naturally the children paid little attention, they were happy to be out on a nature walk and picnic - silica bricks were not on the agenda.

The aerial rope-way was built, the pylons bolted onto concrete plinths which went from the works down to a position on the Cockermouth-Penrith-Keswick Railway, near to occupation bridge No. 27 at Beck Wythop. It was here the company had at last acquired the single track siding and loading area to transport the material away in a quiet and efficient manner

However, the intrusion of this industrial monstrosity in this part of the Lake District was seen by the Friends of the Lake District as another blot on the landscape; they soon registered their complaints to the local authorities. The tall chimney belching its black smoke across the Wythop Woods could be seen for miles around. The Friends requested that the works should be stopped and at the same time, suggested to the local council that while they were about it, perhaps they could also remove the spoil heaps from the derelict mine at Thornthwaite!

A group of ramblers descending from Lord's Seat down to Wythop on the 5th. of August, came through the plant which to all intents and purpose was closed, and only a week later a newspaper report clarified the reason for the lack of activity. The company was in dire financial straits and in order to recoup some finances a sale was held of the plant on the 12th. of August 1939. This was conducted by Messrs. Butcher and the Jung loco was sold to the Buttermere Green Slate Quarries at Honister along with the rolling stock. The sale unfortunately was not enough for survival and so the Cumberland Silica Bricks went into voluntary liquidation on the 28th. of August 1939. It appears that a final call made on the existing shareholders brought a very poor response, a total of just £256. Consequently, the money was not entered onto the company's books but returned, and after the small amount of equity realized from the sale, a percentage dividend was paid out.

Production for the works is not available but three houses were erected by a local builder, George Brantwood. He transported the bricks from the site on his horse and cart and the houses are apparently still standing today although they have been modernized and rendered; one of them is definitely the Hollins at Thornthwaite.

The company certainly invested more than a few thousand pounds in the construction of the huge plant, the laying of the railway, the building of the dam, not to mention the bridge, the aerial rope-way, the negotiation of the rail sidings and the construction of the road. Many people think it was a very elaborate trick to gain money but I do not think so. Surely there are easier ways to make money, and the sheer time and effort that went into the project is here for all to see. No, I think you could write this off as a really bad idea.

Today

If one takes the road via Wythop Mill and continues up to where the road ends just before Wythop Hall, and walks just beyond, to the right can be seen the extent of the foundations extending up the hill. I would imagine that the aerial flight terminus is around where you are standing, the flight descending down to Beck Wythop, roughly half a mile due east, and the rail sidings. The approach can be made up through the forest from the A66 but be warned, this is steep and tough under foot. From your existing point, the large concrete tower is where the narrow gauge rail track came in over the beck, and the dam is to be seen further up stream. The exposure of the silica vein is found by following the forest road east which descends gradually for around 800yds. and here, on the right, is the vein for all to see! After one has seen the size and obvious effort put into the construction of buildings, one must surely think this was more than a pipe dream for a few adventurers, although one eye witness claimed that the kilns collapsed after a few firings!

Miners and Personnel

Because of the number of mines involved within a very small area it has been very difficult to bring about a very accurate individual list, simply because the mining companies operating the various setts would transfer men from mine to mine i.e. Goldscope to Yewthwaite, Barrow to Brandley, Thornthwaite, Rachel Wood and earlier Barf, Beckstones and Woodend. The distance between some of these mines was less than a mile. Every effort has been made to be as accurate as possible.

Miners at Goldscope, Newlands & Keswick

The following is a list of the German miners who came from Europe to work in the mines of Cumberland. Every effort has been made to provide a correct spelling, however many of the documents researched have given different spellings for names thus creating a problem. The names are listed and entered in the first year they appear in records; in some cases men were promoted or changed jobs and mines in which they were employed.

Year	Name	Role	Location
1564	Johan Steinberger	Mining expert	
1564	Daniel Hechstetter	Director	
1564	Hans Loner	Director	
1564	Ludwig Haug	Director	
1564	William Humphrey	Royal Mint	
1564	Peter Schenkel	Buyer	
1564	Jorg Kessler		
1565	Jorg Siber	Miner	
1565	Mr. Nudigate		
1565	Hans Matzler	Miner	Goldscope
1565	Simon Buchberger	Miner	Braithwaite
1565	Hans Reitter	Manager	London
1565	Steffan Kalcher	Miner	
1565	Wolf Binder	Miner	Newlands
1566	Michell Krell	Carpenter	
1566	Balthazar Auer	Carpenter	
1566	Ulrich Frosse	Manager	
1566	Leonard Stoultz	Miner	
1567	Balthazer Moser	Miner	Goldscope
1567	Michall Krempacher	Miner	
1567	Jorg Colmanstetter	Miner	Goldscope
1567	Hans Dierickh	Miner	
1567	Wolf Prugger	Carpenter	
1567	Hans Setzenstoller	Smith	
1567	Andreas Ringseisen	Smith	

Year	Name	Role	Location
1567	Jorg Deufferer	Smelter	Keswick
1567	Peter Holdbeitner	Smelter	Keswick
1567	Thomas Waldner	Smelter	Keswick
1567	Hans Moser	Miner	Goldscope
1567	Caspar Feninger	Sorter	
1567	Israel Waltz	Surgeon/Barber	Newlands
1567	Jobst Stilt	Mines Foreman	
1568	Christopher Gauffner	Smith	
1568	Daniel Ulstat	General Manager	Keswick
1568	Richard Ledes	Bookeeper	Keswick
1568	Rochius Franke	Asst. Manager	Goldscope
1568	Anthony Dediman	Office	Keswick
1568	Hans Hammel	Miner	
1568	Michel Carius	Miner	Goldscope
1568	Wolf Carius	Miner	Goldscope
1568	Wolfgang Hochholzer	Carpenter	
1568	Bernhart Fetchenbach	Smelter	Keswick
1569	Benedict Effendler	Miner	Goldscope
1569	Christopher Bockh	Miner	Newlands
1569	Christian Bockh		
1569	Mathew Scheuher	Miner	Goldscope
1569	Nicholas Fischer	Miner	Goldscope
1569	Hans Krumpuhler	Miner	
1569	Reichart Mitterholzer	Miner	Goldscope
1569	Caspar Clocker	Miner	Newlands
1569	Rupprecht Wurzer	Miner	Newlands
1569	Hans Haring	Mines Foreman	Goldscope
1569	Peter Linsberger	Miner	
1569	Hans Helenstiener	Miner	
1569	Jakob Hofer	Miner	Goldscope
1569	Hans Opperer		
1569	Thomas Eisel	Miner	Goldscope
1569	Jorg Heisel	Miner	Goldscope
1569	Hans Richter	Miner	Goldscope
1569	Gillig Hegler	Miner	
1569	J Dambson		
1569	Jorg Puhler		
1569	Philip Mair	Miner	Goldscope
1569	Hans Mair	Miner	Newlands
1569	Nicholas Schram	Miner	Goldscope
1569	Stefan Nusspaumer	Miner	Newlands
1569	Mathew Scheuher	Miner	Newlands
1569	G. Holger	Miner	Goldscope
1569	Jorg Reichel		
1569	Hans Paindtner	Miner	Goldscope

Year	Name	Occupation	Location
1569	Felix Waldner	Miner	Goldscope
1569	Lienhart Prugger	Miner	Goldscope
1569	Hans Matzler	Miner	Goldscope
1569	Jorg Schwaiger	Miner	Goldscope
1569	Martin Berger	Miner	Goldscope
1569	Michael Krempacher		
1569	Balthazar Moser	Miner	Goldscope
1569	Jorg von Syber	Miner	Newlands
1569	Eberhard Weitgasser		
1567	Martin Ernwallner	Miner	Newlands
1569	Thomas Schopf	Miner	Goldscope
1569	Jorg Silbereisen	Miner	Goldscope
1569	Andreas Torer	Miner	Goldscope
1569	Caspar Feninger	Miner	Goldscope
1569	J Hagrig	Miner	Goldscope
1569	J Hutson	Miner	Goldscope
1569	Hans Dierickh	Miner	Goldscope
1569	Peter Linsbergar		
1569	Hans Hammell		
1569	Ulrich Schlegel		
1569	Simon Buchberger	Miner	Goldscope
1569	Jorg Silbereisen	Miner	Goldscope
1569	Thomas Eisel	Miner	Goldscope
1569	M Oberstiener		
1569	Jorg Staudacher		
1569	Steffan Kalcher	Miner	Goldscope
1569	Hans Unterweger		
1569	Jorg Kossler	Miner	Goldscope
1569	Balthazar Moser		
1569	Wolf Hocholtzer	Miner	Goldscope
1569	Wolf Prugger	Miner	Goldscope
1569	Andreas Reindel	Miner	Goldscope
1569	Lienhart Prugger	Miner	Goldscope
1569	Jorg Schwaiger		
1569	Martin Berger		
1569	Michel Harpfer	Servant	
1569	Gregory Weiss	Housekeeper	
1569	Hans Regauer	Carpenter	
1569	Hans Walsitter	Carter	
1569	Robert Kirkby	Roofer	
1569	Gilbert Warton	Carter	
1569	Jorg Wiser	Sorter	
1569	Stefan Murr	Foreman washer	Goldscope
1569	Martin Kendler	Surveyor	
1569	Christian Bodner	Sorter	

Year	Name	Role	Location
1569	Hans Altschmer	Smelter	Keswick
1569	Sebastian Zaissacher	Smelter	Keswick
1569	Jorg Staidacher	Smelter	Keswick
1569	Ulrich Stampfer	Smelter	Keswick
1569	Ruprecht Schrattenberger	Smelter	Keswick
1569	Hans Plum	Smelter	Keswick
1569	Erhart Greutter	Smelter	Keswick
1569	Bartholomew Fuhrenberger	Smelter	Keswick
1569	Mark Steinberger	Foreman Smelter	
1569	Wolfgang Hund	Blacksmith	Goldscope
1569	Peter Kolseisen	Blacksmith	
1569	Hans Reinbrun	Transport	
1569	Jorg Reichel	Miner	
1569	J Siber	Miner	
1569	H Lancashire	Builder	
1569	H Ladstock	Builder	
1569	R Mason		
1569	T. Youdall		
1570	Hans Merer	Accountant	
1570	Franz Dorn	Foreman Miner	
1570	Thomas Hackel	Miner	
1570	Hans Dempff	Locksmith	
1570	Lienhart Diringer	Carter	
1570	Sebastion Gopler	Carpenter	
1570	Barthel Bollinger	Smelter	Keswick
1571	Christian Bodner	Miner	Goldscope
1571	Wolf Binder	Miner	Goldscope
1571	J Tiffin	Miner	Goldscope
1571	Jorg Marten	Miner	
1571	Robert Banke	Crushing Mill	Goldscope
1571	Jorg Heisel		
1571	Hans Bescht	Carter	
1571	Thomas Wallin	Foreman Smelter	Keswick
1571	Hans Hess	Smelter	Keswick
1571	Gregory Grasendorfer	Smelter	Keswick
1572	Henry Pope	Smelter/Refiner	Keswick
1572	Heinrich Kupferschmidt	Senior Smelter	Keswick
1572	G Fisher		
1572	N Fisher		
1572	T Clark		
1572	T Fletcher		
1573	Jorg Kessler	Miner	
1573	Ruprecht Kaldbucher	Miner	
1573	Franz Wellenberger	Tailor	
1573	Ruprecht Schridt	Smelter	

Year	Name	Role	Location
1573	Fabian Erhart	Foreman Miner	
1573	Caspar Clocker		
1573	Durer		
1573	Peter Linsberger		
1573	Jorg Colmanstetter		
1573	Martin Harris	Brewer	Derwent Isle
1574	Friedrich Schwartz	Agent	London
1574	Hans Haring		
1574	Lienhart Prugger		
1574	Thomas Eisel	Miner	
1574	Hans Moser	Miner	Goldscope
1574	Hans Koller		
1574	Gillig Hegler		
1574	Eberhart Weitgasser		
1574	Starr		
1574	John Scott	Joiner	
1574	J Hudson		
1574	D Stoddart		
1574	Hans Mair		
1574	Hazlitt	Miner	
1574	Bartlem Kornman	Coppersmith	Keswick
1574	Melchior Moser	Coppersmith	Keswick
1575	Celles Rosten	Polisher	Keswick
1575	Hans Rossle	Coppersmith	Keswick
1575	Conrad Zinnagel	Coppersmith	Keswick
1575	Casper Strauss	Coppersmith	Keswick
1575	Lorenz Zeller	Coppersmith	Keswick
1575	Sebastian Schweitzer	Coppersmith	Keswick
1575	Sebastion Dibler	F/man Coppersmith	Keswick
1576	Hans Reinhaus	Coppersmith	Keswick
1575	Thomas Waldner	Foreman Smelter	Keswick
1575	Ulrich.Stampfer		
1575	Ruprecht Schridt		
1575	Hans Altschmer		
1575	R.Bank		
1575	Gillig Hegler		
1575	John Braithwaite		
1575	Robert Banke		
1575	Thomas Reed	Smelter	Keswick
1575	J Banke		
1575	W Griegg		
1575	H Gaskell		
1575	E Gaskell		
1576	Hans Haring		
1576	T Fletscher	Miner	Newlands

Year	Name	Role	Location
1576	Gillig Hegler		
1577	Fabian Erhart	Miner	Goldscope
1577	H Fischer	Miner	Newlands
1577	Balthazar Moser	Miner	Goldscope
1577	E Waterson	Copper House	Keswick
1577	Hans Reinhaus	Coppersmith	Keswick
1577	Caspar Strauss	Coppersmith	Keswick
1577	Andreas Ringseisen	Coppersmith	Keswick
1577	A Damson	Coppersmith	Keswick
1581	Joachim Gaunse	Senior Smelter	Keswick
1606	Hans Clocker		
1609	Mr. Mason	Owner	
1614	Emmanuel Hechstetter	Owner	
1615	Hans Beck	Smelter	
1635	Captain Whitmore	Owner	
1680	David Davies	Surveyor	
1690	Mr. Ewart	Manager	
1692	Thomas Robinson	Owner	
1699	Ralphe Eaton	Miner	
1699	John Fisher	Miner	
1699	John Bonnor	Miner	Goldscope
1699	John Bonnor Jnr		
1699	Thomas Bonnor		
1699	William Bonnor		
1699	Thomas Boon		
1699	William Boon		
1699	Daniel Fisher		
1699	Thomas Bowe Smith	Blacksmith	
1699	John Wilson	Carpenter	
1699	Daniel Bonner	Carter	
1699	Samuel Scott		
1699	Gawen Graeme		
1699	William Ellis		
1699	Joshua Mayson		
1699	Joseph Tickell	Miner	Goldscope
1699	Ewart William	Miner	Goldscope
1700	Thomas Robinson	Manager/Geologist	Goldscope
1702	Baker	Smelter	Goldscope
1702	Myddleton Shaw	Smelter	Goldscope
1702	Thomas Hanson	Mine Foreman	Goldscope
1703	John Scott	Caretaker	Goldscope
1706	E Rolfe	Miner	
1706	J Sickell	Miner	
1707	Clarkson	Miner	
1707	Beach	Miner	

Year	Name	Role	Location
1707	Inman	Miner	
1707	Thornton	Miner	
1713	Thomas Ackersley	Owner	Goldscope
1718	Will Carter	Copper Mill	
1732	Thomas Elder	Copper Mill	
1732	John Christian	Copper Mill	
1732	Henry Simons	Copper Mill	
1739	John Fisher	Copper Mill	
1790	John Tebay	Engineer	
1790	Mr. Barrow		
1818	John Barker	Miner	Dalehead
1835	Isaac Sealby	Owner	Keswick
1835	James Reed	Miner	Loweswater
1835	John Tebay	Engineer	Whitehaven
1845	J Dixon	Miner	
1847	William Clemmence	Engineer	
1847	J Clemmence Jnr	Owner	
1847	John Bowden	Owner	
1847	John Floyd	Owner	
1848	Andrew Richard Clarke	Owner	
1848	Charles Nicholas	Owner	
1848	Patrick Chapman	Owner	
1848	George William Horn	Owner	
1848	Thomas Hart	Owner	
1859	George John May		
1859	Richard David Holland		
1869	Charles Lowden	Manager	
1869	Joseph Pools	Miner	
1872	Henry King Spark	Owner	Darlington
1872	Mr. Newby	Surveyor	
1873	Mr. Davidson	U/Manager	Goldscope
1910	J Burns	Owner	
1912	Thomas Crawford Dennison	Owner	
1913	W. H. Heywood	Owner	
1913	Bennett Johns	Owner	

Miners at Yewthwaite

Year	Name	Role	Location
1793	J. Walker	Miner	
1827	John Tebay	Owner	
1853	John Taylor		
1860	Coultas Dodsworth	Owner	Haydon Bridge
1860	Benjamin Plummer	Agent	Braithwaite
1878	W Hind	Miner	Braithwaite

Year	Name	Role	Location
1878	Mathew Barnes	Engine man	Portinscale
1878	Dixon Barnes	Miner	
1883	E J Hales		
1883	R T Currie		
1883	W Bright		
1883	W A Currie		
1883	W A Bradley		
1883	Henry Burrow Vercoe	Engineer	Portinscale
1883	E C Bradley		
1884	Lt Col Inge		
1884	J Cunliffe		
1884	J Salter		
1884	T Charlesworth		
1890	Joseph Cunliffe	Owner	St. Annes on Sea
1890	Charles Roberts		
1891	Joseph St Patrick Riley	Owner	Salford
1891	H.P. Walker	Secretary	
1891	John Woolcock	Mine Captain	
1891	Samuel Furness	Owner	Didsbury
1912	Mr. Dennison	Miner	
1916	W H Heywood	Miner	

Brandley and Skelgill

Year	Name	Role
1651	Hugh Potter	
1651	Richard Tickell	Miner
1651	John Fisher	Miner
1657	Thomas Tickell	Miner
1657	Col Beale	
1857	Henry Dickinson	Miner
1857	Moses Mawson	Miner
1857	Daniel Dunglinson	Miner
1857	John Bowe	Miner
1857	John Fisher	
1857	Thomas Jones	
1857	James Postlethwaite	
1857	John Clarke	
1857	John Graves	
1857	Joseph Dover	
1857	John Smith	
1857	Moses Dover	
1857	John Dover	

Barrow and Uzzicar

1651	Joseph Hechstetter	Owner
1652	Phillip Wilson	
1655	R Tickell	Owner
1655	Hugh Potter	Owner
1655	Col W Beale	Owner
1655	William Tickell	Owner
1655	John Fisher	Owner
1659	T Tickell	Owner
1699	Rolfe Eaton	Miner
1699	John Fisher	Miner
1699	John Boner	Miner
1699	William Boon	Miner
1699	Thomas Boon	Miner
1699	Daniel Fisher	Miner
1699	Thomas Bonor	Labourer
1699	John Sharp	Blacksmith
1699	Joseph Tickell	Carrier
1699	Thomas Same	
1700	David Davies	Mine Surveyor
1702	Mr. Wilkinson	Miner
1702	John Scott	Miner
1702	Henry Inman	Miner
1702	William Osmond	Miner
1702	J Pratt	Miner
1707	John Scott	Miner
1707	Daniel Fisher	Miner
1707	John Rawlin	Miner
1707	John Thwaite	Miner
1707	Robert Burfield	Miner
1707	Gawen Bow	Miner
1707	John Brough	Miner
1707	Thomas Fletcher	Miner
1737	Thomas Potter	Owner
1755	Isabella Potter	Miner
1755	William Gale	Miner
1755	Robert Peile	Miner
1756	Edward Dobson	Miner
1756	Hugh Workmen	Miner
1756	Charles Longstaff	Miner
1756	Mathew Cowen	Miner
1756	Robert Brown	Miner
1757	Frank Steel	Miner

1757	Nicholas Rough.	Miner	
1757	John Bennett	Miner	
1757	Mr. Harker	Miner	
1770	William Gale	Miner	
1770	John Scott	Miner	
1788	Edward Barron	Miner	Braithwaite
1788	Thomas Bowsher		
1788	William Carruthers		
1788	Thomas Crossthwaite		
1788	Joseph Hodgson		
1788	John Tarleton		
1788	Adam Fletcher		
1788	Stephen Fisher		
1788	James Wilson		
1788	Joseph Boner		
1788	John Coates		
1788	Thomas Spratt		
1788	Joseph Middlefell		
1818	J E Barrow	Owner	
1818	E Barrow	Owner	
1819	John Tebay	Engineer	
1847	Langton	Director	
1847	Samuel Merryweather	Engineer	
1847	Richardson		
1854	Wilkinson	Miner	
1868	Coulthard Dodsworth	Owner	
1868	Benjamin Plummer	Owner	
1874	Henry King Spark	Owner	
1884	Henry B Vercoe	Engineer	
1899	Captain Borlase	Engineer	
1906	Thomas Crawford Dennison	Director	
1906	J F Lobb	Manager	
1927	Mr. Martin		
1929	W T Donovan	Miner	

Ladstock, Thornthwaite & Rachel Wood

* Denotes stoped area named after the miners

1739	W Davies	Miner	Thornthwaite
1813	B Gibson	Miner	Thornthwaite
1819	M Harker	Miner	Thornthwaite
1822	G Bell	Miner	Thornthwaite
1822	T Bell	Miner	Thornthwaite
1823	T Higgson	Miner	Thornthwaite

Year	Name	Role	Location
1841	L Davies	Miner	Thornthwaite
1841	P Crispin	Miner	Thornthwaite
1842	M Collin	Miner	Thornthwaite
1843	E Martin	Miner	Braithwaite
1843	J Spedding	Miner	Thornthwaite
1845	J Bewsher	Miner	Braithwaite
1842	Mr. Clemence	Director	
1842	Mr. Ellice	Director	
1846	Samuel Merryweather	Engineer	
1847	Mr. Richardson	Director	
1847	J J Mallott	Director	
1847	J G Marshall	Director	
1847	H C Marshall	Director	
1847	P Langton	Director	
1847	C Merryweather	Director	
1848	Richard Tangye	Miner	Braithwaite
1849	J Edwards	Miner	Thornthwaite
1850	H Osbourne	Miner	Thornthwaite
1852	H Hewitson	Miner	Thornthwaite
1852	J Davidson	Miner	Thornthwaite
1857	John Phillipson	Miner	
1857	John Sanderson	Miner	
1857	William Cape	Miner	
1857	John Sanderson Jnr	Miner	
1857	Thomas Mitchell	Miner	
1857	John Tickell	Miner	
1857	Thomas Wharton	Miner	
1857	Thomas Bell	Miner	
1857	Thomas Wade	Miner	
1864	I Bowser	Miner	
1870	Charles Loudon	Miner	Braithwaite
1873	F W Crewdson	Director	
1876	W Tyson	Miner	Thornthwaite
1876*	Joseph Kirby	Miner	Braithwaite
1879	John Bell	Chairman	
1879	Walter Blott	Director	
1879	Jaimie Farie	Secretary	
1879	Thomas James Clemence	Director	
1879	Francis McAdams Robertson	Director	
1879	F B Walker	Director	
1879	B M Wright	Director	
1879	Captain Francis	Engineer	
1879	Thomas James	Miner	
1879	J Clemence	Miner	
1881	J Faraher	Miner	

Year	Name	Role	Location
1881	John Mansell	Miner	Thorn Hall
1881*	James Wilson	Miner	Thornthwaite
1881	Jacob Harker	Miner	Thwaite How
1881	John Edwards	Miner	Thwaite How
1881	George Hutton	Miner	Thwaite How
1881	John Jones	Miner	Thwaite How
1881	Joseph Reed	Miner	Thwaite How
1881	John Williams	Miner	Thornthwaite
1881	Lanty Fisher	Office	Powter How
1881*	John Williamson	Miner	Thornthwaite
1883*	F MacDonald	Miner	Thornthwaite
1883	Mr. Robertson	Miner	
1884*	J Bewsher	Miner	Thornthwaite
1887	Mr. Hindmoor	Miner	
1887	Thomas Lancaster	Miner	
1889	Edward Brown	Miner	Keswick
1889	Robert Williams	Foreman	Thornthwaite
1889	J B Lobb	Manager	Seat How
1890*	William Horsley	Miner	Braithwaite
1890	William Barker	Engineer	
1890	Captain Garnish	Manager	
1890	John Nicholl	Engineer	
1890	John Elliot	Miner	
1890*	Joe Hindmarch	Miner	Thornthwaite
1891	Thomas Hougham	Miner	Thornthwaite
1891	Samuel Dykans	Miner	Thornthwaite
1891	William Pearce	Miner	Thornthwaite
1891	Joseph Pearce	Miner	Thornthwaite
1891*	James Emmerson	Miner	Thornthwaite
1891	Walter B Cornish	Agent	Braithwaite
1891	William Holliday	Miner	Braithwaite
1891	Jacob Holliday	Miner	Braithwaite
1891*	William Dixon	Miner	Braithwaite
1893*	Hugh Tonkin	Miner	Braithwaite
1898*	Isaac Grisedale	Miner	Braithwaite
1898	Hugh Pryce	Miner	Braithwaite
1898	Charles Pugh	Miner	Braithwaite
1899	J. Butler	Miner	Thornthwaite
1900*	T. Lewis	Miner	Thornthwaite
1900	R Pattinson	Miner	Thornthwaite
1901	Harry Bennett	Miner	
1901	Harvey Davies	Clerk	
1901*	Mr. Tangye	Miner	
1901	Captain Francis	Engineer	
1904	Captain Johan Hodgson	Manager	

1904	Phillip Waterhouse	Director	
1904	Mr. Waite	Miner	
1904	Mr. Askew	Miner	
1904	Mr. Reed	Miner	
1904	Mr . Bland	Miner	
1904	Mr.Baldwin	Miner	
1904	Mr. Mason	Miner	
1904	Mr.Hicks	Miner	
1904	Mr.Cooper	Miner	
1904	Mr.Pearson	Miner	
1904	T Hodgson	Miner	Thornthwaite
1904	Mr. Cunningham	Miner	Thornthwaite
1904	N Davies	Miner	Thornthwaite
1905*	George Davison	Miner	Braithwaite
1906*	Joseph Dixon	Miner	Braithwaite
1906*	Mr. Drury	Miner	
1906*	Mr. Welch	Miner	
1906*	Mr. Potts	Miner	
1906*	Mr. Thomas	Miner	
1906*	Mr. Satterthwaite	Miner	
1906*	Robert Lindsay	Miner	
1906*	Mr. MacDonald	Miner	
1907*	Mr. Strong	Miner	
1908	J. Thwaite	Miner	Thornthwaite
1909	Arthur Lewthwaite	Miner	Thornthwaite
1909*	Edward Grisedale	Miner	Braithwaite
1909*	John Lowden	Miner	
1909	William Clarke	Miner	Braithwaite
1909*	Thomas William Sander	Miner	Keswick
1909	Robert Sander Snr.	Miner	Keswick
1909	Edward Leck Sander Jnr.	Miner	Keswick
1909	J. P. Dent	Miner	Thornthwaite
1908*	Mr. Todd	Miner	
1908*	Mr Stuart	Miner	
1908*	Mr. Temple	Miner	
1910	J. Thompson	Miner	Thornthwaite
1910	W Blacklock	Miner	Thornthwaite
1911*	Alfred Deviess	Miner	
1922	Thomas Barnes	Miner	Braithwaite

Beckstones, Woodend, Barf & Windy Hill

1532	William Scattergood	Miner	Woodend
1532	Jack Pyzer	Miner	

Year	Name	Occupation	Location
1532	Nicholas Hyde	Miner	
1532	William Smathwaite		
1704	Pilkington		
1756	Anthony Tissington	Miner	Windy Hill
1756	Isabella Potter	Miner	Windy Hill
1756	William Gale	Miner	Windy Hill
1770	Elizabeth Peile	Miner	Beckstones
1770	Robert Piele	Miner	
1808	Joseph Bancroft	Miner	Beckstones
1808	John Bree	Miner	Beckstones
1819	J Tebay	Engineer	
1839	J Walker	Miner	Barf
1848	J Richardson Jnr.		
1848	J Holmes		
1848	J Martin		
1850	W J Laidlow		
1857	Thomas Wade		
1858	T Fuller	Miner	Beckstones
1859	Richard Eales		
1883	W Francis	Engineer	Barf
1888	J Smithson	Miner	Beckstones
1888	W Farr		
1888	T Spink		
1888	W Lingley		
1888	J Hudson		

Glossary of Terms

Adit - A tunnel entering into the hillside, referred to by the German miners as stollen.
Agent - Title given to the day to day manager of the mine.
Ancients - Old miners.
Assay house - A place where the ore is assessed for its richness.
Back filling - Waste rock which is dumped into disused areas of the mine.
Backs - The amount of vein material above the adit to surface.
Bait - Miners lunch.
Ball mill - A revolving steel drum filled with steel balls for reducing the ore to small particles.
Bargain - An agreement between the agent and a group of miners to carry out work for an agreed price.
Battery - A place where copper is beaten into sheets or made into utensils.
Bell-pit - A short shaft sunk onto a mineral vein or coal seam.
Bellows - A type of pump to create a draught to produce a fiercer fire.
Bing - A unit of measurement approx. 896lbs.
Black cawke - Another name for graphite.
Black Jack - Another name for zinc ore.
Blende - Zinc ore.
Bloomery - An early hearth for smelting iron ore.
Bothy - A small hut on the fellside where the miners would live.
Bouse - Ore.
Bouse team - A stone built ore bin.
Brass - A mixture of copper and zinc.
Bronze - A mixture of copper and tin.
Bucking - An early method of crushing ore with a flat hammer.
Buddle - A rotating device to separate very finely crushed ore.
Bunning - Waste material placed on top of the adit roof supports to prevent surface debris falling into the entrance.
Bushel - A measure of 160lbs.
Captain - A title given to the person in charge of the surface and underground workings.
Caulkers - Metal strips fitted to the soles of clogs to prevent wear.
Clogs - Wooden soled footwear used by miners and quarrymen.
Chalcopyrite - A copper bearing mineral.
Charge - The explosive which is inserted into the shot hole.
Charr - Amount equating to 30 pigs of lead.
Chow - Chewing tobacco.
Cistern - A tank of metal or wood for holding large quantities of water.
Coffin level - A tunnel usually hand-chipped in the shape of a coffin and engineered during the 16th. C. prior to gunpowder.

Company - A group of four or five miners working a "bargain".
Copper - Mineral mined in Cumberland by the ancients.
Country rock - The rock of the area bearing the mineral vein.
Crosscut - Tunnel leading to the vein at right angles.
Day - Underground term meaning outside i.e. out to day.
Deads - Waste rock stacked neatly underground to support an area of the mine.
Development - An area of the mine being opened up.
Dialling - The art of taking bearings underground when surveying the mine.
Dressing - Part of the process of reducing the ore extracted from the mine to the size required.
Dressing floor - Usually in the early days a cobbled area where the ore from the mine was dressed.
Drift - A tunnel driven to give access to the vein.
Engine - The early German miners used this description of a waterwheel.
Ergot - a parasite alkaloid, ascomycetes, forming on rye.
Face - The solid rock wall where the charges were placed to drive the level forward.
Fathom - A distance of 6ft.
Fault - An area of displaced ground.
Flats - An area of working where the vein is horizontal.
Flowstone - Secondary mineralization forming on the level walls.
Footwall - the wall forming the lower slope of the angled vein.
Fother - 70lbs. weight measure, although this varies from area to area.
Fuse - The method by which the explosive charge is exploded.
Galena - The ore from which lead is extracted.
Gangue - Matrix consisting of secondary unwanted minerals and dead rock.
Gin - A winding mechanism for de-watering or hauling/lowering into a shaft. The power could be produced by man, horse or water.
Graphite - Pure carbon deposit used for making pencils.
Grizzley - An iron grating for the initial sizing of ore.
Hade - The angle of the vein.
Hanging wall - the wall forming the upper slope of the angled vein..
Headframe - Wooden trestle from which a wheel is suspended to haul up men, ore etc. from the workings below.
Hopper - Wooden chute used for dispatching the ore from the working stopes to the tramming level and ore tubs below.
Horse - A large section of vein material left for support between the hanging wall and footwall.
Horse level - A main tramming level designed to be able to take a horse drawn tubs.
Hund - Early wooden rail wagon.
Hushing - An early method of removing overburden by releasing water down the fell to expose the bedrock and hopefully the vein.
Jackroll - Method of hauling ore up the shaft by hand.
Jaumb - A wedge of rock jutting out from the level wall.

Jiggs - Device for separating waste rock from reduced particles of vein stone in water which is being agitated.
Jumper - A hand-held drill steel.
Kibble - Wood or metal bucket for hauling ore or water; also used as a measurement of weight.
Kolbenbruch - Stamped ore.
Launder - Wooden trunking for transferring water.
Lead - A metal gained from galena.
Leader - The actual vein structure within the lode.
Lease - A legal document agreeing the terms and condition of the mining company's tenancy.
Leat - A trench for carrying water.
Lode - A main vein.
Loth - German term for 1/2 ounce of silver.
Mark - German currency worth around 13s. 3d. in 1600.
Mill - The area on the mine site where the ore is sorted and dressed.
Mine agent - A person who acquires finances and sells ore from the mine, can also be the Mine Captain.
Moiety - Area of ground which has been leased to the company.
Mucking out - Clearing rock from the face after blasting.
Muntz metal- Discovered in c1832, resists the action of sea water and prevents barnacles.
Old Men- Early miners sometimes referred to as the ancients.
Outbye - To travel out of the mine.
Packwall - Waste rock stacked beside the tunnel walls to support them.
Partnership - A group of workmen headed by a spokesmen to arrange bargains for working.
Pillar - Section of rock left in situ to support the roof of the mine.
Pit - General term to describe a coal mine or iron mine in Cumberland.
Plug & feather- Miners tools for splitting rock.
Plumbago - Another name for graphite.
Polisher -A person who finished off the copper utensils.
Portal - The entrance to the level.
Pricker - A copper or iron needle inserted through the stemming into the charge to insert the fuse.
Prop - Timber used to support the mine working.
Quintal - 100lbs. in weight.
Rise - A vertical shaft connecting the workings.
Robbing the mine - Removal of some or all of the pillars when it is known the mine is about to close.
Royalty - An area of land defined by the lease or a percentage to be paid to the landowner for the weight of mineral extracted and sold.
Run-In - An underground area where the roof or walls have collapsed.
Sett - Area of land that the miners are allowed to operate.
Shaft - Usually a vertical or steeply inclined tunnel, used for hauling ore and men.

Shot - Detonation of explosive.
Shot-firer - Person who fires the shots.
Shot hole - The hole bored to take the shot (gunpowder, dynamite etc.).
Skirt - Edge of the vein visible in level walls.
Slimes - Fine slurry waste created by the process of milling the ore.
Smelter - A place where ore was melted down.
Solar - Sheet of iron placed at the face prior to blasting so that the ore can be shovelled up easily.
Sole - Floor of the level.
Spoil - Rubbish from the mine and the mill.
Sprag - Method of securing a mine tub by inserting a metal spike through the wheel.
Stamps - Vertical timbers with iron shoes for crushing ore, using a waterwheel as power.
Stemming - Clay or other material used to pack the charge into the drilled hole.
Stemple - Large horizontal timber used to support the stope walls and create false floors.
Stone mill - An orepass made of large cobbles.
Stope - Working area of the mine where the vein stuff has been removed.
Stringer - Small workable vein leading off main lode.
Sump - A blind shaft in the sole of the level usually to catch surplus water.
Tailings - Waste material from the milling process.
Take-note - A short term agreement to mine prior to a lease.
Tallow - Animal fat candles.
Tally stick - Notched piece of wood used to record the number of tubs or kibbles dispatched to surface - for piece work payment.
Tamping - Pressing the powder and stemming firly into the shot-hole.
Trammer - Man or boy who removes mine tubs from the mine.
Trenching - Method of cutting horizontal trenches across the open fellside in the hope of exposing the vein.
Trial - A small surface excavation or short tunnel to prove the vein.
Tributing - An early method of mining, the miner working a certain section of the mine and being paid for ore removed.
Truck system - method of payment by credit from the company.
Quintall - 112lbs. i.e. around a hundred weight
Vein - Mineral bearing fissure in the rock.
Vugh - A cavity in the vein containing mineral in crystal form.
Wad - Local name for graphite.
Water blast - A method by which water is introduced down a shaft into the mine workings for ventilation of the mine.
Wedge - Early iron tool for splitting rock.
Wheeler - Miner who pushes a wheelbarrow.
Workings - General term to describe the underground system of a mine.
Yorkers - Twine tied around the trouser leg just below the knees to stop dirt going up.

Production Figures

In the area covered by this book there were three major working setts. Due to the various mines of the Newlands Valley, the companies often lumped the production figures together thus making a complete list, including the larger mines of Goldscope and Yewthwaite and also the much smaller workings. The same thing happened with the other setts of Braithwaite and Coledale, and likewise the Thornthwaite sett. We have wherever possible tried to produce an accurate set of individual figures.

We have attempted to list the production figures for each of the individual mines, however because many of the workings operated in a sporadic nature, incomplete records are unattainable. Also, some of the companies operated more than two or three mines in the area at the same time and amalgamated the production figures. Consequently the production and prosperity, the success or failure of an individual mine has been lost for ever. Tonnage figures have been rounded up for the sake of simplicity and it should also be noted that silver percentages have been omitted as these were not available in most cases. Indications of market prices have been included to give the reader some idea of the overall values.

DALEHEAD COPPER MINE

These production figures could include work done at the Longwork but production at Dalehead for these early dates is:

Year	Tonnage
1806	31
1807	36
1808	96
1810	29
1823	20
1824	7
1825	15
1829	30
1832	11
1841	11
1843	1
1844	4
1845	4
1846	4
1848	53

CASTLENOOK LEAD MINE

Year	Tonnage
1860	4
1863	30

NEWLANDS VALLEY
GOLDSCOPE MINE PRODUCTION FIGURES
NV INCLUDES NEWLANDS VALLEY

	Lead	Copper
1567		1
1568		15
1569		40
1570		62
1571		51
1572		60
1573		60
1574		27
1575		5
1576		29
1577		14
1578		3
1579		18
1580		8
1581		33
1582		
1583		40
1584		53
1611		98
1619		23
1624		18
1629		15
1630		10
1632		16
1646 NV	149	
1647 NV	140	
1649 NV		
1650 NV	140	
1651 NV	316	
1652 NV	106	
1653 NV	246	
1654 NV	44	
1655 NV	22	
1656 NV	3	
1657 NV	36	
1658 NV	35	
1659 NV	26	
1663 NV	26	
1665 NV	9	

Year	Value	
1679 NV	306	
1680 NV	152	
1681 NV	181	
1682 NV	103	
1683 NV	128	
1684 NV	248	
1685 NV	176	
1686 NV	86	
1687 NV	118	
1689 NV	144	
1690 NV	78	
1691 NV	8	
1693 NV	113	
1696 NV	2	
1698 NV	7	
1699 NV	261	
1700 NV	165	
1701 NV	74	
1702 NV	60	
1703 NV	141	
1705 NV	141	
1706 NV	40	
1707 NV	93	
1708 NV	77	
1710 NV	10	
1811	32	
1822 NV	419	
1825 NV	15	
1828 NV	62	
1831 NV	35	
1832 NV	61	10
1836 NV	36	
1837 NV	68	
1838 NV	40	
1847		8
1848		8
1849		8
1850		8 last copper mined
1851	14	
1852	18	
1853	266	
1854	505	
1855	456	
1856	422	
1857	351	

1858	535	
1859	391	
1860	415	
1861	480	
1862	480	
1863	350	
1864	250	
1865	150	
1866	36	
1870	93	
1871	105	
1872	138	
1873	86	
1877	42	
1878	38	
1919	25	
1920	26	

YEWTHWAITE MINE

1577	15	
1791	34	
1793	6	
1806	14	
1807	9	
1808	14	
1809	78	
1810	14	
1811	6	
1824	4	
1827	2	
1829	4	
1834	2	
1836	11	
1843	1	
1844	2	
1850	35	£380
1851	9	
1852	130	
1853	64	£860
1854	35	£470
1855	45	
1856	18	
1865	100	
1866	343	

1867	350
1868	331
1874	1
1875	72
1876	60
1877	36
1878	25

COBALT MINE

1822	2	
1823	3	
1825	2	
1845	2	
1848	33	
1849	24	£12 a ton

* Recently ore has been analyzed from this site and cobalt is present.

STONYCROFT LEAD MINE

1848	21
1849	22
1854	78

BARROW & UZZICAR MINE

1649	12
1650	6
1651	105
1652	35
1653	21
1654	2
1655	2
1657	52
1658	36
1659	26
1660	26
1662	26
1663	8
1699	24
1701	76
1702	73
1705	3
1726	1

Year	Amount	Price
1727	2	
1728	2	
1729	1	
1753	9	
1754	14	
1755	25	
1756	19	
1757	16	
1758	21	
1759	23	
1761	7	
1762	3	£5 a ton
1764	5	
1766	2	
1767	18	£6 10s. 0d. a ton
1769	5	
1770	2	
1808	1	
1810	4	
1811	4	
1829	1	
1832	62	
1833	7	
1834	34	
1835	101	
1836	46	
1837	21	
1838	40	
1840	5	£14 a ton
1841	17	
1842	11	
1843	1	
1844	11	
1845	21	£9 15s. 0d. a ton
1846	4	
1847	1	
1848	21	
1849	22	
1853	69	
1854	78	
1855	19	
1856	8	
1857	2	
1886	76	20
1887	55	5

1888	59

1650-1848	4,260 tons WSH
1888 1854	523 tons WSH

LADSTOCK MINE

1877	75 zinc
1878	65
1879	24

BARF, WINDY HILL, WOODEND, BECKSTONES

1532	no return	£15 13s. 4d.
1704	no return	
1754	no return	
1756	15	
1757	4	
1758	8	
1759	8	
1762	1	£5 a ton
1763	1	
1764	1	
1765	4	
1773	14	
1806-1848	21 WHS	
1836	14	
1839	3	
1849	4	
1857	1	

THORNTHWAITE AND RACHEL WOOD MINES

	Lead		Zinc	
1829	1			
1835	68			
1836	68			
1837	21			
1838	40			
1845	14			
1876	4			
1883	6			
1888	74	£9	95	£4 a ton
1890	325		197	
1891	940		251	

1892	747	376
1893	250	125
1894	110	36
1895	167	108
1896	246	202
1897	228	250
1898	255	418
1899	192	520
1900	132	388
1901	107	290
1902	24	151
1903	128	639
1904	285	798
1905	321	1099
1906	441	982
1907	532	746
1908	372	525
1909	229	650
1910	623	986
1911	890	904
1912	540	840
1913	360	567
1914	350	700
1915	300	500
1916	220	450
1917	200	450
1918	150	460

1870 - 1918 Blende - 15,682 tons: £90,673. Lead - 10,987 tons: £111,515. Average lead price: £10 3s. 0d., blende: £5 15s. 5d.

Bibliography

Abrahams Israel, Joachim Gaunse.
Adams John, Mines of the Lake District Fells, 1988.
Anon. Chartered Company of Mines Royal, Burt R., P. Waite, Michael
Anon. Copper through the Ages, 1934.
Anon. Engineering & Mining Journal, Thornthwaite Mine, Vol. 6, 1912.
Atkinson Ray Burnley, Mineral Statistics Northern England, 1981.
Baron John, All About the English Lakes, 1925.
Blake George, Mining in the Middle Ages, Transactions of the Midland Institute XCV1, 1888.
Bott G., Keswick, the Story of a Lake District Town, 1994.
Bouch C. M. L. & Jones G. P., The Lake Counties 1500-1830, 1968.
Castleden R., British History, A Chronological Dictionary of Dates, 1994.
CATMHS Newsletter No. 5.
CATMHS Newsletter No. 20.
Clapham Sir John, A Concise Economic History of Britain from the earliest times to 1750, 1963.
Collingwood W.G. German Miners at Coniston 17th Century. CWAAS 1909.
Collingwood W G Elizabethan Keswick, 1912.
Collingwood W.G. The Keswick and Coniston Mines 1600. CWAAS 1928.
Collingwood W.G. Lake District History 1925. Titus Wilson & Son, Kendal.
Collingwood W.G. Leaving of the German Miners, FRCC No. 3, 1930.
Crosthwaite Fisher, The Crosthwaite Registers, CWAAS Vol. 11, 1876.
Crosthwaite Fisher, Colony of German Miners at Keswick, CWAAS Vol V1, 1883.
The Romans in Westmorland, CWAAS Vol 111, 1878.
Day J, The Costers: Copper-Smelters and Manufacturers, Newcomen Society, Vol. 47, 1974.
Darby H.C. Historical Geography of England before 1800, 1936.
Donald M. B., Elizabethen Monopolies, 1961.
Donald M. B. Elizabethan Copper, The History of the Mines Royal, 1955.
Eastwood T., Memoirs of the Geological Survey, VolXX11 The Lead and Zinc Ores of the Lake District, 1921.
Eastwood T., Dewey H., Memoirs of the Geological Survey, Vol. XXX Copper ores of the Midlands, Wales, the Lake District and Isle of Man, 1925.
Engineering and Mining Journal, Thornthwaite Mine, Vol. 94 1912.
Fell A., Early Iron Industry of Furness.
Grant Doug, The Sixth Duke of Somerset, CWAAS 1985.
Greaves W. & Carpenter J.H, A Short History of Mechanical Engineering, Longmans,1969.
Hall Caine, Son of Hagar, Eveleigh Nash & Grayson Ltd.
Hamilton Henry, The English Brass and Copper Industry to 1800, 1976.
Hammersley George, Daniel Hechstetter the Younger 1600-1639. 1988.

Hammersley G., Cost Accounting at Keswick 1598-1615, The German Connection. 1990.
Harrison W., A Description of England (in Holinshed's Chronicles) 1587.
Harris J. R., The Copper King, Thomas Williams of Llanidan, 2003.
Holland Eric, Coniston Copper, 1986.
Hoover H. C., De Re Metallica, 1950.
Jenkins Rhys, German Colony in the Lake District, 1938
Jones C., Goldscope CATHMS.
Kendal and District Mine Research, Newsletter June 1984.
Kendall J. D., History of Mining in Cumberland and North Lancashire.
Lefebure M., Cumbrian Discovery, 1977.
Lefebure M., Cumberland Heritage, 1970.
Lipsom E., Economic History of England Vol. 1 1929, Vol. 2 1934, Vol. 3 1931.
Marshall J. D., Davies-Shiel M., Ind. Archaeology of the Lake Counties, 1969.
Millward R. Robinson A., The Lake District, 1970
Oxford Dictionary of National Biography, Vol47, Oxford Press ,London, 2004
Peters E. D. The Principles of Copper Smelting, 1907.
Postlethwaite J., Mines and Mining in the English Lake District, 1877.
Raistrick A., Jennings B., A History of Lead Mining in the Pennines,1965.
Rawnsley H. D. Past and Present English Lakes, James MacLehose & Sons, 1916.
Rees William, Industry before the Industrial Revolution Vols. 1 & 2, 1968.
Robinson Thomas, Anatomy of the Earth, 1694.
Robinson Thomas, Natural History of Westmorland and Cumberland, Freemans, London,1709.
Rorig Fritz, The Mediaeval Town, 1964.
Rowse A. L., The England of Elizabeth, 1950.
Salzman L. F. English Industries of the Middle Ages, 1923.
Shaw W. T., Mining in the Lake Counties, 1970.
Simons E. N., Metals, 1967.
Sopwith T., An Account of the Mining District of Alston Moor Weardale and Teasedale, 1833.
Taylor R, Ramblers Guide to the Vale of Newlands, C1950
Tyler Ian, Force Crag, Blue Rock Publications,
Tyler Ian, Greenside, Blue Rock Publications,
Tyler Ian, Honister Slate, Blue Rock Publications,
Tyler Ian, Seathwaite Wad, Blue Rock Publications,
Tyler Ian, Thirlmere Mines, Blue Rock Publications,
Tyler Ian, Cumbrian Mining, Blue Rock Publications,
Verlagshaus R., Schwaben Tirol, Vols. 1 & 2, 1989.
Victorian History of the County of Cumberland, Dawsons, London, 1968.
Wallace W., Alston Moor, Its Pastoral People its Mines and Miners,1890.
Wildridge J. D. J., Wythop Silica Brick, CIHS Nos. 19/20.
Wildridge J. D. J., Mines of Windy Hill and Barf, Northern Mines 1972.
Willis G., Copper and Brass, 1968.
Winchester Angus, Landscape and Society in Mediaeval Cumberland, 1987.